Hebrews

Stay in the Game

Darrin Yeager

Frames of Reference LLC

Hebrews
Stay in the Game

Copyright © 2023 Darrin Yeager
All rights reserved. No part of this book may be reproduced in any form, known now or in the future, without written permission of the copyright owner, except for brief quotations in reviews or other materials.

https://www.dyeager.org/

ISBN 979-8-9889650-1-5
Published by Frames of Reference LLC

The integral sign with alpha and omega limits logo is a trademark of Frames of Reference LLC.
Unless otherwise noted, Bible passages are from the King James Version of the Bible.
Passages marked NKJV taken from the New King James Version of the Bible copyright ©1979, 1980, 1982 by Thomas Nelson Inc. Used by permission. All rights reserved.
Scripture quotations marked New Living Translation (NLT) are taken from the Holy Bible, New Living Translation, copyright © 1996. Used by permission of Tyndale House Publishers, Inc., Wheaton, Illinois 60189. All rights reserved.
31 27 09 20 03

Table of Contents

Foreword		v
Preface		ix
1	Introduction	1
	Authorship	3
	Why Study a Letter to the Jews?	5
2	The Basis for Our Rest	7
3	Jesus Superior to Angels	17
4	Danger of Drifting	25
5	Jesus: Qualified Redeemer	39
6	Danger of Unbelief	47
7	Danger of Dull Hearing	55
8	Danger of Dormancy	73
9	Danger of Infancy	81
10	Danger of Departing	91
11	A High Priest After Melchizedek	107
12	The Work is Done	117
13	The New Covenant in Force	125
14	Danger of Despising	135
15	The Hall of Faith	149
16	Stay in the Race	165
17	Stay True	177
A	Fluff	187
B	The Scientific Method	193

		Scientific Method Defined	193
		Why Does It Work?	194
		Biblical Examples	194
	C	Trust the Math	199
	D	Frames of Reference	207
	E	Which Bible Translation?	211
	F	Deutero-Isaiah Hypothesis	225
	G	Post-Modern Philosophy	227
	H	Buzzword Bingo	231
		Heresy	231
		Apostasy	232
	I	Five Bible Commentators You Should Listen To	235
		1. Chuck Smith	235
		2. Jon Courson	235
		3. Walter Martin	236
		4. Chuck Missler	236
		5. John Loeffler	236
References			237

Foreword

Aside from tripping over two precious barn kittens, the first thing you may notice as you enter my stable is a large print hanging on the wall — three horses in a full gallop, running as hard as they can. Their environment is not ideal. It is dry, the soil's hard, no water can be seen for miles. Barren. Unforgiving. Desolate.

Paul tells us in Hebrews to "run with perseverance the race marked out for us." Until eight months ago, my race had always been easy. Unknown to me, the terrain would quickly change as I did not realize my life would soon mirror the image on the wall — running wildly through desolate and unforgiving terrain.

Despite undesirable conditions, the horses depict strength, determination, and perseverance, qualities reminding me of my Morgan mare, Maggie — a horse steadfast in the midst of life's adversity. She has been my closest, most trusted friend running beside me, showing me an escape to an otherwise cruel world.

It all started November 21st, 2012. My husband and I lost our beloved dog of ten years. For some people it would have been "just a dog," but for us, Happy was a member of the family. We were devastated. Little did we know, the turmoil and heartbreak was just beginning.

A month later while working in our stable, a pregnant mare kicked me six times. One kick included a blow to the back of my head, causing short term memory loss and information overload. When the physician came to run tests, he informed me if the horse were shod, the blow to my head would have been fatal.

That was a major turning point in my life, and I knew God was trying to get my attention. Housebound and bedbound left me constantly praying, seeking His will for my life He so graciously spared. I was left hopeful for the future and thankful I was still here to be the wife and mother He called me to be.

As my hope grew, so did the turmoil. A week after my accident, my mother was pinned by a draft horse, tearing all the cartilage surrounding her ribs. She was housebound and bedbound, just as I was. The bad news escalated as the days progressed, and the new-found hope dwindled.

Eight days after my mother's accident, my cousin died of pancreatic cancer. Ten days later, my sister-in-law passed away very unexpectedly at the young age of 44.

The hope that began as a flame dwindled, and was finally snuffed out, replaced by bitterness and depression growing rampantly inside me. I began to withdraw. I didn't make time for friends. I just wanted to be left alone and wallow in self-pity. I didn't understand why a loving God would allow so much persecution to happen to a God-loving family. To cope, I turned to Maggie for comfort. She was the only one who seemed to get it, providing me with an escape and carrying me onward when I was ready to give up.

Unfortunately, Maggie could not prevent the news we received four short days after my sister-in-law died. The news of one of my most treasured family members informing me they had cancer hit like a ton of bricks, harder than any horse could kick. Hearing those words and being completely caught off guard filled me with emptiness, fear, and utter despair. I curled in a ball and sobbed like a baby, pushing away anyone trying to provide comfort. I begged God to make it all go away. I yelled at Him...

> *Why are you doing this to us? You promised you would never, ever give me more than I can handle, yet here I am Lord. I am broken, I am depressed, I want to die, God. Why didn't you just let me die when I had the chance? I can't do this anymore.*

I continued in my fit of rage for quite some time. I ended my prayer asking "Why can't you just tell me, God? Why can't you just tell me how it's all going to end?" And for the first time in 34 years, God spoke loud and clear. He said, "Why can't you just trust me?"

The next day as I was on the back of my horse, I knew I was guilty of not putting 100% of my trust in a faithful, loving God. He was hurting with me. That evening, I made a commitment that I would trust Him fully, that I would lay it at His feet and allow my baggage to be used for His glory.

Foreword

Over the next few months, three more family members passed away. My nephew was incarcerated, my kids' cat died, and my grandmother was in a near fatal car accident. The last tragedy took place on August 14th, as I went out with a friend early morning to turn horses out. She noticed Maggie bleeding severely, blood flowing with a vengeance, leaving behind her a trail stained in dark red. Somehow Maggie managed to cut her foot, severing the heel bulb and cutting through the coronet band, barely missing a major artery by mere centimeters. I was devastated.

Most equine enthusiasts know that leg or hoof issues are not something to ignore. I knew I wouldn't be able to ride for quite some time and didn't know what Maggie's future would hold. My heart sank. During the past eight months of constant depression, Maggie was my rock. She provided the relief I needed after every disappointment entering my life. When I rode, I felt free, I felt safe, I felt every little hurt and reminder of what was happening in my life slowly disappear.

The night after Maggie hurt herself, I prayed for a full recovery. I prayed that God would hurry up and heal her so she in a sense could heal me. That night I was awoken at 3:45am. I heard the words "remain in me." Like a broken record, it kept repeating, "remain in me, remain in me." I asked God what He was trying to tell me and it all became clear. He said Maggie was the one I had ran to, through every disappointment, through every tragedy over the last eight months, when I should have run to *Him*. He said He had to remove her for a while, so that He could be my priority. He wanted to be first, He wanted to hear my cries, He wanted to provide me with that escape, and that sense of comfort and peace no one else could.

Someone once told me that God gives His toughest battles to His strongest soldiers. Sometimes we don't want to be soldiers because we choose to only see the pain and suffering involved in battle. We want to give up, rather than fight the good fight. God sees our battles as potential for new life, as we are being renewed day by day. Our light and momentary troubles are achieving in us an eternal glory far outweighing any trial we will ever encounter.*

God is the same yesterday, today, and tomorrow. He equips us as He runs beside us, carrying us through our times of heartache. And with God (not a pony), we can run just like those horses illustrated on my stable's wall — with strength, determination, and most of all, perseverance.

~ **Lindsey Bowers Tatum** September 2013

---

* 2 Corinthians 4:16

Preface

I'M A BIT OCD. WHEN WORKING, I USE A CALCULATOR to determine *exactly* how much weight, how high, or how far a job requires. While performing some construction, the task required moving bricks, and down at the local store I discovered they weighed 38 pounds each. Doing the math (knowing the job required 72 bricks), resulted in a total weight of 2,736 pounds.

Using a half-ton truck, those bricks require 3.42 trips. Nuts. Getting to the store requires a thirty minute drive (one disadvantage to small-town living — supplies can be a way off), this will take all day! Well, a friend who completed similar construction told me he finished in one trip.

How, I asked, did you borrow some farmer's truck? Nope, he carried it all in an old Nissan truck, saying "those weight limits are just recommendations."* Somehow he made it home, and I've learned being so OCD† isn't always good — his practical experience trumped my slide-rule.

I've never forgotten that, and if he tells me yeah, it'll handle it, that's good enough for me — I'm all-in. I'll be scared like a turkey on Thanksgiving, but I'm still all-in. Over the years I've learned to trust his opinion on similar matters. I've learned the hard way when you have no clue what you're doing, find someone who does know and listen to them. What could this possibly have to do with anything, you might ask. A legitimate question.

I first met the Tatums with a group watching soccer, just after the birth of their first child. The quiet types (I can relate to that),

---
* Please, do not ignore manufacturers' recommendations. Those limits exist for a reason.
† I really have CDO, as someone told me it's the same as OCD, but with the letters in alphabetical order *as they should be*.

it's hard to have a deep conversation during a sporting event (with the social skills of a grapefruit, talking wasn't on my agenda anyway). They were associates of my trusted friend who somehow managed to avoid destroying his truck, and since I *did* know his character, the fact he associated with them was good enough for me. Character by proxy, you might say.

That was years ago, and it turns out he knew of what he spoke — the Tatum family is of highest character. Before anyone points out their flaws, that does not mean they don't make mistakes, as we all do. No, that simply means these are people you want living next door, the ones you can count on when your back is to the wall. They simply won't quit — no matter how much they want to.

Allow me to digress a bit, and you'll discover why Lindsey Tatum's horse appears on the cover. Every teacher or speaker has phrases or words associated with them. I frequently use the same phrases over and over (and over), trying to make sure nobody forgets them.

- At 3 AM you've got what you've got.
- You may not get a Lexus, an ice cream, *or a pony.*

One Sunday while teaching, a trouble-maker sitting in the front row (actually one of our elders) waited ... waited ... waited to pounce. Then it came when I said "God doesn't guarantee you a pony," and that guy in the front row lept up out of his chair, jumped up to the podium, and placed on it a small toy pony, saying "now you've got one, brother." Needless to say, the church roared.

I'm glad people remember those words, and I'll keep using them. Over and over. And over. Like Peter, I will not be negligent to remind you of these things, even though you already know them. If that's good enough for Peter, I think the rest of us should follow the example.

The pony idea came to mind while I pondered ideas for the book's cover. I thought of Lindsey Tatum, as she's what you might call a horse guru. Personally, I try to stay away from things that are bigger, stronger, and can chase me down and kick me in the head, but I understand not everyone feels the same. As a caretaker of horses, she surely must have pictures I could use, so before I could think better of it, I messaged her about it and went off to work.

Had a weird idea this morning. Looking for ideas for the cover for my next book and thought of using a horse or pony.

> *Might you and the kids be interested? The title is "Stay in the Game, but you still don't get a pony."*
>
> *I'd include Jamie, but I think he shares my aversion to being in the same city as a horse.*

What I got back was not what I expected, to be sure. Not that she would turn me down, but quite a story exists *behind* the story.

> *Would love it!! I need to email you about something that happened last night when I have more time. God literally woke me up at 3:45 this morning.*

3 AM? That grabbed my interest *fast* — I'm always talking about 3 AM — and coincidence is not a kosher word. She laid out a story I didn't know half of. I've learned (the hard way) when strange things happen, it's usually the Lord getting involved, hitting me in the head with a clue by four.

Many people go through tough times, and many think they're all alone. Jamie and Lindsey have been through quite a bit in the last year, and their character and faith enabled them to make it through. You might be going through something right now, so remember, somebody has clawed over the same ground you have — you are never alone.

The Tatum's story illustrates my main message — stay in the game. Never quit, never give in, never surrender. After all, it's not going to get easier, as I'm sure the Tatums will tell you.

> *I have fought a good fight, I have finished my course, I have kept the faith.*   2 Timothy 4:7

And now, as Paul Harvey would say, you know *the rest of the story.*

Chapter *1*

Introduction

IF YOU READ "GET BACK IN THE GAME," YOU recall Zechariah and Haggai both spoke concerning rising off the couch and getting in the game. Too many Christians sit in pews week after month and never allow the Word to make a difference in their lives — sure, it works Sunday (and usually Wednesday too), but when the rubber meets the road at 3 AM they're woefully unprepared to handle the situation. Like an airplane running out of fuel at 30,000 feet, they nosedive into the ground in a spectacular fireball — it ain't pretty.

However, placing too much emphasis on work can lead to an erroneous conclusion — a Christian must continually work without a break (and if truly doing the Lord's work won't get tired), which leads to the b-word ... burnout. Yes, the time has come to get off the bench and join the game (as it's the fourth quarter and we rapidly approach the two-minute warning), but it's also a time to *rest*. What? Aren't those ideas contradictory? Nope.

In order to work, you must rest, but not sitting on the couch eating Bon-Bons while watching MTV. No, the rest you require involves answering a simple question — who is Jesus? You're told frequently to rest in Christ, but what does that mean? More specifically, who is this Jesus you should rest in? If you don't know who He is, how can you rest in Him?

That's what concerns the writer of Hebrews. If you have the desire to work for the Lord, you must understand work and rest, and understand rest does not mean cessation of activity. During a pastor's conference a speaker said if you can do anything else besides ministry, do it. He spoke about pastors, the idea if being a pastor isn't the driving force in your life, if it's not what you can't wait to get out of bed to do, it might just be you *should* do something else.

Lest you think that strange, it comes straight from the Bible, as Jeremiah started the idea. You can imagine poor Jeremiah, as he watched the country he loved slowly slide down into the tar pit of abandoning God. Sadly, the only thing man learns from history is man learns nothing from history, as J. Vernon McGee notes:

> *You and I are living at a time which is probably like the time of Jeremiah. Ours is a great nation today, and we have accomplished many things. We have gone to the moon, and we have produced atom bombs. Although we are a strong nation, within is the same corruption which will carry us down to dismemberment and disaster. It is coming, my friend.**

Not exactly the most encouraging situation, so you can imagine each time Jeremiah spoke for the Lord and something unpleasant happened to him, eventually the thought occurred, hey, why don't I stop speaking what the Lord says? Whenever I do, a disaster follows. Only one problem with his plan — it didn't work.

> *Then I said, I will not make mention of him, nor speak any more in his name. But his word was in mine heart as a burning fire shut up in my bones, and I was weary with forbearing, and I could not refrain.* Jeremiah 20:9

Jeremiah *couldn't* do anything else, God lit a burning fire deep in his bones, and he simply could not contain it. That's the fire you need. If you can do *anything* else, do it, an idea applying to more than pastors, it applies to any gifts of the spirit; if you dread performing your "ministry," perhaps the Lord called you in other areas. Simply put, you're not resting — yes Virginia, you can rest while working.

Our fellowship has a guy who plays piano a little, and if he didn't do what he did his head would explode (sorry for the picture). It's his nature, what drives him, what he enjoys, and what he's good at. Another person would require canceling "American Idol" if they ever appeared on it, for nobody with a better voice will ever be found; God reached down and changed vocal chords to pure gold. Someone else casually mentioned they had a few minutes between Wednesday and Sunday so taught themselves how to play bass.

---

*   McGee (1982a, page 351)

Introduction

Musicians can't comprehend how non-musical the average person is; I tried for years to play guitar, never making it past … well, I never made it *to* beginner status. The result was … less than satisfactory (to be an understatement).

Musicians demonstrate God's gifting and the burning passion deep inside. They work at it, but at the same time the music simply flows out — they can't help it. Like Jeremiah, the Lord gave them a passion and a gift they can't contain. Yet those abilities aren't typical. I use musicians as examples because they seem strange to me, as someone struggling to play the radio. They have no choice, they can't hold back even if they wanted to. Like filling up a balloon, eventually the pressure *must* release, or it explodes.

Naturally, even possessing the burning passion, you still get tired. If you're tired, but motivated, that's good. You *will* get tired in your service for God. You need rest, but we must define the type of rest required if you're going to be effective for God. Not rest as in watching TV while eating Bon-Bons, we're talking about spiritual rest. It's comfort. It's knowing who He is, and your relationship with Him. It's not inactivity. Hebrews concerns rest; many Christians don't avail themselves of the rest God provides, and struggle in their efforts instead.

Authorship

Before we jump into the book, we must discuss a small side issue — the authorship of the book, as it's an unsigned letter. Many Bibles label it "The epistle of Paul to the Hebrews," but that's a guess (one I happen to agree with).

Why would Paul not sign it? As you travel through Acts, you notice every time Paul spoke to the Jews it didn't turn out well. They tried to kill him, started riots, and generally were less than receptive to his message. For that reason, if Paul authored a letter to the Jews, he would not necessarily want it associated with him.

It also won't mention apostolic authority, rather the arguments originate from the Old Testament and are presented as a lawyer in a courtroom — much like Romans. If you've noticed a style similar to Romans, it could be the same author used a common style when writing both.

A casual reading reveals Pauline style — long sentences, detailed arguments, lofty subjects, and more. That's not proof, but it matches Paul's other letters, and some of what Hebrews contains appears in Paul's other writings.

> *For when for the time ye ought to be teachers, ye have need that one teach you again the first principles of the oracles of God, and are become such as have need of milk, and not of solid food. For every one that useth milk is unskillful in the word of righteousness; for he is a babe.* Hebrews 5:12–13

That sounds similar to Paul's instruction to Corinth, does it not? Once again, that doesn't *prove* Pauline authorship, but it supplies a strong hint; another hint of Paul's authorship comes from Peter:

> *And account that the longsuffering of our Lord is salvation, even as our beloved brother Paul also according to the wisdom given unto him hath written unto you; As also in all his epistles, speaking in them of these things; in which are some things hard to be understood, which they that are unlearned and unstable wrest, as they do also the other scriptures, unto their own destruction.* 2 Peter 3:15–16

As the apostle to the Jews, Peter mentions two ideas hinting of a Pauline letter to the Jews (if not Hebrews this means Paul wrote a letter not preserved for some reason):

1. Peter says Paul wrote to you (Jews).

2. "Some things are hard to understand."

If you've read the book of Hebrews, you know sections still cause big debates, as the letter contains some of the most debated and difficult passages in the Bible. The author also mentions Timothy, and we know Timothy traveled with Paul. As J. Vernon McGee says of the authorship:

> *... there is abundant evidence that Paul was the author. Both internal and external evidence support the authorship of Paul. The writer had been in bonds (Hebrews 10:34). He wrote from Italy (Hebrews 13:24). His companion was Timothy (Hebrews 13:23). The writing is Pauline. Also, in my opinion, Peter identifies Paul as the writer (see 2 Peter 3:15–16).**

Finally, the book closes with "I have written a letter unto you in few words"; classic Pauline style — after thirteen difficult chapters, he laments he wrote in few words!

---

*   McGee (1982b, page 503)

While not conclusive, more evidence points to Paul's pen than others, so most likely the author is either Paul or unknown. Others disagree with Paul's authorship, and that's not a big deal. If God needed us to have a definite answer to the authorship, He would have told us. The authorship of Hebrews adds to the list of battles not worth fighting; like the identity of the two witnesses in Revelation, we apparently don't need to know; the message demands attention, not the author.

Why Study a Letter to the Jews?

While living as New Testament Christians, one tragedy arises from Christians discarding the Old Testament. Yes, it's true we're freed from Mosaic Law, but that does not mean we should not study it, as Paul told the Corinthians those lessons from the Old Testament were for our learning.

As we learned from Zechariah, we face similar problems to the Jews. This time it's legalism, religiosity, and a failure to rest in Christ for His completed work. Does that sound familiar? Many Christians suffer from the same disease, so Paul's letter to the Hebrews provides us the solution to the malady, exactly as it did for first century Hebrews.

Hebrews demonstrates Jesus' superiority over religion. Enter the rest God designed, and stop working for it. It's not Jesus plus anything, it's Jesus. Period. Sure, you know that; we're saved by faith, not works. Yet how often do we labor and toil instead of resting?

Don't just do something, stand there.

Chapter 2

The Basis for Our Rest

As we jump into the book, the first few verses present three types of rest Christians commonly struggle with, involving rest for your spirit, not your body. If you understand these three, you'll be relieved of many problems facing other Christians.

> *God, who at sundry times and in diverse manners spoke in time past unto the fathers by the prophets.*   Hebrews 1:1

Similar to Moses writing in Genesis, Paul presents no arguments for God's existence, he simply assumes you understand. Unfortunately, man attempts to satisfy his thirst for proving God exists with various philosophical proofs, most of which fail to appease the god-denier.

Ontological — The argument states if you can imagine in your mind a perfect, ultimate, greatest possible being — but that being didn't exist — then that being would *not* be perfect and ultimate, since it lacks a trait (existence) without which it could not be perfect. If that sounds like philosophical mumbo-jumbo similar to asking how many angels can dance on the head of a pin, yeah, it sounds that way to me too, so we'll move on.

Cosmological — Since the universe exists, it must be caused by something, and that something must be caused by something, and so on. Eventually a first cause must exist, as infinite chains of causes can't exist; that first cause is God.

Teleological — The universe appears as an ordered, designed system, thus it must have a designer. Design implies a designer; if you're handed a watch, you don't believe it magically and spontaneously appeared, you understand a team of engineers designed it, while precision machinery constructed it. Similarly, the ordered universe must have a designer, God.

The argument (while not a proof) certainly has merit. Science and other disciplines work because we inhabit an ordered and designed universe. If you purchased a computer program, would you think it resulted from design, or chance? Obviously design, since we call random, non-designed features in computer programs *bugs*. Nobody uses a computer program and believes it came from anything other than skilled and talented programmers.

Yet when considering the universe, suddenly the atheist shifts thinking — while not denying the designed nature of software, the atheist looks at the ordered, designed universe and proclaims poof! This came from nothing! No designer. Is that a logical position to take? Design and structure implies a designer.

TRANSCENDENTAL — An argument from morality and logic, which exist universally *apart from the cosmos*. Those values existed before, and will continue after, the universe exists. Again, this does not *prove* God exists, but it does leave the atheist in a bit of a quandary. If no god exists, how do you define morality? A question posed to Richard Dawkins, the face of modern atheism.

> *"What defines your morality?" I asked with genuine curiosity.*
>
> *There was an extended pause as Dawkins considered the question carefully. "Moral philosophic reasoning and a shifting zeitgeist." ...*
>
> *I asked an obvious question: "As we speak of this shifting zeitgeist, how are we to determine who's right? ...*
>
> *"Yes, absolutely fascinating." His response was immediate. "What's to prevent us from saying Hitler wasn't right? I mean, that is a genuinely difficult question. But whatever [defines morality], it's not the Bible. If it was, we'd be stoning people for breaking the Sabbath."*
>
> *I was stupefied. He had readily conceded that his own philosophical position did not offer a rational basis for moral judgments. His intellectual honesty was refreshing, if somewhat disturbing on this point.**

Like the interviewer, we give Dawkins credit for admitting atheism provides no rational basis for morality. What Dawkins de-

---

*   Taunton (2007)

scribes yields nothing more than majority rules (zeitgeist*). That does not mean atheists can't *be* moral, or act in moral fashion, but atheism provides no basis for morality. Ultimately, morality comes from the God they seek to deny.

Are any philosophical arguments for God acceptable? Not really — if the supernatural exists, it (by definition) can't be deducted by ordinary means, so attempts to prove the existence of God won't be satisfactory. Interestingly, one idea my philosophy professor *did* find persuasive was CS Lewis' discussion of Jesus, although it's not actually a proof for God.

> *I am trying here to prevent anyone saying the really foolish thing that people often say about Him: "I'm ready to accept Jesus as a great moral teacher, but I don't accept His claim to be God." That is the one thing we must not say. A man who was merely a man and said the sort of things Jesus said would not be a great moral teacher. He would either be a lunatic—on a level with the man who says he is a poached egg—or else he would be the Devil of Hell. You must make your choice. Either this man was, and is, the Son of God: or else a madman or something worse. You can shut Him up for a fool, you can spit at Him and kill Him as a demon; or you can fall at His feet and call Him Lord and God. But let us not come with any patronizing nonsense about His being a great human teacher. He has not left that open to us. He did not intend to.*[†]

Since Jesus claimed to be God, He either was or wasn't. If He was, we should acknowledge Him as such. But if not, if He knew He didn't speak the truth, He was a liar. If, however, He honestly thought He was God (but wasn't), that means He was mentally challenged, or delusional. In either case, He lacks the power to save Himself, much less all mankind, so anyone trusting in Him remains lost, as well as being a fool.

It's not profitable to try to prove God's existence, and don't expect to persuade people lacking a belief in God. Of course, atheists claiming God *doesn't* exist (and thus are more enlightened

---

[*] Zeitgeist means spirit of the age, or what society determines to be right and wrong at a specific point in time. Previously "bad" actions could thus later be good, and vice-versa. No absolute morality exists, which is why Dawkins asks what prevents us from saying Hitler was right. You can think of it as value relativism in a society void of absolute morality.

[†] Lewis (1969, page 55–56)

and intelligent than their religious counterparts) find themselves trapped by a logical problem of their own creation.

Atheism will always be (by definition) illogical for the simple reason you can't state God does not exist unless you possess all knowledge. If you don't know everything in the cosmos (and outside it), God can exist outside your knowledge, unknown to you. Atheism fails to follow logic, holding an illogical (and unprovable) position; its followers accept it on faith, without proof, logic, or reason. Only by possessing *all* knowledge can a person with certainty state no god exists.

Nobody's saying you can't *believe* there is no God, only if you choose to make that statement you're taking it on *faith*, not reason, critical thinking, or logic; don't confuse logic with *proof.* None of this proves God does or does not exist, only the atheist claim "there is no God" equates to immature gibberish devoid of logic and critical thinking — you're free to believe nonsense if you wish, but don't call it reasoned and logical.

You're left with the basic dilemma — you can't prove or disprove God — you can only examine the evidence you have, and arrive at a reasonable conclusion. Either God exists, or we evolved from slime. You don't get another option.* Unfortunately, evolution doesn't work, as it violates the laws of Physics, having no scientific evidence (that means repeatable, published, experimental evidence) for its foundations (matter comes from nothing, non-living goo becomes alive, and so on).

Thus, a god (little g) must exist. The question: which one? That's what I call the confusion of religion — a topic we'll focus on shortly, so hang on as we return to Hebrews. God has been clear on what He expects. Not only in the prophets and Old Testament, but creation itself, as Paul notes elsewhere.

> *Because that which may be known of God is manifest in them; for God hath shown it unto them. For the invisible things of him from the creation of the world are clearly seen, being understood by the things that are made, even his eternal power and Godhead; so that they are without excuse.*
>
> Romans 1:19-20

God spoke by the prophets many times. What happened? People mocked and rejected their words (and thus by extension, God), and persecuted the prophets themselves. God finally sent

---

*   Some propose a third option: space aliens deposited us here. Aliens, however, either evolved or were created, so you're right back to square one.

His Son, and we all know He wasn't treated much differently from any Old Testament prophets.

> *Hath in these last days spoken unto us by his Son, whom he hath appointed heir of all things, by whom also he made the worlds;* Hebrews 1:2

Worlds in Greek is not cosmos, but aion, referring to time or age. It's broader in scope than simply the physical universe.

In regard to creation, Paul makes an unqualified, clear statement as Moses did. It wasn't from the goo to the zoo to you, as evolution remains unscientific; actual science requires something called the scientific method. In short, you make a guess, then design and perform experiments to either confirm or disprove your guess. The scientist then modifies the guess depending on experimental results. So what proof (experimental evidence) exists for the following foundational evolutionary concepts?

1. Matter coming from nothing.

2. Goo suddenly becoming alive.

3. Monkeys transforming into humans.

If you can't provide reproducible experimental data for those guesses, it's not science, *by definition*. Worse, those ideas fly in the face of what we *do* know about the universe. Matter coming from nothing runs into problems with Einstein's $E = mc^2$ concept. Everyone has seen the equation (at least if you ever watched "The Twilight Zone"), but few understand what it means — energy equals mass times the speed of light squared. That might not mean much to you, but one critical idea follows from it: energy can change from one form to another, but can't be created — it's a zero sum game.

For example, if you live in a cold climate, you might use a wood stove to keep warm. Each day you shove blocks of wood inside, and what do you obtain? The wood turns to ash, as the matter of the wood turns to energy (heat).

If you approached a scientist to claim Einstein's equation didn't hold you'd be laughed out of the room, save one class — biology. In that class, evolution ignores one of the most famous scientific laws. Somehow, sometime, someway, something violated Einstein's law — a violation without experimental evidence or actual observation, as evolutionists cast aside any scientific laws they must for their guess to work.

That's not science. For what reason would you believe the laws of Physics don't apply? Only because your theory requires it. That's not the only area of evolution casting aside scientific principles for the guesswork of the unproven; consider abiogenesis or spontaneous generation of life. Has spontaneous generation of life from non-life *ever* been observed? Nope. Once again, if you took a bucket of slime to a scientist, and told him if he simply waited, eventually an entire ecosystem would appear, you'd be laughed out of the room ... unless that room is a biology class.

Ordered rules exist for the universe — which we don't normally see broken — but we're going to *assume* sometime in Mr. Peabody's wayback machine they *were* broken long enough for goo to appear from nothing and come alive. Right. And they say religious people have blind faith?

As we discuss rest, many people struggle with evolution, trying to cram it into the Bible. But it won't fit, and the attempt causes much unrest we find in the church. Yet some try, claiming the creation in Genesis 1 could be ages; each day, they argue, could be billions of years, thus showing God used evolution to create. This idea goes by the name day-age theory, and to some extent it contains truth, as the Hebrew word for day can also mean age or time period.

Before entropy existed no decay occurred, thus no method to detect passage of time, because dating methods rely on decay or similar idea coming from entropy. The problem with the day-age theory (trying to cram the square peg of evolution into the round hole of the Bible) isn't in Genesis, but Exodus.

> *Six days shalt thou labor, and do all thy work; But the seventh day is the sabbath of the Lord thy God; in it thou shalt not do any work, thou, nor thy son, nor thy daughter, thy manservant, nor thy maidservant, nor thy cattle, nor thy stranger that is within thy gates; For in six days the Lord made heaven and earth, the sea, and all that in them is, and rested the seventh day; wherefore the Lord blessed the sabbath day, and hallowed it.* Exodus 20:9-11

Context makes clear the day spoken of contains 24 hours. You're free to accept or reject that as you wish, but the Bible speaks clearly: God created in six 24 hour days, not billions of years. Don't try and meld the unscientific idea of evolution with the rock-solid ground of God's Word.

Finally, discussions surrounding the age of the universe always fail to take relativity into account. What reference frame are you considering? Time is not absolute — you can't actually speak of a period of billions of years. Absolute time periods only exist in a specified reference frame, a certain quantity that may or may not be equal in other reference frames.*

I spent years requesting evidence claimed to exist for evolution. Nobody could provide it,† so in May 2010 I finally gave up, and wrote evolution: case closed, saying "Thus, we're putting this discussion on the back burner until they ... you know, actually have *science* behind them we can discuss." It's been a few years, and nobody provided actual scientific evidence for the first steps in the evolutionary process. Until they do, relegate their unsubstantiated ideas to philosophy class.

The first rest you must realize remains simple: Genesis 1:1: "In the beginning God created the heaven and the earth." Period. You believe it, but do you rest in it?

> *Who, being the brightness of his glory, and the express image of his person, and upholding all things by the word of his power, when he had by himself purged our sins, sat down on the right hand of the Majesty on high;* Hebrews 1:3

The Greek for express image implies character, appearing only here in the New Testament. Everyone wants to see god and be "spiritual," with everyone pointing this way to god, that way to god, I'm a guru and can really show you the way. Those same gurus reject Jesus as creator and Lord, thus they'll never find God as Jesus represents the express image of God.

In John 14, Phillip expresses the same problem everyone shares today (nothing ever changes, does it?). Frustrated by vague and unsuccessful attempts to find God, he said to Jesus show us the Father, and that's good enough for us. Jesus provides one of those strange responses, saying if you've seen Me you've seen the Father, why do you ask then to see the Father?

---

* Generally, we *are* all in the same reference frame, so for most purposes it can be ignored, which is why in normal conservation we don't discuss it. However, when talking about vastly different conditions of gravity, mass, and velocity (such as the big bang), those relativistic effects must be considered.

† Evidence requires use of the scientific method, meaning reproducible, peer-reviewed laboratory experiments. I received lots of name-calling, but nothing meeting the demands of the scientific method.

The second rest ... if you're struggling to find God, look to Jesus. Much of Hebrew's remainder will involve Jesus as superior — to angels, to Moses, to the priesthood, creation, and everything. If you don't understand Jesus as superior and the express image of God, you'll miss the rest God wants you to have.

Paul mentions Jesus as "upholding all things by the word of His power," something quite similar to what he told the church at Colosse.

And he is before all things, and by him all things consist.
Colossians 1:17

Consist in Greek means holding together, which may not mean much without a sidebar on Physics. Recall your high school Physics? Sure you do ... inside the atom exist protons and neutrons. But wait, like charges (protons) repel each other. So what holds it together? Well, it's something called the "strong nuclear force." Which, as Paul told you, is Jesus — right now Jesus personally prevents each atom in the universe from flying apart.

Peter reminds us "the heavens shall pass away with a great noise, and the elements shall melt with fervent heat, the earth also and the works that are therein shall be burned up." What's that? The biggest atomic explosion ever. An atomic weapon contains only a few pounds of material — can you imagine the power released when the entire cosmos explodes? Of course, that means it requires that much power to hold it together right now. How big is your God?

He by Himself — third rest. You don't add anything. It's not Jesus plus. Many people struggle with works verses faith. But frequently they don't follow through to its logical conclusion. If you believe you do something to either get or maintain salvation, that means Jesus' work on the cross was both insufficient and incomplete for salvation. That's not a good place to be.

Jesus sat down? Why? Was He tired? Similar to God creating in six days and resting on the seventh, He didn't rest because He was tired, but because nothing remained to do. The work completed, thus no reason exists to stand.

In the first three verses, Paul presents three types of rest Christians frequently don't have.

1. God created heavens and earth.

2. Jesus represents the express image of God.

3. He by Himself purged our sin.

So why rest? We'll discover Christ superior to Moses, Law, humanity, and more in the following chapters.

Chapter 3

Jesus Superior to Angels

WE'VE DISCUSSED REST, HOW REST ISN'T A cessation of activity. What we're getting at is rest in Christ. But that begs the question, who is Jesus? *Why* should you rest in Him? With so many people shouting "this way to god," you're left with the confusion of religion. Can you possibly *know*?

The Confusion of Religion

In the next section Paul demonstrates Jesus' superiority over angels. That, of course, means He's not one of them, an idea some groups reject. As we'll discover, the problem stems not from denying Jesus is God — everyone remains free to accept or reject Him as they wish — the problem arises when they *also* state they accept the Bible. Contrary to the popular teaching of value relativism, absolute right and wrong *do* exist — even fake TV characters know it, as a famous TV doctor said:

> *Right and wrong do exist. Just because you don't know what the right answer is—maybe there's even no way you could know what the right answer is—doesn't make your answer right or even okay. It's much simpler than that. It's just plain wrong.**

In medicine, you're either right or wrong. Heal the patient or kill him. No middle ground exists, no passing the buck, no value relativism. You don't want your doctor to say, "well, antibiotics

---

*   "House" (the TV Show) Season One, Episode 121 "Three Stories"

being the best way to treat an infection may be truth for you, but I think jumping up and down yelling 'I'm cured' while eating grapefruit is truth." You'd certainly run away from such medical absurdity, would you not?

Claiming Jesus isn't God — but one of the angels — remains a common idea among various groups. From a created being to Satan or Michael's brother, denying Jesus' deity is popular. The question is not is it popular, but is it *true*.

If someone says Jesus isn't God that's their choice — they're free to accept or reject Him as they wish. However, people should understand when their positions (like atheism, liberal theology, social justice, etc.) create logical problems. The only way to escape the absurdity those ideas create comes from cognitive dissonance (or what Orwell called DoubleThink) — the ability to hold conflicting positions simultaneously, and yet believe both.

Cognitive dissonance allows the atheist to make the absurd statement "there is no god" while boldly proclaiming to be the pinnacle of logic and intelligence. It allows the social justice promoter to claim social justice is integral to the Gospel, ignoring Paul's clear definition in 1 Corinthians 15 (and his warning concerning alternate gospels in Galatians). It allows the value relativist to—at the same time—declare no absolutes exist ... absolutely (the liars paradox).

Those illogical ideas allow someone to feel comfortable denying reality, while reasonable analysis proves them to be illogical and absurd. The *only* way the human brain can accept contradictory ideas comes via cognitive dissonance. Here's where groups denying the deity of Jesus (while claiming to accept the Bible) run into cognitive dissonance. Take them to Isaiah:

> *In the year that king Uzziah died I saw also the Lord sitting upon a throne, high and lifted up, and his train filled the temple. Above it stood the seraphim; each one had six wings; with two he covered his face, and with two he covered his feet, and with two he did fly. And one cried unto another, and said, Holy, holy, holy, is the Lord of hosts; the whole earth is full of his glory. And the posts of the door moved at the voice of him that cried, and the house was filled with smoke. Then said I, Woe is me! For I am undone; because I am a man of unclean lips, and I dwell in the midst of a people of unclean lips; for mine eyes have seen the King, the Lord of hosts.* Isaiah 6:1–5

Ask them who that is, and they'll respond, "why, that's Jehovah God!" Right? Right! Now flip over to John's gospel.

> *But though he had done so many miracles before them, yet they believed not on him; That the saying of Isaiah the prophet might be fulfilled, which he spoke, Lord, who hath believed our report? And to whom hath the arm of the Lord been revealed? Therefore they could not believe, because that Isaiah said again, He hath blinded their eyes, and hardened their heart; that they should not see with their eyes, nor understand with their heart, and be converted, and I should heal them. These things said Isaiah, when he saw his glory, and spoke of him.* John 12:37–41

This passage contains many pronouns, but backing up a bit it's clear John refers to Jesus; your Bible likely references back to Isaiah 6 as Isaiah seeing the Lord's glory.

But we already established Isaiah saw Jehovah God, thus ... Jesus *is* God. Immediately when these facts become known you'll see cognitive dissonance kick in. They simply can't let go of their idea Jesus isn't God, yet they accept the Bible — ideas unable to be held at the same time. You can say Jesus isn't God, or say you accept the Bible, but you can't have both. It's simply not possible. But wait (as the late night infomercials say), there's more.

> *Who hath wrought and done it, calling the generations from the beginning? I the Lord, the first, and with the last; I am he.* Isaiah 41:4

Who's that? That's Jehovah God, right? Right!

> *Thus saith the Lord the King of Israel, and his redeemer, the Lord of hosts: I am the first, and I am the last, and beside me there is no God.* Isaiah 44:6

Who's that? That's Jehovah God, right? Right!

> *I am Alpha and Omega, the beginning and the ending, saith the Lord, who is, and who was, and who is to come, the Almighty.* Revelation 1:8

Who's that? That's Jehovah God, right? Right! Well ... sort of. Your Bible likely prints this verse in red-letter, indicating words of Jesus. However, for the sake of argument we'll let it slide and agree it's Jehovah God. Notice in all these verses Jehovah God says He's the first and the last, right? Right!

> *And when I saw him, I fell at his feet as dead. And he laid his right hand upon me, saying unto me, Fear not; I am the first and the last; I am he that liveth, and was dead; and, behold, I am alive for evermore, Amen; and have the keys of hell and of death.* Revelation 1:17-18

Who's that? They'll follow the pattern and bleep out it's Jehovah God, but likely miss the rest. The first and last, but dead and now alive? When did God die? Oops — they've got problems right here in River City. Only Jesus Himself fits that description, but it's already established the first and the last is God, thus Jesus *is* God. And they proved it themselves! No way out of this exists. You can't have two firsts, or one isn't actually first; it must be the same entity.

We've got a problem. Jesus from the Bible *is* God, yet they stand at the door saying He isn't, *and* they accept the Bible. It's a perfect case of cognitive dissonance, as both statements can't be true at the same time. Notice we're not saying which *is* true (that's a discussion for another time), only pointing out to any group saying Jesus is not God, yet they believe the Bible, find themselves in a hopelessly illogical position.

At least one of their ideas *must* be wrong. If I say the sky is green, and you say it's yellow, at least *one* of us is wrong (maybe both), but both *can't* be right since they contradict each other. That's the position they find themselves in. Finally, take them to Paul's letter to the Galatians:

> *I marvel that ye are so soon removed from him that called you into the grace of Christ unto another gospel, which is not another; but there be some that trouble you, and would pervert the gospel of Christ. But though we, or an angel from heaven, preach any other gospel unto you than that which we have preached unto you, let him be accursed.* Galatians 1:6-8

If at least one is wrong, *and* Paul warns about alternative gospels he didn't teach, which idea should you drop? The one in the Bible, *or* the one coming by a prophet, angel, or radical political philosophy *after* the Bible? This is unarguable logic, not an opinion or analysis of fact. At no point did this discussion say Jesus is—or is not—God. It only proves without cognitive dissonance you must choose between denying the deity of Jesus and accepting the Bible as true.

This "middle ground" (much like CS Lewis' trilema) doesn't leave open the possibility for what so many people like to live by.

Jesus Superior to Angels

Sure, I'm a Christian and go to church, but Jesus? Nah, He's not really Lord, He's the man upstairs. After all, I'm a pretty good guy, so I don't really need to confess Jesus as Lord, right? You can't believe the Bible and deny the deity of Christ. At least one of those ideas *must* be abandoned.

Do *not* call them a cult, don't argue with them, because at this point they'll be quite frustrated. Remind them you're on their side, you admire their knocking on doors, but they hold two positions that can't both be true *at the same time*. You won't tell them which to believe, but at least one of those ideas they claim to hold *must* be false.

Other groups claim Jesus was resurrected a spiritual being, not physical. This isn't a new heresy, as early in the first century the Gnostics taught since matter is evil, Jesus couldn't be an actual physical person, He was resurrected a spiritual being because all matter is corrupted. Really? For those groups, try John 2.

> *Then answered the Jews and said unto him, What sign showest thou unto us, seeing that thou doest these things? Jesus answered and said unto them, Destroy this temple, and in three days I will raise it up. Then said the Jews, Forty and six years was this temple in building, and wilt thou raise it up in three days? But he spoke of the temple of his body.*
> John 2:18-21

What? Jesus said He'll raise up His *body* again in three days. Sorry Gnostics. Finally, for those who don't believe Jesus claimed to be God, recall a verse in John 10 as once again, the Jewish leaders desire to stone Jesus.

> *The Jews answered him, saying, For a good work we stone thee not, but for blasphemy; and because that thou, being a man, makest thyself God.*
> John 10:33

Why? Because Jesus claimed to be God. At least the Pharisees understood what Jesus *claimed* to be. They might have rejected it, but they understood the claim, something many people today miss. So the question is Jesus claimed to be God, do you believe it?

Whenever you're talking to *anyone* the question that counts is who is Jesus? Get them to define terms. The Jesus many people talk about is *not* the Jesus of the Bible. Specifically, He can *not* be a "good teacher," as CS Lewis said He's either Lord, Liar, or a Lunatic, but not a good teacher. Since He claimed to be God, that option isn't available. When you talk to people, *get them to define Jesus.* That's the name of the game. You'll discover people might sound thoroughly orthodox, but when you finally pin them down, they do not believe in the Jesus and Gospel of the Bible. Why does this matter? Paul spends quite a bit of time telling you the nature of Jesus.

Paul's Argument Jesus Superior to Angels

Jesus claimed to be God. Paul certainly accepted that. But he writes to the Hebrews, so he presents an argument from the Old Testament. Paul specifically says Jesus is above the angels, thus that means He's not one of them. You don't worship angels. Some guys tried in the Bible, but it's not allowed.

> *And I fell at his feet to worship him. And he said unto me, See thou do it not! I am thy fellow servant, and of thy brethren that have the testimony of Jesus. Worship God; for the testimony of Jesus is the spirit of prophecy.* Revelation 19:10

> *And I, John, saw these things, and heard them. And when I had heard and seen, I fell down to worship before the feet of the angel who showed me these things. Then saith he unto me, See thou do it not; for I am thy fellow servant, and of thy brethren the prophets, and of them which keep the words of this book. Worship God.* Revelation 22:8–9

Yet you *should* worship Jesus, which tells you He's not an angel. That should be enough proof, but common sense isn't so common anymore. Travel to Luke 19:28–40 for what we call Palm Sunday. Luke mentions the Pharisees wanted to stop the crowd, but why? Because they proclaimed Jesus as Messiah and God, and surely they didn't want the crowd blaspheming, did they? Paul's first point, Jesus is above the angels.

> *Being made so much better than the angels, as he hath by inheritance obtained a more excellent name than they.* Hebrews 1:4

Many people hold the mistaken idea a great battle exists between God and Satan, as if they're equals. Satan is an angel, while Paul spends the rest of the chapter showing Jesus is *superior* to angels, thus they're not equal. Satan's two great deceptions are either to deny he exists, or he does exist but is equal to God so the outcome is in doubt. Nobody disagrees Satan is an angel; Paul demonstrates Jesus' superiority over angels, thus the supposed battle between Satan and Jesus isn't much of an event.

> *For unto which of the angels said he at any time, Thou art my Son, this day have I begotten thee? And again, I will be to him a Father, and he shall be to me a Son?* Hebrews 1:5

The Bible can use first-begotten not as time, but prominence. In Jeremiah 31:9 the Lord says I am a father to Israel, and Ephraim is my firstborn, but when you look back in Genesis who was Joseph's first — by time — born?

Manasseh.* Recall when Joseph brought his two sons for Israel to bless, he placed Manasseh on his left so Israel would use his right hand to bless him, but Israel crossed his hands, meaning Ephraim will be firstborn in prominence, even though he was born second. Be careful. Firstborn can mean time, but it can mean prominence.

When did God say "This is my son"? Twice. At the baptism of Jesus (Matthew 3:17), and transfiguration (Matthew 17:5) the Father proclaims Jesus as His son.

The second part of the verse comes from 2 Samuel 7:14 — a chapter speaking of the covenant with David, and in verse 16 David's house and kingdom will be established forever. Paul establishes the idea when verses aren't directly speaking of the Messiah, they can have a secondary meaning about the Messiah. Many times when the Bible contains secondary meanings, they aren't known until after the event occurs. Paul (and other New Testament writers) reveal Old Testament writings secondary prophecies about Jesus.

> *And again, when he bringeth in the first-begotten into the world, he saith, And let all the angels of God worship him. And of the angels he saith, Who maketh his angels spirits, and his ministers a flame of fire.* Hebrews 1:6–7

If all the angels are to worship Him, that means He's above them (since the lesser worships the greater), thus He can't be an angel. The first chapter of Hebrews proves devastating to those groups claiming Jesus as one of the angels.

---

* Genesis 41:51-52, 48:12–19

> *But unto the Son he saith, Thy throne, O God, is for ever and ever; a scepter of righteousness is the scepter of thy kingdom. Thou hast loved righteousness, and hated iniquity; therefore God, even thy God, hath anointed thee with the oil of gladness above thy fellows.* Hebrews 1:8–9

He rules by righteousness forever, something to remember as society continues to degrade. When things aren't going your way, when life is tough, when it seems like the bad guys win, remember God hates evil and loves righteousness, and the current state of the universe will not be permanent.

> *And, Thou, Lord, in the beginning hast laid the foundation of the earth; and the heavens are the works of thine hands. They shall perish; but thou remainest; and they all shall wax old as doth a garment; And as a vesture shalt thou fold them up, and they shall be changed; but thou art the same, and thy years shall not fail.* Hebrews 1:10–12

Jesus was involved in creation back in Genesis. What angel was involved in creation? None. Paul continues to present argument after argument proving Jesus not only can't be an angel, but He rises above all in prominence, power, and, of course, deity.

Notice Paul agrees with Peter in 2 Peter 3:10 when he states the cosmos will "wax old as a garment" — a statement of entropy as everything trends to chaos and disorder.

> *But to which of the angels said he at any time, Sit on my right hand, until I make thine enemies thy footstool? Are they not all ministering spirits, sent forth to minister for them who shall be heirs of salvation?* Hebrews 1:13–14

Paul concludes his list of differences between Jesus and the angels as He's treated differently in several ways.

- To no angel did God say "This is my Son."
- Angels are not to be worshiped.
- Angels are not on the throne.
- Angels are not involved in creation.
- Angels are not on the right hand of the Father.

Angels exist simply as ministering spirits. Thus, Jesus is not only *not* an angel, He is superior to all of them. You can rest in that.

Chapter 4

Danger of Drifting

PAUL PROVIDES HIS FIRST OF SEVERAL WARNINGS, as rest does not mean cessation of activity or apathy, it means staying focused in the game and on the prize, but without worry or anxiety. Remember, you *can* rest while working.

> *Therefore we ought to give the more earnest heed to the things which we have heard, lest at any time we should let them slip.*
> Hebrews 2:1

Different translations render drift away in place of slip, as Zodhiates notes the definition means "To float by or drift past as a ship, or to flow past as a river. Figuratively to slip away, suggesting a gradual and almost unnoticed movement past a certain point."*

Many in the church drift away. Drifting usually begins slowly and unnoticeably, but picks up speed until you realize you're going over the cliff. Of course, then it's too late to change course and avoid disaster.

How did we get here? Where a popular pastor doesn't want to focus on salvation, but recasting the foundations of Christianity? Drifting. Slowly at first, then picking up speed until what they should anchor to disappears over the horizon. Drifting begins with liberals — not Democrats, but liberal theology.

Drifting involves the foundations of Christianity, not minor issues. The inerrancy of the Bible, deity of Christ, virgin birth, atonement of Christ on the cross, existence of hell — all are pillars

---

*   Zodhiates (1992a, page 1113)

of Christianity. What the church frequently fights over — pre-tribulation rapture verses post-tribulation, baptism, and more, are disagreements on minor points; sometimes people engaging in these issues call others heretics as an insult, all while ignoring actual fundamental doctrine.

How do you know the difference between heresy and minor disagreements? The Bible speaks clearly on the gospel (1 Corinthians 15), thus if someone points to a different gospel (social justice), they—by definition—promote heresy. Baptism? If groups want to argue over dunking forward or backward, those details aren't covered in the Bible; the difference boils down to technical implementation, not foundational doctrine.

For some reason, the church readily swallows godless perversions of the gospel—in clear contradiction to Paul—while arguing over minor issues not detailed in the Bible. This should not be. How did the church drift so far away? Or more simply, what *is* liberal theology?* Let's begin the discussion with the following:

> *Now, I've heard from a bunch of folks who are eager to point out that most modern scholars are doubtful that the apostle Paul actually wrote the pastoral epistles ...*
>
> *The epistles were never meant to be interpreted and applied as universal law ... It is not the details found in the letters that we should seek to imitate, but rather the attitudes.*†
>
> *... a postmodernist is more comfortable with the both/and perspective, allowing multiple truths to exist in tension. It recognizes the significance of subjective reality on our understanding of truth, and as such, challenges more rigid doctrines, dogmas or policies that value uniformity of thought over pluralistic coexistence.*‡

Notice the buzzword phrases?

- "Pluralistic coexistence"
- "Subjective reality"
- "Multiple truth"

---

* We'll lump many groups under one banner: progressive, post-modern, social gospel, liberal, common good, etc. They're not the same, but they generally share a similar post-modern foundation, which causes all the problems.

† http://rachelheldevans.com/mutuality-let-women-speak

‡ http://www.redletterchristians.org/is-postmodern-christianity-dead/

Danger of Drifting

- "Challenge rigid doctrine"
- "Most modern scholars"

Those express standard liberal theology positions. In broad respects, liberal theology can be called value relativism or postmodernism; the rejection of absolute truth (or reality). If I say the sky is orange, and you say it's yellow, liberal theology allows us both to hold "truth" — as we individually see it. How absurd is liberalism? It claims multiple truths can exist: $2 + 2 = 4$ and—at the same time—$2 + 2 = 5$.

It really works as absurd as it appears, no matter how much verbiage liberals wrap around it to appear scholarly. Our old friend cognitive dissonance rescues people holding liberal theology from the insanity of contradictory positions, and yet believing both as "true."

Liberal theology misses *all* Scripture is given by God, and profitable for doctrine (2 Timothy 3:16). If that be true, then statements like Paul's letters were never meant to be applied universally, or multiple truths exist *must* be false. Those statements contradict Paul, and can't both be true at the same time. Either God inspired Paul's writing or not; Peter also puts Paul's work on par with scripture.

> *... our beloved brother Paul also according to the wisdom given unto him hath written unto you ... which they that are unlearned and unstable wrest, as they do also the other scriptures, unto their own destruction.* 2 Peter 3:15–16

When liberal theology redefines what God inspired Paul and Peter to write, it casts aside God's Word. What remains then? Can we do whatever is right in our own eyes? Once declared the Bible isn't *all* God's inerrant Word, then someone — using some method — must decide what is (and is not) God's Word. Who gets that task? What method will they employ? And why should their method be used over others?

Some cast aside certain sections of Paul's instruction to modernize it or make it fit with popular culture. When encountering such people, mention the warnings against sexual immorality only applied for those days in the first century; the writers never envisioned current society, so if a husband wants to have an affair or visit prostitutes, it's acceptable!

You'll quickly notice the deer-in-the-headlights look, for they can't accept that idea, but the method used to justify modern adultery uses the *same* method liberals use to cast aside parts of the Bible they don't like — modernizing or allegorizing. However, our friend cognitive dissonance soon rescues them, as their color returns when they manage to reject one idea (adultery), but embrace another (rejecting other parts they don't like), using *exactly* the same logic — so-called "modernizing."

Christianity transforms into a fight over who gets to perform the picking and choosing, what method they'll use, and why their "scholarship" rises above others, leaving nothing behind but value relativism. For example, liberals promote the strange idea Isaiah didn't actually write the book bearing his name. Two Isaiahs? No, someone else says, there were three (I think they were Larry, Moe, and Curly). Moses didn't actually write the first five books bearing his name (documentary hypothesis). And on and on it goes — the result nobody believes anything. The make-up-your-own Bible leads to denominations denying basic Biblical truth, as an article on the Episcopal church notes.

> *... it is flexible to the point of indifference on dogma, friendly to sexual liberation in almost every form, willing to blend Christianity with other faiths, and eager to downplay theology entirely in favor of secular political causes.**

A denomination believing everything, and yet nothing. You can imagine a pastor involved in liberal theology devoid of absolute truth could proclaim:

> *I don't know whether or not God exists in the first place, let me just say that.*
>
> *God is a mystery to me. ... That God is an emptiness out of which everything comes.*†

Those thoughts appear in an interview with Unitarian minister Marilyn Sewell and famous atheist Christopher Hitchens. Notice when she says:

> *I'm a liberal Christian, and I don't take the stories from the scripture literally. I don't believe in the doctrine of atonement (that Jesus died for our sins, for example).*‡

---

* http://www.nytimes.com/2012/07/15/opinion/sunday/douthat-can-liberal-christianity-be-saved.html
† http://www.portlandmonthlymag.com/arts-and-entertainment/category/books-and-talks/articles/christopher-hitchens/
‡ ibid.

Atheist Hitchens replies:

> *I would say that if you don't believe that Jesus of Nazareth was the Christ and Messiah, and that he rose again from the dead and by his sacrifice our sins are forgiven, you're really not in any meaningful sense a Christian.**

Stunning. Atheist Hitchens appears to posses a superior grasp of Christian theology over the liberal Unitarian. How did the church arrive at the place where leaders deny foundational tenets of Christianity? This isn't a minor point, as the atheist correctly states, denying Jesus' atonement means you're not really a Christian. Potlucks over truth?

> SEWELL: *I don't believe that you have to be fundamentalist and literalist to be a Christian.*
>
> HITCHENS: *Well, I'm sorry, fundamentalist simply means those who think that the Bible is a serious book and should be taken seriously.*†

Liberal theology denies and casts aside the Bible (at least parts they don't like), while the fundamentalist‡ takes it seriously. Why does it matter? Besides the obvious problem of abandoning and failing to teach basic Christian doctrine, it matters because the atheist says:

> *If we want to change the mind of the believer then the most effective way is to drive a wedge between their arguments for the existence of God (i.e., natural theology) and the other things they believe based in the Bible.*
>
> *...And so first we must make them liberals, then agnostics and then atheists. If we attempt to argue them from Christianity to atheism in one fell swoop we will not do it.*§

---

* ibid.
† ibid.
‡ Fundamentalist, like apostate and heretic, remains a loaded word many people sling around as an insult. Heresy means "A religious belief opposed to the orthodox doctrines of a church. ... The rejection of a belief that is a part of church dogma" Agnes (2007, page 667), while apostasy means "An abandoning of what one has believed in, as a faith, cause, or principles" Agnes (2007, page 66). The problem exists with those not understanding the definitions of apostate, heresy, and fundamentalist, not the words themselves.
§ http://debunkingchristianity.blogspot.com/2010/03/how-to-undercut-christianity-at.html

Liberal theology paves the path to hell — yes, that's a strong statement, but it's time to end the fear of speaking the truth, and the truth remains simple: liberal theology ends up far from Christianity. The goal of at least one atheist (and likely many others) is accomplished via liberal theology, for the simple reason it *sounds* Christian, without actually *being* Christian.

If the Bible is the inerrant Word of God liberal theology contains nothing but nonsense. And if the Bible isn't God's Word (and thus not inerrant), why bother with it all? We should all be atheists, because the Bible provides nothing more than quaint stories and mythology. In the end, liberal theology rejects God but lacks the guts to admit it.

Don't drift away, because at 3 AM will you stand for a Jesus you don't know, aren't sure is actually the God of the Bible (which isn't God's Word anyway), doubt He really existed, deny His death and resurrection provide atonement for your sin, and hell exists as nothing more than a figment of popular culture or mental illness?

If you're not under power (of Christ), you're subject to whims of people around you, or falling for the morality of what Dawkins called zeitgeist, simply meaning majority rules. "Thou shalt not follow a multitude to do evil (Exodus 23:2)."

Notice the Bible doesn't allow majority rule — right is right and wrong is wrong. Correct theology won't be found by a popularity contest any more than mathematicians vote on what $2+2$ equals (everyone once believed the world was flat. Didn't make it true). Scientists have been duped by Piltdown man and other deliberate hoaxes, and even those with the best intentions have made horrible mistakes. It matters not if everybody—or nobody—believes something, or if someone with a PhD behind their name states something. The issue will always be truth, not popularity.

When teaching this section, Jon Courson related a story involving a vacation his family experienced on the Colorado river. When they were out on a boat the engine blew up, and when he told his sister to throw out the anchor, she did ... but it wasn't attached to anything, and only sunk to the bottom. Useless. After relating the story, Jon noted how important anchors are to the Christian life.

> *It's important to have an anchor connected to the boat if you're on the Colorado river—or the Wellington river. Perhaps you've never heard of the Wellington, but I guarantee you've heard of the river into which it flows: the Niagara. Posted at the*

Danger of Drifting

point where the Wellington empties into the Niagara, is this sign: Do you have an anchor? Do you know how to use it?*

When I had family living in Bremerton Washington (home of a Navy port), occasionally the USS Nimitz would arrive for repairs or maintenance. Nimitz-class carriers are incredible machines; next to the Saturn V rocket,† perhaps the most advanced machine ever created. The Nimitz can cruise at 35 mph for decades without stopping, from its over 250,000 horsepower engines, while displacing 100,000 tons.

No matter how awesome the ship is, when the Nimitz arrives in port, whatever they anchor to must be stronger than the ship. You can't simply toss a line around it and hope it holds; whatever power the ship possesses, the anchor must hold greater.

The same with people. You must anchor to something stronger than yourself. Money, power, and a Lexus won't cut it as anything you obtain will be, by definition, weaker than yourself. You face the same question boaters on the Wellington face: Do you have an anchor? Do you know how to use it? The answer to the first is yes, the Bible you hold provides an anchor. The second question many pew-warmers fail.

Liberal theology *can't* provide an anchor since it refuses to acknowledge truth or even the inerrancy of the Bible, always arguing over what parts apply today, and what parts can be ignored. Naturally, drug addicts ignore warnings on that, adulterers and others ignore commands on those areas, others ignore structure in the church, organization of marriage and family, or replace the gospel with radical political ideology.

Liberal theology is so convenient, you can make up whatever you want, and justify it however you want. Once you travel down the dark path of liberal theology two things *always* happen:

1. You're on the road to atheism.

2. Strange ideas like social justice, common good, universal salvation, etc. infect the church and replace God's Word.

You must anchor, or you'll fall for anything. We're talking about the s-word nobody likes to mention in polite company: stubbornness. I broke my arm during Taekwondo training — I

---

*   Courson (2003, page 1456)
†   If you're under 30 you probably have no idea what that is. Go ahead and Google it, we'll wait.

did something I shouldn't have, and got injured because of it. I managed to finish the session, not discovering the extent of the injury until the next morning, when an X-Ray revealed a bone not exactly where it should be (had the extent of the injury been known training certainly would have ceased). When it occurred, the pain was severe, but not intolerable. Pausing for a moment to collect my thoughts, I returned to training. Yet in those few moments, I faced the following choices:

1. Go down. Give in. Quit.

2. Keep going in spite of the pain.

I ended up finishing the session; that may sound quite deranged, but I'm certainly not the only one ever to do such a thing, as during the 2012 Olympics a United States sprinter broke his leg halfway through his race.

> *Manteo Mitchell felt the pop in his leg and knew it wasn't good. "It felt like somebody literally just snapped my leg in half," he said. The American sprinter had half a lap to go in the first leg of the 4x400-meter relay preliminaries Thursday and a choice to make: keep running or stop and lose the race. To him, it was never much of a choice.*
>
> *... he credited something more than simple adrenaline for pushing him the rest of the way around the track. "Faith, focus, finish. Faith, focus, finish. That's the only thing I could say to myself," he said.**

Like Manteo, I tend to be stubborn, so I chose to continue — you can call that stiff-necked as well. Do you know where the first instance of stiff-necked occurs in the Bible? Exodus 32, with Moses on the mountain and the people complaining to Aaron they don't know where Moses went. In Moses' absence they conjure up the bright idea of building a golden calf, which should be obvious wasn't a great idea. But then, liberal theology and abandoning God's Word never provides satisfactory results.

Meanwhile, back up on the mountain...

> *And the LORD said unto Moses, Go, get thee down; for thy people, which thou broughtest out of the land of Egypt, have*

---

* http://summergames.ap.org/article/us-runner-finishes-olympic-relay-lap-broken-leg (accessed Aug 9, 2012)

Danger of Drifting

> *corrupted themselves. They have turned aside quickly out of the way which I commanded them: they have made them a molten calf, and have worshiped it, and have sacrificed thereunto, and said, These be thy gods, O Israel, which have brought thee up out of the land of Egypt. And the LORD said unto Moses, I have seen this people, and, behold, it is a stiff-necked people.* Exodus 32:7–9

That episode didn't turn out very well — from that and other events we conclude stubbornness should be avoided, yet don't make the mistake stubbornness is *always* wrong. Sure, many times it is, but we do have examples where stubbornness turned out to be a good thing, and prevented drifting. Recall Daniel chapter 1, as Daniel enters captivity. He's only a teenager at the time, but the first chapter reveals Daniel "purposed in his heart not to defile himself."

That's stubborn and stiff-necked, but in a good way, as he prepared himself for what lay ahead. A myth exists for unprepared people that when crises comes, they'll rise to the occasion. Few things are further from the truth (well, maybe "I'm from the government, and I'm here to help you"). You'll rarely rise to the occasion, you'll sink to whatever level of training and forethought you've previously had; you've noticed ill-prepared people panic during crisis, have you not?

For Taekwondo, I mentally picture everything that might occur — every kick is a knockout, every evasive action works perfectly, and every counter technique to the opponent's succeeds (of course, sometimes the mind is willing, but the body is weak, but that's the reason for physical training — to get those two as close together as possible).

What line won't you cross? How far will you allow yourself to drift before you return? You must anchor before the storm arises, as once the wind blows, the ability to prepare disappears. A quote attributed to many golfers says "The more I practice, the luckier I get" — be prepared *before* you need it. People performing well under pressure likely do so because they've already considered the situation beforehand. When faced with crisis at 3 AM you've got what you've got. You won't rise to the occasion, you'll sink to your level of preparation. What condition is your training program in?

Training provides positive static stability. Stability means the ability to return to equilibrium once disturbed (if you've seen Mythbusters, you've seen them perform stability tests). But a difference exists between *positive* static stability and *negative*.

While both function equally in non-crisis modes, what happens to each when something pushes them away from their ideal?

Imagine a bowl, drop in a marble and if you disturb it, it eventually settles down at the bottom again. That's positive static stability. No matter how you push the marble around, it eventually settles at the bottom stable position. But turn the bowl upside down, put the marble on the bottom of the bowl, and it may stay there, but if moved, it falls off the side, not returning. That's negative static stability; when serious social occasions arise, it's over the edge (we call that panic and unpreparedness).

Thus, you want *positive* static stability, which provides automatic corrective force returning you to the stable position. In the Christian life, positive stability comes from preparation — learning the Bible for yourself, so when that 3 AM call arrives, you don't look around for someone to bail you out.

Finally, notice anchoring requires continuous and willful action; doing nothing leads to drifting. If you wait too long to anchor, the Niagara falls sneak up (as if you could miss the warning of the roaring sound of water), and you *will* go over and crash on the rocks below. Remember, those falls live around the corner whether you believe so or not.

You can take offense, or take action, but you can neither change the laws of Physics, nor spiritual laws. It's God's sandbox, and the falls always exist, even if denied by liberals. The only question is will you heed the warnings? What happens if you ignore this warning? Paul continues.

> *For if the word spoken by angels was steadfast, and every transgression and disobedience received a just recompense of reward; How shall we escape, if we neglect so great salvation; which at the first began to be spoken by the Lord, and was confirmed unto us by them that heard him;*   Hebrews 2:2–3

Questions for liberals. If you know what God said and willingly reject or recast it, how do you think you will avoid the truth and responsibility for your actions? In chapter 10, Paul states it's fearful to fall into the hands of the living God. How much more when you willfully and deliberately turn away from what you know to be true? You earn your reward — either a reward for good actions, or a punishment for poor actions. Either way, your actions trigger a response you can't control.

We have a problem these days, and it's people worrying about being offended instead of concerned about truth. Truth remains

Danger of Drifting

truth whether you like it or not. $2 + 2$ still equals 4,* whether or not you like it, believe it, or are offended by it. When Jesus said "I am the way, the truth, and the life: no man cometh unto the Father, but by me" that's what He meant.

The danger of drifting remains — stay anchored, because you are responsible. Burying your head in the sand will not provide good results.

A warning comes in Numbers 16 with the rebellion of Korah. Korah and his guys complain to Moses, whining who put you in charge? It's rebellion against God-given authority, which could be the topic of a book itself, as it comes in many forms. In Numbers 16 they rebel against Moses, and Moses doesn't get upset or angry. He simply replies, okay, tomorrow we'll see if you're right or not — will liberal theology changing God's Word work, or does absolute truth remain in spite of a liberal's wishes?

> *If these men die the common death of all men, or if they be visited after the visitation of all men, then the Lord hath not sent me. But if the Lord make a new thing, and the earth open her mouth, and swallow them up, with all that appertains unto them, and they go down alive into sheol; then ye shall understand that these men have provoked the Lord.*
>
> Numbers 16:29–30

That's what happens — they receive their reward after abandoning God's Word (as many do today) and substituting their own heretical ideas (like "modernizing Christianity for the 21st century"). The Bible provides other examples of people rejecting God's Word and warning, instead substituting their own not-so-bright ideas for God's Word.

- Ananias and Sapphira (Acts 5). "Why hath Satan filled thine heart to lie to the Holy Spirit? ... And Ananias hearing these words fell down, and gave up the ghost: and great fear came on all them that heard these things."

- Herod (Acts 12). Pride and failure to give glory to God when the crowd shouts "voice of a god, and not of a man. ... And immediately the angel of the Lord smote him, because he gave not God the glory: and he was eaten of worms, and gave up the ghost."

---

*   Except for sufficiently large values of 2, as the math joke goes.

- Belshazzar and the writing on the wall (Daniel 5) — "the joints of his loins were loosed, and his knees smote one against another. ... In that night was Belshazzar the king of the Chaldeans slain."

If we have the advantage of these examples (and we do), and Paul told us (1 Corinthians 10:11) they were for *us* as examples (and they are), what happens if the church avoids the warnings, substituting its own value-relativistic ideas? Did any of those examples end well for the people promoting false ideas?

Drifting isn't the only danger on the river; neglect means "to become apathetic," "to have an attitude of indifference," "to have no care or concern for it." These are people who have salvation; salvation is in their possession, but they are becoming indifferent to it.* They drift away not from willful abandon, but from apathy, and eventually could arrive at a place where they deny the existence of God — an atheist pastor or one who denies the foundations of Christianity until nothing remains but good works and potlucks. Like someone sucking out the chocolate of an M&M, liberal theology removes foundational principles, leaving behind an empty shell, and it can't satisfy.

Sometimes neglect isn't apostasy, but being too casual. You can make two errors; the first treats God as unapproachable (we should come boldly to the throne of grace), the second treats God too casually (God said to Moses take off your shoes, you're standing on Holy ground). It's neither too casual, nor too formal, but a correct attitude we require.

Apathy and concerns over daily life crowd out service for God, and we forget we're supposed to be in service for God, not worrying about our Lexus. Paul somehow maintained the correct attitude throughout his life, as he compared the Christian life to running a race.

> *Know ye not that they which run in a race run all, but one receiveth the prize? So run, that ye may obtain.*
> 1 Corinthians 9:24

It's maximum effort. Not a sprint, but a marathon — continual, steady effort over an extended period. When you're finally on your deathbed, you want to be like the athlete saying at the end of the game "that's all I had." Don't run the Christian life weighted

---

*   Missler (2008, page 38)

down by junk providing no value; you don't show up for a race with boots, but lightweight shoes.

Remember back in Haggai? "Thus speaks the LORD of hosts, saying: 'This people says, "The time has not come, the time that the LORD's house should be built."' Then the word of the LORD came by Haggai the prophet, saying, "Is it time for you yourselves to dwell in your paneled houses, and this temple to lie in ruins?"*

We must understand time is short. Don't put off what you can do. We always have many excuses — that's a form of drifting too. Once again, the Bible provides examples of what *not* to do. Moses tried to avoid the call. Jonah famously tried to duck it. Jeremiah didn't like it. We always have excuses. Chuck Missler says never underestimate the ability of a person to rationalize.

Early in life, it's college, and we're so busy, but after graduation, then it's you and me, Lord. Oh wait, it's kids, once they're grown a bit, it's you and me, Lord. But the job is tough, as soon as I get past this rough stretch, it's you and me Lord. Then mom and dad have Alzheimer's and they're old, so we must take care of them, but then it's you and me Lord...

Before you realize what happened, you're sucking oxygen on your death bed wondering where time went. *So teach us to number our days, that we may apply our hearts unto wisdom (Psalm 90:12).*

First you get back in the game, then you must persevere to stay in the game, with the goal always being as Paul: "I have fought a good fight, I have finished my course, I have kept the faith (2 Timothy 4:7)." Our goal should be to have that written on our headstone.

> *God also bearing them witness, both with signs and wonders, and with diverse miracles, and gifts of the Holy Spirit, according to his own will?*   Hebrews 2:4

The Lord in previous verses obviously referred to Jesus (the author mentions those of us that heard Him), but in addition, God the Father bears witness with three things.

SIGNS AND WONDERS — The sign is the message, and a wonder is amazement.

DIVERSE MIRACLES — Dunamis or power. The reference verse is 2 Timothy 1:7 "For God hath not given us the spirit of fear; but of *power*, and of love, and of a sound mind."

GIFTS OF THE SPIRIT — Not talent, but a gift of the spirit. Many musicians have talent, but few posses the gift. As a radio station

---
*   Haggai 1:2–4 NKJV

manager, I receive music samples. Sometimes when you listen to it — even if it sounds good — it's a bit off as many musicians look at ministry as a job, not a calling.

To summarize, you can be a Christian but drift so far you become ineffective, and if you're not careful and corrective, you'll ride over the falls and crash on the rocks below. Nobody *wants* that to happen to them, but if you're not careful, it will as truth remains truth whether you like it or not.

Four tough verses, reminding us God has spoken, and we won't be unaccountable if we drift away, so stay anchored to the rock. It's really that simple, but tough to apply every day.

Faith, focus, finish. Faith, focus, finish.

Chapter 5

Jesus: Qualified Redeemer

WE'VE COVERED SEVERAL IDEAS: THREE reasons why Christians fail to rest, the superiority of Jesus over angels, and the danger of drifting away from what you know. Paul now shows Jesus as the qualified redeemer, showing the Jews Jesus is the Messiah they wait for.

For unto the angels hath he not put in subjection the world to come, whereof we speak.   Hebrews 2:5

We're going to discuss *why* Jesus had to be both man and God, a strange idea people might struggle with. It's vital to understand, as you can't deny either without denying salvation; cults frequently deny one or the other. Early Gnostics denied His humanity, today's heretics deny His deity.

Paul does not use the Greek word cosmos, rather he uses a word referring to the earth, thus the earth environment to come must be the future millennial kingdom. Man in general has dominion over the earth and creatures (from Genesis 1:26 and Psalm 8); global warming and its worship of mother earth conflicts with Biblical teaching. We are to be good stewards, but not place earth above human needs.

Christians should be good stewards of the earth; I don't want toxic sludge in my water either, but a difference exists between stewardship and worship; global warming extremists pass far beyond proper stewardship and into worship of mother earth, to the point man serves the earth, not the other way around.

But one in a certain place testified, saying, What is man, that thou art mindful of him? Or the son of man, that thou visitest him? Hebrews 2:6

The verse before in Psalm 8 reads "When I consider thy heavens, the work of thy fingers, the moon and the stars, which thou hast ordained, what is man." Man exists as a tiny speck of water and chemicals, inhabiting the surface of a piece of dust revolving around an insignificant star, swirling in a cosmos so vast it defies ability to grasp.

Consider the heavens; a light year being 5.9 Trillion miles or 5.9×10^{12} miles. That's a *huge* number, but compare it to the Federal deficit — we used to call staggeringly large numbers astronomical numbers, maybe we should call them economic numbers. Either way, it's hard to fathom the scope of our universe.

The cosmos being billions of light-years across, containing 10^{86} particles, yet God counts the hairs on your head. You're not forgotten, you're never abandoned. If God tracks each sub-atomic particle in the universe, do you think He could forget His children?

Thou madest him a little lower than the angels; thou crownedst him with glory and honor, and didst set him over the works of thy hands; Thou hast put all things in subjection under his feet. For in that he put all in subjection under him, he left nothing that is not put under him. But now we see not yet all things put under him. Hebrews 2:7-8

As we previously saw, God gave man dominion over the earth. What did Adam do with it? He blew it, and now Satan runs the show. For those who think Satan isn't in charge of the earth, recall the temptation of Jesus — if Satan didn't posses what he offered, what temptation would exist? Yes, Satan has vast influence on the earth.

Yet a strange phrase found in insurance policies — if you read your policy (and you should), you'll find it references "acts of God," when it should read something else, since Adam ceded the title of the earth to Satan way back in the Garden.

Since man blew it, he's incapable of fixing the situation as it requires a perfect sacrifice to fulfill the penalty. The sacrifices of the Old Testament covered sin, but couldn't pay the price required for it. God gave the Law so we would know our sin, that's all. Sadly, by the time Jesus arrived the Pharisees believed the Law could make them righteous before God. Jesus in the sermon on the mount destroyed that idea, but His message fell on deaf ears.

Jesus: Qualified Redeemer

While Satan may have run of the earth temporarily, all things ultimately come under authority of Jesus — that's only fair, since He created it, and paid for it. We don't see everything correct right now, but rest assured, at some future point (which comes closer every day), a righteous rule will emerge.

> *But we see Jesus, who was made a little lower than the angels for the suffering of death, crowned with glory and honor; that he by the grace of God should taste death for every man.* Hebrews 2:9

For God's LAW to be fulfilled, sin requires a sacrifice, and that sacrifice must be perfect. This is where Jesus as fully God yet fully man comes in. He must be *both* to fulfill the job duties. But first, what is the LAW, and how does it differ from the law and Law?

- law — Lowercase law refers to government law — speeding, murder, taxes, etc. Obviously Christians should follow this, as Paul notes in Romans 13. The only exception would be if a law conflicts or goes against God. For example, a law against prayer. See Daniel 6 for an example.

- Law — The Law with one capital normally refers to the Mosaic Law. Not everyone uses this convention, so normally we'll use the term Mosaic Law to avoid confusion. Galatians (3:24–25) informs us Christians aren't bound by (Mosaic) Law.

- LAW — It's less common, but God's universal LAW can be noted by using all capitals. The LAW refers to God's eternal, never changing standards. It existed in the Garden of Eden, under Abraham, Moses, in the New Testament, and today. For example, murder is wrong. When Cain killed Abel in Genesis 4, it was the LAW he violated, not the law (as no government existed), or the Law (as it was pre-Moses).

Jesus must be fully God to satisfy the requirements for a perfect, sinless sacrifice. Since sin tarnishes everything since the fall, nothing on earth can meet the requirement. Jesus must also be fully man; it's important because the redeemer must be a relative.

Some people have wondered why the book of Ruth exists in the Bible, but it's an example of the kinsman redeemer. Ruth lost her land, but discovered Boaz. In chapter 3 Ruth tells Boaz he's a kinsman, and can redeem the land. Boaz informs her a nearer kinsman exists, and by rights he has first choice to redeem it.

By chapter 4 Boaz confronts this guy, who declines, thus Boaz the hero can perform the role. But notice Boaz can't simply redeem for himself since a nearer relative exists. That's the role of the kinsman-redeemer. It *must* be the closest relative. In legal terms, standing.

- Fully God = sinless — the perfect sacrifice.

- Fully Man = closest relative. Able to perform the service.

Both able and acceptable. The kinsman-redeemer must have *both*. Jesus meets *both* requirements — a man to be the kinsman redeemer, *and* fully sinless to be the perfect sacrifice required for Adam's sin. Deny either and we're still trapped in sin.

> *For it became him, for whom are all things, and by whom are all things, in bringing many sons unto glory, to make the captain of their salvation perfect through sufferings.*
> Hebrews 2:10

The captain is leader — some translations use author, while perfect has more of a flavor of complete or finished. The work is done, nothing exists you can do to add to it. It's not Jesus+ to obtain salvation, thus baptism for example has nothing to do with salvation.

Figuring all that out provides rest. Many Christians struggle with various issues, and are thus not at rest. Part of rest (and remaining combat-ready) means discovering you don't add anything to the salvation equation. It's not Jesus + stuff = salvation, with the stuff being baptism, works, or anything else.

If you want to stay in the game, you need to rest. That doesn't mean quit working, but to understand salvation and the relationship between Jesus and salvation. Hint: If it's anything like Jesus+, you'll *never* find the rest you're looking for, and you will fail to be combat-ready.

You can paraphrase this as Jesus the leader of our complete salvation through His death and resurrection and not anything we do. It's interesting liberal, progressive "Christians" move away from this basic tenet of salvation.

As we previously saw, some work to modify fundamental Christian concepts to move Christianity from its foundation of personal salvation. Obsessive? No. That's like saying football is obsessed with touchdowns. Not obsession, which has a negative connotation, rather it's the definition. If you remove Jesus' death from salvation, you've got nothing. Jesus' death providing salvation *is* the definition of Christianity. It's not obsession, but definition. If you deny that, not much remains (well, potlucks, but how many of those can you really do?).

> *For both he that sanctifieth and they who are sanctified are all of one, for which cause he is not ashamed to call them brethren,* Hebrews 2:11

You're not a friend of God because you want to be or *you* choose to be, but because *He* chooses you to be. Most people use Windows on their computer, but I gave it up a long time ago for Unix. The biggest complaint about Unix (what you might better know as Linux, though there is FreeBSD, AIX, etc) being it's not very user friendly. Unix people respond, Unix isn't unfriendly, it's just picky about who its friends are.

The Lord isn't so much — He chooses sinful man, provides for salvation, and then calls you brethren and friend, *none* of which He had to do, and none of which we earned. It would have been easier for the Son to say to the Father, this creation didn't work out, let's scrap it and try over. Would He be wrong? After all, can the clay talk back to the potter?

> *Saying, I will declare thy name unto my brethren, in the midst of the church will I sing praise unto thee. And again, I will put my trust in him. And again, Behold I and the children which God hath given me.* Hebrews 2:12-13

Those come from Psalm 22 and Isaiah 8:17–18. Notice how Paul takes Old Testament passages and applies them to Jesus. Some people deny the prophet's writings applied to Jesus, but that ignores the precedent as New Testament writers, under inspiration of the Holy Spirit, applied prophetic writings to Jesus.

Some passages and prophecies have primary and secondary meanings, or near and far fulfillment. Simply put, a passage always contains an exact meaning, but may also provide secondary prophetic meanings later. Be careful, it has to be in context, and that context is Genesis to Revelation.

> *Forasmuch then as the children are partakers of flesh and blood, he also himself likewise took part of the same; that through death he might destroy him that had the power of death, that is, the devil.* Hebrews 2:14

As the perfect sacrifice He could do that since He meets the requirements. Salvation comes from no other, as Peter said "Neither is there salvation in any other: for there is none other name under heaven given among men, whereby we must be saved (Acts 4:12)."

Notice it's not Jesus' teachings providing salvation (though they were good), nor His example (though we should follow), nor His miracles (only a testimony for who He is). It's only the death and resurrection of Jesus defining *the* Gospel, as Paul wrote in 1 Corinthians 15.

It's curious some groups de-emphasize the cross, instead focusing on "following Jesus," which sounds so spiritual. When you actually dig in to their ideas, you'll find they don't only diminish Jesus' sacrifice, they eliminate it, substituting good works for salvation. Following Jesus then becomes strange political strategy, having nothing to actually do with Christ or the Gospel.

As Paul said, "For the preaching of the cross is to them that perish foolishness; but unto us which are saved it is the power of God."* Take away Jesus' teachings, miracles, and examples, but keep the cross, and salvation remains. But take away the cross, keeping everything else, and we're still dead in our sin.

It's not those other ideas aren't important or useful, but they are *not* the Gospel, as Paul said in 1 Corinthians 15 "Moreover, brethren, I declare unto you the gospel which I preached unto you ... For I delivered unto you first of all that which I also received, how that Christ died for our sins according to the scriptures; And that he was buried, and that he rose again the third day according to the scriptures."

That's the Gospel. That's what destroys him who has power of death, and death itself. That's the good news, not social justice or other perversions. Those are heresy and poison, plain and simple. Even if heretical teachers mix 99% correct doctrine with 1% heresy, you're still dead if you swallow it. Being *mostly* non-heretical won't cut it.

> *And deliver them who, through fear of death, were all their lifetime subject to bondage.*   Hebrews 2:15

The soul that sins, shall die; the wages of sin is death. No way out exists. From the moment of birth you begin to die. Nobody escapes it. It's only a question of when. Some people live in terror of death and spend their life looking for immortality. That's the

---

*   1 Corinthians 1:18

bondage you were born into. That's the legacy of Adam. In one man, all sinned. In one man, we're all saved.

> *For verily he took not on him the nature of angels, but he took on him the seed of Abraham.* Hebrews 2:16

As we've talked about the confusion of religion previously, another verse causing problems for those who say they accept the Bible as the Word of God, yet claim Jesus was an angel and not God. Jesus specifically was not an angel.

> *Wherefore, in all things it behooved him to be made like his brethren, that he might be a merciful and faithful high priest in things pertaining to God, to make reconciliation for the sins of the people.* Hebrews 2:17

He's not some vague nebulous entity, He can relate to you, because He lived as a man. Two mistakes can be made, the first being too casual and forgetting who you're addressing (the creator of the universe), while the other extreme views God as some stand-offish entity having no idea what you're going through.

The high priest idea will be developed later in Hebrews, so we'll keep moving.

> *For in that he himself hath suffered being tempted, he is able to help them that are tempted.* Hebrews 2:18

Smoking is perhaps one of the toughest habits to quit. I knew a guy who (like many) smoked for most of his life. At one point part of his lung had to be removed. He tried to quit, did the gum (packs a day), and more. One day when I saw him I asked about how the stop smoking thing was going. He said not too bad, since he started again. Probably not an uncommon story.

If you've tried to quit, but gave in the next week, do you know how it feels a month later? Nope. Only someone who made it as far as you can relate to your situation on day 372. Since Jesus *never* gave in to temptation, He can relate to anyone facing anything, at any time.

That's Jesus, and that's why His never giving in means He can relate to you.

> *Wherefore, holy brethren, partakers of the heavenly calling, consider the Apostle and High Priest of our profession, Christ Jesus.* Hebrews 3:1

You've seen Jesus superior to angels, how He's fully God and fully man, how He can relate to you. Consider how a total man can relate to you, while as fully God He possesses the qualities required to be the perfect high priest.

Understanding Jesus is fully God, yet as fully man He relates to us, enables the rest and peace everyone seeks. Next section, the danger of doubting, and how that prohibits entering God's rest He wants you to have.

Chapter 6

Danger of Unbelief

MANY CHRISTIANS STRUGGLE WITH DAILY LIFE, asking "where is this abundant life Jesus promised? Is this all there is? Why is life so hard, and bad things happen to good people?" This chapter Paul explains one (but not the only) possible reason.

> *Wherefore, holy brethren, partakers of the heavenly calling, consider the Apostle and High Priest of our profession, Christ Jesus.*
> Hebrews 3:1

We've seen Jesus superior to prophets, and superior to angels. Paul confronts the final superiority He must possess for the Jews: He's superior to Moses. To the Jews, of course, Moses is venerated (writing the first five books, exodus from Egypt, etc). Yet notice he wasn't allowed to enter the promised land (Numbers 20) because he made a big boo-boo.*

Apostle simply means one who is sent. Whenever we hear apostle we think of the twelve, but it's a bit broader than that. It's someone sent from God with His message. You could say he represents God to man. "Thus saith the Lord..." In contrast, the high priest performs service in the temple, offers sacrifices, and generally performs an interface between man and God — he represents man to God.

Thus, an apostle *and* high priest represents two-way communication with God.

---

* Moses misrepresented God, which He takes *very* seriously. Moses related God was angry with the people when He wasn't.

> *Who was faithful to him that appointed him, as also Moses was faithful in all his house.* — Hebrews 3:2

Recall in the garden as Jesus prayed to the Father, if it be possible, let this pass by, *nevertheless*, not my will, but yours. That's faithful. Not what I want, but what He wants. It's dedication to the mission above all else, denying personal comfort.

How many one-off activities do Christians allow to consume (and that's a carefully chosen word) us? Sure, some are necessary for life, but how faithful to God are we when those activities' seductive call arrives? The church diverts to discussions over baptism, tribulation, Bible versions, and so on. Sure, some of those might be important, but are we faithful to the primary mission?

Moses was faithful. Recall Exodus 32 while Moses was on the mountain and his second in command Aaron had the bright idea to create a golden calf; God said that's it, let's have a do-over, and I'll create another nation. In short, God said wipe 'em out, and I'll create a new people.

After all the problems Moses experienced leading millions of people through the wilderness, he didn't agree — yeah, these people are a pain, let's start over with a better group. Instead Moses intercedes for the people. Moses might have had an easier time with a different group, but he remained faithful to them, even when they didn't deserve it.

It's the idea of standing with someone, no matter what. Husbands and wives should share a similar bond, a bond that says no matter the evidence, if they say so that's good enough. Remember a difference exists between evidence and proof. Facts are facts, but interpretation differs. Your fingerprints may be on the bloody knife (fact) but it may or may not mean murder (interpretation).

It's having the stuck-like-glue mentality: you can't fire me and I'm not going to quit. Ever. That's the attitude Moses had. He certainly could have had an easier life if he *wasn't* so faithful.

> *For this man was counted worthy of more glory than Moses, inasmuch as he who hath built the house hath more honor than the house. For every house is built by some man, but he that built all things is God.* — Hebrews 3:3–4

The Jews venerated Moses, but he only cared for the house. Paul switches to the builder: Jesus. If Moses held so much honor among the Jews (yet was only a caretaker), how much more should they venerate the builder of the house itself?

And Moses verily was faithful in all his house, as a servant, for a testimony of those things which were to be spoken after; But Christ as a son over his own house, whose house are we, if we hold fast the confidence and the rejoicing of the hope firm unto the end.   Hebrews 3:5-6

The difference between a caretaker and owner — if the caretaker (Moses) was faithful and venerated by the Jews, how much more should the owner and builder (Jesus) be? Paul presents a simple — yet unavoidable — conclusion.

The phrase "if we hold ... unto the end" can cause problems. We could plunge into a debate of Calvinism vs Arminianism and argue over which is correct.* But "if" has more of a flavor of "since"; it's not a condition, rather a sign.

You can tell who the good guys are because they don't waver. They may stumble, they may have problems (like Moses), they may even have stiff penalties for their actions (like Moses), but they never abandon ship. As Peter said, where would we go?

J. Vernon McGee says cults exist because they're God's strainer, sifting out churches and people who aren't actually believers, yet desire to appear religious. We've seen examples of those (liberal theology, social justice) who deny almost all of Christianity, yet still desire to appear under the banner of Christianity. They fail to hold fast, in fact, they willfully abandon foundational principles.

Thus, Jesus is superior to the venerated Moses; another part of history provides the second warning in this letter, that of unbelief or doubting.

Wherefore as the Holy Spirit saith, Today if ye will hear his voice, Harden not your hearts, as in the provocation, in the day of trial in the wilderness, When your fathers put me to the test, proved me, and saw my works forty years. Wherefore I was grieved with that generation, and said, They do always err in their heart, and they have not known my ways. So I swore in my wrath, They shall not enter into my rest.   Hebrews 3:7-11

Everyone knows the story, how the Jews left Egypt on a few weeks journey to the promised land. Upon arriving, they send in

---

* They *both* are right in what the assert, but wrong in what they deny. Einstein's relativity explains how both are correct *at the same time*. It's another of those centuries old paradoxes disappearing when you study Physics and apply it to your Bible.

spies to search out the land. Most of them come back and say it's too hard, we can't do it. Only two of them said, sure, it's hard, and will be a battle, but let's get off the couch and get in the game! The same problem exists in today's church. Sure, service for God is tough. Service seems to get last place as too much other stuff intrudes. Paul told Timothy a soldier doesn't worry about things not relating to his duty to his boss.

The Jews grumbling begins. Oh, you brought us out here in the desert to die! Think of the children! And the Lord says, you want to die? I can arrange that. God gives them what they want — you don't want to enter God's blessing, you don't have to. God doesn't *force* anyone to do what He wants. If someone doesn't want to be saved, they don't have to be. If someone doesn't want to perform as God calls, He finds someone else.

Oh, and by the way Jews, the children you worried about will enter in and engage the battle you're unwilling to.

Two guys come back with the report, sure, some obstacles exist, but God can handle it. Caleb and Joshua weren't listened to, and as a result the Jews spent 40 years wandering around. Wouldn't it have been easier to do as the Lord said? Sure, life is tough — nobody said it wasn't.

You might be saved, but wondering where the abundant spirit-filled life Jesus promised is. The promised land isn't heaven as some might say. How can we be sure? Giants live in the land, battles, and yes, sin. It represents walking in the spirit, or as we've said many times — staying in the game. Contrast the wilderness they chose with the promised land God provided.

- Wilderness is dry, barren, and death.

- Promised land flows with milk and honey, but giants and battles as well.

Recall Joshua and the battle of Jericho. Perhaps the most bizarre battle plan (save Gideon's) in the Bible. Everyone knows the story, they march around the city, and one day blow trumpets and the walls come down. But did you ever think what it must have been like around the table as Joshua informed his generals of the battle plan? God was on their side, so as long as they remained committed, God went before them in battle.

After mighty Jericho, a puny little city called Ai comes up. It's so tiny the military generals say don't bother sending everyone, just send a small group and they'll take it. Perhaps they were too

Danger of Unbelief

proud of their last victory, or were guilty of getting in front of God, instead of following. Either way, they met defeat.

Why? They had sin in the camp, and didn't follow God's directions. With God, nothing is impossible; without God, nothing is possible — odds or resources don't matter. Jericho was a large city defeated by following God's orders, the small city of Ai easily defeated the Jews because they failed to follow directions.

With that background Paul's readers would certainly already know, he provides the application.

> *Take heed, brethren, lest there be in any of you an evil heart of unbelief, in departing from the living God.* Hebrews 3:12

Could that be us today? Dry, barren, working on our own instead of allowing God's power to move. We're stuck in Ai instead of conquering Jericho.

Departing means apostasy. It's a willful abandonment of truth, exactly what we see in many churches and groups today. You know, the fully buzzword-compliant ones. The ones denying the inerrancy of the Bible. The ones modernizing. The ones failing to speak the truth for fear of bothering someone.

Yep, those people are exactly what Paul cautions about. Don't let an evil unbelief creep in, which will cause you to depart from God. It can become so bad nothing substantial remains — only potlucks. Like an M&M with all the chocolate sucked out, it may *look* like an M&M, but won't really satisfy.

> *But exhort one another daily, while it is called Today, lest any of you be hardened through the deceitfulness of sin.*
> Hebrews 3:13

Eventually apostasy results in hardening. People spend so much time denying truth, they arrive at a place where they can no longer accept truth. That's when you'll see bizarre arguments denying basic truth, or phony gospels of social justice replacing the true Gospel. Those people become hardened through deceit.

Who does Paul address? Christians. Can you become hard-hearted? It appears so, or Paul wouldn't have warned against it. That doesn't mean losing salvation, but return to what Paul always obsessed over: running the race well. You can run the race, but be bogged down in other things, and ultimately fail to finish well.

Paul told Timothy "I have fought a good fight, I have finished my course, I have kept the faith." To do that you must cast aside unbelief and enter the promised land, not equating the abundant spirit-filled life with easy. Service for God is tough. God isn't concerned with easy, but *character*.

> *For we are made partakers of Christ, if we hold the beginning of our confidence steadfast unto the end.*   Hebrews 3:14

That "if" once again you can read as since. It's a sign, not a condition; it identifies those who haven't (and won't) abandon the truth.

> *While it is said, Today if ye will hear his voice, harden not your hearts, as in the provocation.*   Hebrews 3:15

Today means today. Don't put it off. Paul says the Old Testament doesn't contain stories for history's sake, those stories exist for us to learn from.* Don't repeat the mistakes from the past.

> *For who, when they had heard, did provoke? Did not all that came out of Egypt by Moses? But with whom was he grieved forty years? Was it not with them that had sinned, whose carcases fell in the wilderness? And to whom sware he that they should not enter into his rest, but to them that believed not?*   Hebrews 3:16–18

A reminder of the lesson they should have learned, and even if they hadn't learned, would be familiar with. The Jews had faith to leave Egypt (world), but not enough to enter the promised land victorious. Why? They didn't believe it. So what happened? God gave them what they wanted. They wanted to die in the wilderness, and they did.

You don't want to enter the promised land? You don't have to. It's not salvation, or heaven, but walking by the spirit. You'll still have battles, but would you rather fight at Jericho or Ai?

> *So we see that they could not enter in because of unbelief.*   Hebrews 3:19

It's easy to make the mistake of unbelief; if I'm not living the abundant life Jesus promised it's because I'm not reading 300 chapters a day, witnessing to 50 people per hour, and fasting 300 days a year. That's works.

---

*   Romans 15:4

Failure to enter was also not because of a golden calf. You could make a list of all the problems the Jews had wandering in the desert, but those aren't listed here. We *all* make mistakes. Paul doesn't say they entered not because of mistakes or sin, the simple answer is they didn't believe it.

God delivered Israel from Egypt by the blood of Passover and water of the Red sea as the Egyptian army drowned behind them. On to the promised land! As Lee Corso says, not so fast, my friend. They were saved, but failed to accept God's promise. Instead of entering the spirit-filled life, they wandered in the wilderness. Yes, you can be saved, but not victorious.

God says, here it is, and we say I'll believe it when I see it, while God says no, you'll see it when you believe it. It's not a question of reality or whether it exists or not — just because someone doesn't believe something doesn't make it untrue. Truth doesn't care. That promised land waits for you to enter. The only question: do you believe it enough to enter? Or do you prefer to wander in the wilderness, powerless?

What's holding you back from the spirit filled life isn't a list of sins. Sure, habitual sin is a problem and must be dealt with (see Ai). But it's not listed here. If you're struggling with something, that's not keeping you out. Even Paul had problems as he relates in Romans 7 "For I know that in me (that is, in my flesh) dwelleth no good thing: for to will is present with me; but how to perform that which is good I find not. For the good that I would I do not; but the evil which I would not, that I do."

That's Paul's lament as he finds himself in chapter 7. But everyone knows chapter 8, and it begins "There is therefore now no condemnation to them which are in Christ Jesus."

They didn't believe what God told them. Nothing more, nothing less. If you're dry, dusty, and wandering in the wilderness, maybe you need to return to basics. God said it, believe it. It's not about an easy life, as we'll definitely have battles — God never promised everyone a Lexus and a pony. Just the opposite, in fact. Remember Jesus saying in this world you *will* have tribulation?

> *Now unto him that is able to do exceeding abundantly above all that we ask or think, according to the power that worketh in us.*   Ephesians 3:20

Exceedingly more than we ask for, or even think. Do you believe it? Or are you stuck in unbelief? The choice is yours. God won't force you to live in the promised land any more than the Jews.

Your choice, but choose wisely as only one path allows you to stay in the game. We should all strive to be as Paul wrote to Timothy: I have fought the good fight, I have finished my course, I have kept the faith. Never give in. Never quit. Never surrender. Or, as you should be used to by now: Stay in the game!

Life is hard. We'll all have tough times. But at 3 AM you've got what you've got — either an empty toolbox leading to cataclysmic defeat from failure to be prepared, or an unshakable commitment leading to unquestionable victory. It's your choice — do you want to fight like Chuck Norris or be slaughtered like a pig?

Chapter 7

Danger of Dull Hearing

Last chapter we discussed unbelief, the danger of missing God's promises simply because you don't believe them. This chapter Paul warns of dull hearing — just because you've heard everything he's said doesn't necessarily mean you're *applying* it. When 3 AM rolls around, either you discover you can apply what you know (and fight like Chuck Norris), or the nightmare of reaching in your toolbox and finding nothing (ending up like the pig). No other possibility exists.

We call people who, at 3 AM when crisis arrives, are unable to answer the bell *casualties*. Don't we all want to stay in the game despite adversity? Then we must listen to Paul — the guy who knows adversity.

> *Let us therefore fear, lest, a promise being left us of entering into his rest, any of you should seem to come short of it.*
> Hebrews 4:1

Paul spends two chapters discussing unbelief, so it's a big deal. Unfortunately, too many Christians keep a pew warm week after month and learn …nothing. And lest I bore you with repetition, when 3 AM rolls around, do you want to answer the bell or be slaughtered like a pig? It's still your choice.

For those who might think these warnings only apply to slackers, and once you become spiritual these warnings won't apply, notice Paul includes himself in the warning as he says "let *us*" fear. No matter where you are in your Christian life, the warning of dull hearing applies.

In fact, mature Christians might be in *more* danger than younger ones. Oh yes, I've read Hebrews, I know what it says. Sure, I've been to church for dozens of years. Danger. It's then you've become hard of hearing. You'll *never* reach a point where you've learned it all. Never. Stay focused and alert.

You mean a Christian can miss the rest God provides? It appears so. How many right now aren't resting? Why not? Is it due to failure to believe what God said? Unbelief is the opposite of faith. What is faith?

> *...means that persuasion is not the outcome of imagination but is based on fact, such as the reality of the resurrection of Christ, and as such it becomes the basis of realistic hope.**

Faith isn't blind trust. It's based on a realistic analysis of facts. Paul continues in chapter 11 to state "without faith it is impossible to please him," so whatever faith is, it's something we'd better figure out.

I frequently drive across a bridge. As I drive across, I have faith that bridge will carry me to the other side. As a mathematician and scientist, I understand structural calculations, the strength of concrete and steel, and principles of design. Thus, as I approach, I have a reasonable expectation that bridge will function as the engineers intended.

Yet I *never* examined the design for the bridge. I've never seen the stress calculations, nor tested the strength of the concrete. I have a reasonable expectation (Biblical faith) in that bridge, because of what I *do* know. It's not proof, however.

On the contrary, suppose I came to the bank of the river, and for some reason the bridge didn't exist. Foolishly driving off the embankment would be blind faith, as no expectation exists of somehow teleporting to the other side. I have faith in the bridges' engineering, while driving off the embankment is stupid.

We need to cast off unbelief and rely on faith. When you do, you'll discover the rest Paul speaks of. That does not mean an easy life with a Lexus, ice cream, and a pony, it means the ability to hang in a firefight because you know in whom you've trusted, and He is able to keep that which you trust to Him.

> *For unto us was the gospel preached, as well as unto them; but the word preached did not profit them, not being mixed with faith in them that heard it.*   Hebrews 4:2

---

* Zodhiates (1992b, page 1162)

Not everyone hearing the Gospel responds. You're free to accept or reject as you wish. Just hearing the Word does not profit, rather, the person responding to the Word — mixed with faith — prospers.

Recall the parable of the soils in Matthew 13. Some heard and grew, some ignored, some sprouted and were choked out. Different reactions, but notice the same seed fell on each soil. Nothing was wrong with the seed, rather different results come from different reactions.

If we want to be productive and fruitful, when tough times come two choices exist. Quit, or dig in. It's time to stay in the game — mixing faith with the Word enables you to do that. One of my favorite stories comes from the gospels as the disciples find themselves in a ship when a storm arises.

> *And when he was entered into a ship, his disciples followed him. And, behold, there arose a great tempest in the sea, insomuch that the ship was covered with the waves; but he was asleep. And his disciples came to him, and awoke him, saying, Lord, save us; we perish.*
>
> *And he saith unto them, Why are ye fearful, O ye of little faith? Then he arose, and rebuked the winds and the sea; and there was a great calm. But the men marveled, saying, What manner of man is this, that even the winds and the sea obey him!* Matthew 8:23–37

Ever feel like those disciples on the boat? Lord, it's a crisis, and you're asleep! Don't you care? Where are you? Were they ever in any danger? Of course not. Yet (here's the lesson), *did they act like it?* Negative. Are you in any danger? Remember, that does not mean an easy (or even long) life. You can be persecuted and killed, die a long and suffering death from cancer, but that does not mean God forgot you. Your eternal security remains secure, and that's the important part.

It's commonly taught Jesus' rebuke of their faith (or lack thereof) meant they didn't understand who Jesus was, and when they would arrive at a fuller understanding, problems like these would vanish. Not true, for the simple reason they woke Him up. They weren't concerned by anyone else sleeping, they woke up the one guy they knew could handle the situation.

What faith did they lack? Faith in His plan. In Mark 4:35 Jesus said let's go over to the other side. He did *not* say let's go out to the middle of the lake and drown. They knew who He was, but lacked faith — the reasonable expectation knowing who He is He had the ability to carry out what He said.

Fear leads to unbelief, doubt, and despair. The dark side are these. If you want to be successful, you must cast them off. Another example comes from Peter walking on water in Matthew 14.

> *And straightway Jesus constrained his disciples to get into a ship, and to go before him unto the other side, while he sent the multitudes away. And when he had sent the multitudes away, he went up into a mountain apart to pray; and when the evening was come, he was there alone. But the ship was now in the midst of the sea, tossed with waves; for the wind was contrary.*
>
> *And in the fourth watch of the night Jesus went unto them, walking on the sea. And when the disciples saw him walking on the sea, they were troubled, saying, It is a spirit; and they cried out for fear.*
>
> *But straightway Jesus spoke unto them, saying, Be of good cheer; it is I; be not afraid. And Peter answered him and said, Lord, if it be thou, bid me come unto thee on the water. And he said, Come. And when Peter was come down out of the ship, he walked on the water, to go to Jesus.*
>
> *But when he saw the wind boisterous, he was afraid; and beginning to sink, he cried, saying, Lord, save me. And immediately Jesus stretched forth his hand, and caught him, and said unto him, O thou of little faith, wherefore didst thou doubt? And when they were come into the ship, the wind ceased.* Matthew 14:22–32

Faith or foam, it's your choice. Earlier they lacked faith in His plan — what He said, He meant. You must mix action with faith. Peter tried, and started to sink as he believed what he saw instead of what he knew. That wasn't the only time Peter needed to mix faith with action; Acts 12 explains faith as Peter finds himself in prison.

> *Peter therefore was kept in prison; but prayer was made without ceasing by the church unto God for him. And when Herod would have brought him forth, the same night Peter was sleeping between two soldiers, bound with two chains; and the keepers before the door kept the prison.* Acts 12:5–6

It's a bad situation. Hopeless. No chance of escape.

> *And, behold, an angel of the Lord came upon him, and a light shone in the prison; and he smote Peter on the side, and raised him up, saying, Arise up quickly. And his chains fell off from his hands. And the angel said unto him, Gird thyself, and bind on thy sandals. And so he did. And he saith unto him, Cast thy garment about thee, and follow me.*
> Acts 12:7-8

Peter had to act on what he knew and heard — it took faith for that. Peter had to change his faith to action. Failing that, he'd still find himself chained in prison. The chains of your hopeless situation are gone. Do you act like it? Many times we don't, but never forget faith does not mean you'll get a Lexus and a pony.

In verse 9, Peter didn't believe it, yet acted anyway. Sometimes you might not 100% believe what you've been told, but again, faith doesn't mean that. It means you have a reasonable expectation based on what you do know, and faith requires you to act on that, as Peter did.

If Peter hadn't acted on what he saw, he'd still be in prison. Sure, he could have engaged in a scholarly discussion about it: that's a good theological point (chains represent the spiritual battle in each of us), and maybe I see how that might work out. He could have gone round and round for hours in his head.

No, Peter GET UP! Get moving!

Later in the chapter, notice the response of those praying for Peter's release. They're deep in prayer when Peter arrives at the door free from prison. They send the servant girl away, saying stop bothering us, we're praying for Peter!

Lesson for the day: when you ask the creator of the universe to intervene, expect results. Maybe not what you want, maybe not when you want, maybe not how you want, but at some point you will see a response. Chuck Missler says never underestimate a person's ability to rationalize. In other words, failure to use what you *know* to be true. That's unbelief.

> *For we which have believed do enter into rest, as he said, As I have sworn in my wrath, if they shall enter into my rest; although the works were finished from the foundation of the world. For he spoke in a certain place of the seventh day in this way, And God did rest the seventh day from all his works.*
> Hebrews 4:3-4

Those who believe enter rest. But if you're one of those "modernizing" the Bible and deny it says what it says, rest will elude you. You're free to accept or reject any of what the Bible says, but people look silly claiming when God said xyz He actually meant abc. Or worse, certain parts (that only they or other scholars can determine) don't apply today.

Ask those so-called scholars who gets to decide what is—and is not—God's Word. Why should we accept their method over others? Notice they deny parts they don't like (that seems to be their criteria). Scholars constantly fight over what God really said, so are never at rest, only constantly arguing.

Why did God rest the seventh day? Was He tired? No, He rested because there was nothing left to do. Rest comes when you realize nothing remains to be done — He did it all. Rest also eludes those holding a Jesus+ view of salvation, the idea they must do something to get (or maintain) their salvation. Those people find themselves forever searching for rest, but never able to obtain it. In contrast, I'm not resting because life is easy, I'm resting because I know in whom I have trusted. There's nothing left for me to do.

> *And in this place again, If they shall enter into my rest. Seeing therefore it remaineth that some must enter therein, and they to whom it was first preached entered not in because of unbelief, Again, he limiteth a certain day, saying in David, Today, after so long a time; as it is said, Today if ye will hear his voice, harden not your hearts.*   Hebrews 4:5–7

We return to the Jews' example upon leaving Egypt. They failed to enter the rest simply because they didn't believe it. Rest was always available to them, but they chose not to accept it. God won't *force* you to enter rest (that's kind of a contradiction anyway), you're free to strain and struggle if you wish. After all, the Jews made exactly such a choice. Should we not learn from the past?

We can learn from an interesting concept in law known as the pardon. You might not know a pardon holds no power or usefulness if the person won't accept it; two US Supreme Court cases affirm this legal concept.

> *A pardon is a deed, to the validity of which delivery is essential, and delivery is not complete without acceptance. It may then be rejected by the person to whom it is tendered, and if it be rejected, we have discovered no power in a court to force it on him. ...A pardon may be conditional, and the*

condition may be more objectionable than the punishment inflicted by the judgment.*

SCOTUS (the US Supreme Court) held a conditional pardon — even if in a capital crime — may be rejected. After all, they may not like the conditions, and accepting a pardon implies guilt. The key point SCOTUS held — you can't be forced to accept something, *even if it's beneficial to you.* Legally, you can reject a pardon of a death sentence, and you can also reject God's offer of rest.

When should you cast aside unbelief? Today! The Lord makes many promises; people don't find them because they refuse to believe them. You'll see it when you believe it, not the other way around. Cast off unbelief now, and don't become hard-hearted as each day hardens the heart a bit more. Never forget Paul speaks to Christians, thus it's those the warning applies to.

Without faith, it is *impossible* to please God. The Jews failed the faith requirement, and thus wandered powerless. It was by their choice, however, they wandered powerless. If they accepted God's Word on faith, history would have been quite different.

> *For if Joshua had given them rest, then would he not afterward have spoken of another day. There remaineth therefore a rest to the people of God.* Hebrews 4:8-9

A rest *is* available to you, but like the Jews, you must believe it exists. It's not a cessation of activity, but a restful spirit in times of crisis. It's faith in God's plan that no matter what transpires, His Word will occur. Not blind trust, but a reasonable belief based on facts and experience. At 3 AM you've got what you've got. We *all* have crises in life; some stumble, some prosper through, some thrive and inspire others. Those making it through discover rest by faith, those failing do not.

> *For he that is entered into his rest, he also hath ceased from his own works, as God did from his.* Hebrews 4:10

If you're trying by your own efforts, you'll never find much rest. It's all about Him.

> *Let us labor, therefore, to enter into that rest, lest any man fall after the same example of unbelief.* Hebrews 4:11

---

* United States v. Wilson — 32 U.S. 150 (1833), see also Burdick v. United States — 236 U.S. 79 (1915)

Labor? To rest? Yep. Simple ideas, yet incredibly hard to put in practice. You must work at resting. No, that's not an oxymoron, as rest (in the Biblical sense) doesn't mean lack of activity, it reflects a state of mind and spirit. It doesn't mean easy street either. It means having the ability to stay in the game.

The vast majority of cars sold now come with automatic transmissions. For us old-timers, if you recall when you first tried to drive a manual transmission, it wasn't very restful, was it? But after you get the hang of it, you can sing with the radio and talk at the same time, because you're resting and you believe you can do it — no doubt exists. Of course, some people never rest — we call them clutch killers.

> *For the word of God is living, and powerful, and sharper than any two-edged sword, piercing even to the dividing asunder of soul and spirit, and of the joints and marrow, and is a discerner of the thoughts and intents of the heart. Neither is there any creature that is not manifest in his sight, but all things are naked and opened unto the eyes of him with whom we have to do.*   Hebrews 4:12–13

Frequently used for witnessing, it applies to Christians. If you think you're getting by with something, you're wrong. As you read your Bible, you'll come to sections proving a bit uncomfortable, sections you'd rather ignore. Perhaps that means it's time to reflect and consider your actions.

Unless, of course, you want to join the ranks of heretics who, when they arrive at a part of the Bible they don't like, ignore it or claim it's not for today (we group all those under the banner of liberal theology). You know, that part doesn't mean what it says, or it's not meant for today. This verse still applies to those people as well, as all things are open to God.

Paul speaks of thoughts and intents, *not* actions or results. Too often we're worried about results instead of intents. The end does not justify the means. In fact, you're not responsible for results at all — that's God's problem. You *are* responsible for your effort and intent. Remember the sermon on the mount. The whole idea centered around intent, not necessarily actions or results.

> *Seeing then that we have a great high priest, that is passed into the heavens, Jesus the Son of God, let us hold fast our profession. For we have not an high priest which cannot be touched with the feeling of our infirmities; but was in*

Danger of Dull Hearing

all points tempted like as we are, yet without sin. Let us therefore come boldly unto the throne of grace, that we may obtain mercy, and find grace to help in time of need.
Hebrews 4:14-16

The Greek word for boldly means to speak freely. In the military when you're called on the carpet and required to give an answer, a certain protocol exists — some things you simply don't say. So you request permission to speak freely and break that decorum. No such problem exists with God, He says you're always allowed to speak freely.

God says let your requests be made known to Him. But He doesn't say you'll get your way. He doesn't say you'll understand. He doesn't say you'll receive instant gratification. He doesn't promise a Lexus. Or a pony. Or ice cream. Only that He has your best in mind.

When we talk about faith, unbelief and such, we always assume if God is a good God, then when we're healed, start the new job, and life is good that means God is good. But when the test comes back terminal? When a nail punctures your tire, is your first thought "Praise the Lord"? Does His character change if we don't get our way? Of course not. Only our attitude. It matters not if you're healed or not, God's character will not change. He doesn't stop being good and loving because the answer to your request comes back negative.

Consider this; perhaps it's not the strong and prayerful receiving a positive response, rather the weak who can't handle adversity. Paul prayed three times for healing, and he received the response "My grace is sufficient for you." As a tower of faith, even in tough times, Paul could live with the trouble and not have it impact his faith.

Similar to the eating of meat in Romans 14 and 1 Corinthians 8:7-9, notice it's not the one *refraining* from eating having stronger faith, it's the one who does eat, knowing no problem with it exists. We commonly get that backward, and see people holding a long list of rules, and think, my, look at them, they don't do all those things, how spiritual.

Paul flips common wisdom around — the one appearing weak by eating actually has stronger faith. I think a similar idea can happen with healing also. Not always, but it's something to think about. Some simply haven't grown to the point where they can maintain their faith in times of trials — God might choose them to heal. Why are some healed, and others not? Nobody knows, but what right does the clay have to speak back to the potter?

> *Content. That's the word. A state of heart in which you would be at peace if God gave you nothing more than he already has. Test yourself with this question: What if God's only gift to you were his grace to save you. Would you be content? You beg him to save the life of your child. You plead with him to keep your business afloat. You implore him to remove the cancer from your body. What if his answer is, "My grace is enough." Would you be content?*
>
> *But there are those times when God, having given us his grace, hears our appeals and says, "My grace is sufficient for you." Is he being unfair?**

Romans 8:28 says "And we know that all things work together for good to them that love God, to them who are the called according to his purpose." It does *not* say you'll understand. That's what we want, but don't always get. So we pray and request, and sometimes even beg. If God is God, then He knows more than you. We arrive at a philosophical question called the problem of evil. More simply, why does God allow bad things to happen to good people? We begin with ideas everyone can agree on.

1. God is good, all-knowing, and all-powerful.

2. Evil exists.

Everyone should agree on those; even the atheist denying God exists would agree on the characteristics of God, if He were to exist. Continuing on with the thought:

1. A perfectly good being would want to prevent all evils.

2. An omniscient being knows every way in which evils can come into existence.

3. An omnipotent being who knows every way in which an evil can come into existence has the power to prevent that evil from coming into existence.

---

*   Lucado (2005, page 131)

4. A being who knows every way in which an evil can come into existence, who is able to prevent that evil from coming into existence, and who wants to do so, would prevent the existence of that evil.*

Since evil *does* exist, therefore, the philosopher proclaims, God can't exist. Not just *doesn't* exist as the atheist claims, but can't. It's impossible for such a being (whether the Christian God or some other) to exist. You should be ready to give every man an answer. That doesn't mean being a philosopher, but each Christian should hold some basic knowledge to defend their faith. That also means handling tough questions like the problem of evil. After all, left unchallenged, this logical deduction means God can't exist.

Step number four causes the problem. For if an all-knowing, all-powerful, all-loving God has some reason to allow evil to exist, the argument falls apart. What possible reason could a God of that nature have to allow evil to exist? In other words, why not create a cosmos where no one has the possibility to do evil? Why not create a utopia where we all live happily ever after?

Simply put, the only way to know why God would allow evil is if you were God yourself and had the same knowledge He had. Of course, if you *were* God, then trying to prove God doesn't exist is a bizarre proposition, is it not? The nature of God isn't at issue — by definition He is all-knowing and benevolent — rather, the atheist makes the mistake thinking he possesses the same knowledge and experience as God — an error attributed to hubris.

Another answer exists as well. Sure, God *could* create a cosmos where you had no choice but to follow Him and live in His presence, but if such a universe existed the (potential) atheist would be the first to shake their fist at God and proclaim "you gave me no choice — that's not fair!" And he'd be right — forced love represents a contradiction.

So God gives you a choice, you can do good or evil, accept Him or reject Him, live in heaven or not. It's all your choice. By allowing you to make that free will choice, it also means you have the capability to choose poorly, or do evil things. God respects your choice and does not force Himself on anyone. If you don't want Him, fine. If you do, fine. You're a free agent and can choose your own destiny. So yes, God *could* prevent you from doing evil, but then you'd be nothing more than a puppet. So God allows you to choose, knowing some will choose Him, others won't.

---

*   http://www.iep.utm.edu/evil-evi/

Additionally, one more error arises with the problem of evil, and that involves the nature of God. Being all-powerful does *not* provide the ability to do anything. Read that again, and be sure it sinks in — being all-powerful does *not* provide the ability to do anything. All-powerful God can't do at least three things. First, He can't learn. If you know everything, no possibility exists of learning. Second, He can't lie. It's against His nature. Third, He can't make you love Him. Love implies a voluntary choice, you can't be forced to love someone.

Finally, the eternal question — why do bad things happen to good people? The simple answer — there are no good people. All have fallen short. God doesn't grade on a curve, and being better than the next guy won't cut it. But, as Paul moves on he provides another answer.

> *Who comforteth us in all our tribulation, that we may be able to comfort them which are in any trouble, by the comfort wherewith we ourselves are comforted of God.*
>
> 2 Corinthians 1:4

Many times when someone else has gone through the same situation, you must be humble enough to say "I need help," which isn't always easy to do. Don't suffer alone, it's likely someone else has crawled through similar territory, no matter how dry and barren. Maybe there's really nothing you can do. All you can say is I've been there. I get it.

God isn't worried about you driving a Lexus, He's concerned about character — those words we don't like to talk about anymore: duty, honor, commitment, responsibility. We don't see much of those anymore, in fact, we're so used to politicians lying it hardly registers. But character matters. Sometimes you need something you can't get any other way. Since that's what God focuses on, a small temporary inconvenience pays for eternal fitness.

Lest you think that's crazy, it's Paul, not me:

> *For our light affliction, which is but for a moment, worketh for us a far more exceeding and eternal weight of glory;*
>
> 2 Corinthians 4:17

Paul and light affliction don't go hand in hand. They tried to kill him on more than one occasion. Every ship he sailed on went down. He had medical problems, legal problems, problems in the city, problems in the country, yet Paul finished his letter to Timothy with:

Danger of Dull Hearing

> *But watch thou in all things, endure afflictions, do the work of an evangelist, make full proof of thy ministry. For I am now ready to be offered, and the time of my departure is at hand. I have fought a good fight, I have finished my course, I have kept the faith.*
> 2 Timothy 4:5–7

What do you do in times of crisis? How do you stay in the game? Paul said come boldly to the throne, to find grace to help in time of need. That's it. No magic answers. I don't have special words to make it go away, and nobody else does either. In the darkest times of life, you face two choices: quit or dig in. I've seen many people quit, and they don't fare well. Stay in the game. Never give in, never surrender.

One week during our Wednesday church service a tragic event occurred as a train struck and killed a person in the middle of our town (and only a few hundred yards from our building). As it turns out, video from the train revealed the person walked to the middle of the tracks, closed their eyes, and waited to be hit. Suicide by locomotive.

Depression and desperation perhaps caused this person to end their life. Everyone at some point feels alone and troubled (that's part of the human condition), yet not everyone feels the need to invoke a permanent solution to a temporary problem. Why? I certainly can't solve the world's problems (and won't even try), but I've learned over the years one simple truth: You are not alone.

Oh sure, it may (likely does) *feel* like that, but it's not true. Elijah certainly suffered from depression; after the high point of Mt. Carmel and defeating the prophets of Baal, what happens in the next chapter? The queen has it out for him, and he becomes depressed and pouts.

> *I have been very jealous for the Lord God of hosts. For the children of Israel have forsaken thy covenant, thrown down thine altars, and slain thy prophets with the sword; and I, even I only, am left; and they seek my life, to take it away.*
> 1 Kings 19:10

What was his problem? He bought the lie he was all alone. Hiding, depressed, and feeling all alone, the Lord responds to Elijah "Yet I have left me seven thousand in Israel, all the knees which have not bowed unto Baal." To paraphrase God's response: You are not alone. Even the giant of the New Testament — the apostle Paul — struggled with problems, at one point proclaiming:

> *For we would not, brethren, have you ignorant of our trouble which came to us in Asia, that we were pressed out of measure, above strength, insomuch that we despaired even of life.*   2 Corinthians 1:8

Paul? Despaired of life? Burdened beyond measure? Beyond strength? Yep. You are not alone. Yes, sometimes it feels like it, but you're not. If you have feelings of hopelessness and despair, do one more thing before giving up: reach out (in person) to a friend, counselor, pastor, or someone else you trust. Sure, you think it won't work, sure you might believe it's a waste of your time, definitely they won't understand what you're going through. Do it anyway.

After all, if you're right, will tomorrow differ from today? That same black cloud still looms overhead waiting for you — you've lost nothing. Yet if you're wrong, tomorrow could be quite different from today. Reject permanent solutions to problems, no matter how difficult those problems are. *Behold, I am the Lord, the God of all flesh: is there any thing too hard for me?**

So what do we do when the rubber meets the road?

- The test comes back positive — it's cancer. Aggressive. Inoperable. Terminal.

- The phone rings — your wife had a heart attack. She's gone.

- Alzheimer's slowly takes the ability to function away.

- The job paying the bills suddenly disappears.

What then? Sure, I realize I'm not alone. Sure, I understand I need to stay in the game. But how exactly am I supposed to do that? Think back to December 1944, during the battle of Bastogne. It's wintery cold — the coldest in decades. Hitler makes a final push, with a focus on Bastogne.

The Allies rush to defend it.

On December 22nd, the Germans ask the surrounded Americans to "honorably surrender"; General McAuliffe responds with one word: **NUTS!** When pressed for a way to translate the one-word reply into German, the interpreter said it roughly means "Go to hell, and if you continue to attack we'll kill every %#*! German entering the city."

Two days later, the General—on Christmas eve—pens a memo:

---

*   Jeremiah 32:27

Danger of Dull Hearing

> *What's merry about all this, you ask? We're fighting — it's cold — we aren't home. ...We have stopped cold everything that has been thrown at us from the north, east, south and west ...The Germans actually did surround us, their radios blared our doom. Allied troops are counterattacking in force. We continue to hold Bastogne ...**

Perhaps it's been a tough week (or month, or decade). Broke. Sick. Cold. Doom. Despair. You're trying to hold on to the last piece of ground you've got, and you're tired of fighting. You are never alone, even as you sit silently in your foxhole.

The enemy sends a message demanding your total surrender — you can sit out the final years of the war in a prison camp, but relatively comfortable. Either that, the enemy says, or you'll be destroyed, your carcass strewn over the frozen tundra, if any large pieces remain.

NUTS!

Never give in. Never quit. Never surrender. Sure, service for God is tough, but you're not called to cigar-smoking in an easy chair, you're called to be a soldier. And that's tough — in any weather. Recall another lesson from Christmas past:

> *These are the times that try men's souls. The summer soldier and the sunshine patriot will, in this crisis, shrink from the service of their country; but he that stands by it now, deserves the love and thanks of man and woman. Tyranny, like hell, is not easily conquered; yet we have this consolation with us, that the harder the conflict, the more glorious the triumph.†*

Cancer? Sickness? Poverty? Peril? All part of the life — you won't find retirement in the Bible. Daniel continued to be called, long after he "retired" from official service. You're *never* too young, too old, too sick, too broke — too anything. It's time to dig in, because the battle will be long, hard, and tiring. *Count on it.* God didn't say *easy*, he said *soldier*.

STAND UP! It's time to get off the couch, and get back in the game. Life isn't easy. Yes, the battle is hard. Yes, you'll take enemy fire. Yes, sometimes you'll be cold. Yes, others (even "Christians") will criticize you. That's the way it is.

---

*   https://web.archive.org/web/20141230205014/http://www.history.army.mil/books/wwii/Bastogne/bast-20.htm (accessed Sep 14, 2013)
†   Thomas Paine, "The Crisis"

> *The credit belongs to the man who is actually in the arena, whose face is marred by dust and sweat and blood; who strives valiantly; who errs, who comes short again and again, because there is no effort without error and shortcoming; but who does actually strive to do the deeds; who knows great enthusiasms, the great devotions; who spends himself in a worthy cause; who at the best knows in the end the triumph of high achievement, and who at the worst, if he fails, at least fails while daring greatly ...**

You continue to serve until you draw your last breath. All the problems you face ...NUTS! Get help, learn, study, commit, and soldier on ...because it's 2:59 AM you're not a superhero, and it's time to fight.

During WWII, Winston Churchill delivered many bold speeches to inspire the people. At that time the war wasn't going well, and frankly, it wasn't hard to conceive Germany gaining total control of Europe. Standing in their way lay a stubborn Brit.

> *I would say to the House, as I said to those who've joined this government: "I have nothing to offer but blood, toil, tears and sweat." We have before us an ordeal of the most grievous kind. We have before us many, many long months of struggle and of suffering. You ask, what is our policy? I will say: It is to wage war, by sea, land and air, with all our might and with all the strength that God can give us; to wage war against a monstrous tyranny, never surpassed in the dark and lamentable catalogue of human crime. That is our policy. You ask, what is our aim? I can answer in one word: victory. Victory at all costs, victory in spite of all terror, victory, however long and hard the road may be; for without victory, there is no survival.*†

> *Hitler knows that he will have to break us in this Island or lose the war. If we can stand up to him, all Europe may be free and the life of the world may move forward into broad, sunlit uplands. But if we fail, then the whole world, including the United States, including all that we have known and cared for, will sink into the abyss of a new Dark Age made more sinister, and perhaps more protracted, by the lights of perverted science.*

---

* "Citizenship in a Republic" Theodore Roosevelt April 23, 1910
† "Blood, Toil, Tears" House of Commons, May 13, 1940

Danger of Dull Hearing

> *Let us therefore brace ourselves to our duties, and so bear ourselves that if the British Empire and its Commonwealth last for a thousand years, men will still say, This was their finest hour.**
>
> *Even though large tracts of Europe and many old and famous States have fallen or may fall into the grip of the Gestapo and all the odious apparatus of Nazi rule, we shall not flag or fail.*
>
> *We shall go on to the end, we shall fight in France, we shall fight on the seas and oceans, we shall fight with growing confidence and growing strength in the air, we shall defend our Island, whatever the cost may be, we shall fight on the beaches, we shall fight on the landing grounds, we shall fight in the fields and in the streets, we shall fight in the hills; we shall never surrender, and even if, which I do not for a moment believe, this Island or a large part of it were subjugated and starving, then our Empire beyond the seas, armed and guarded by the British Fleet, would carry on the struggle, until, in God's good time, the New World, with all its power and might, steps forth to the rescue and the liberation of the old.*†

For the people living through WWII, only one option existed: victory. No quitting, no surrendering. Sadly that attitude has been lost, as many currently think it's too hard, I quit, somebody bail me out! Many Christians do the same thing. It's time to saddle up folks, because it's not going to get easier.

You probably know everything I wrote in the last pages, but do you believe it? Do you act like it? We *must* be wary of becoming dull of hearing, which leads to unbelief. When times are tough, where will you go? I've spent the better part of a decade trying to find alternatives. Atheism, evolution, eastern philosophy — none of them stand up, and I've taken the best shots from those groups claiming I'm wrong.

When the enemy arrives at 3 AM demanding your surrender, you've got what you've got. No bestseller books, no faith guru, no magic beans, no easy answers, nothing. You come boldly, to do that you must have faith, not in a genie granting wishes, a Lexus, and a pony (with ice cream), but a loving God who knows you and has your best future in mind.

---

* "Their Finest Hour" Parliament at Westminster, June 18, 1940
† "We Shall Fight on the Beaches" House of Commons, June 4, 1940

For I know the thoughts that I think toward you, saith the Lord, thoughts of peace, and not of evil, to give you an expected end.
Jeremiah 29:11

Whew! That's a tough section. But if you want to stay in the game it's time to fill up that toolbox and make sure you not only know what we've covered, but you apply it. Grab your lunch-box and hard-hat, and get to work.

Because at 3 AM, you've got what you've got.

...And it's 2:59 AM.

Chapter 8

Danger of Dormancy

For every high priest taken from among men is ordained for men in things pertaining to God, that he may offer both gifts and sacrifices for sins; Hebrews 5:1

A priest represents man to God. One duty involved offering sacrifices to God on a person's behalf. Post-cross, Christ performs that role, as the curtain of the temple was torn in two, it signified everyone's uninhibited access to God. As Paul still speaks to a Jewish audience, the idea of a priest would be instantly identifiable to them.

A sacrifice appears quaint and easy to read, but doesn't create the necessary impact. We toss around familiar words like sacrifice, without stopping to consider what they imply. How did we get in this mess, and more important, what is required to rescue us from it? When we lost our beloved 16-year-old dog, it made a big impression, but the dog provided one final lesson. Sin stinks. Allow me to digress a bit, and let's travel back to Genesis.

On the fifth day God created Dachshunds, and all manner of dogs, and God saw that they were good.
Genesis 1:21, Yeager translation

Back in the garden, death, disease, and entropy didn't exist. Everyone had a pony. Ice cream didn't make you fat. Puppies played joyfully with all. Life was good. But enter the villain, stage far-left.

Now the snake was more cunning and deceitful than any family-friendly pet that God had made, and he slithered up to the woman and said "Did God say you shall not eat of any tree?" And the woman said "we shalt not eat of the tree in the middle of the garden, lest entropy and decay enter the cosmos, and my puppy die." Then the slimy snake lied to her face saying, "your puppy shall not die" ...

Well, you know the rest of the story. It doesn't end well for them, and they get tossed out of paradise. That's not the end, of course, we still pay for that mistake long ago. Death. Disease. Decay. It's ugly. It begins with Satan and his deception in the garden ... and ends thousands of years later with my dog: diabetes, kidney failure, blind, and deaf. He took my dog, the sick bastard. Maybe not directly, but the events he set in motion ended in the 21st century with the death of my dog.

The physicist understands what happened — entropy entered into the world, better known as decay, death, and sin. We can't do anything about it, it's a normal force of the fallen cosmos we inhabit. Still, my dog is gone. Sin is ugly, gross, and like "The Blob" (for you old-timers) oozes around and takes the life of everyone it comes in contact with. Death. Disease. Chaos. It killed my dog.

Fixing the situation requires a sacrifice. Sin is ugly and nasty, and requires a permanent solution — sacrifice, a word we glibly toss around. Nobody in the Old Testament would have that problem; the sacrifices offered provided a constant reminder of the fruits of sin: decay, death.

Consider Passover. Imagine each family keeping a lamb for a week or so — it becomes a family pet, and all the kids love it (like a dog). One day you slit its throat and watch the blood drain out in a pool on the floor and the life slowly ebb away from such a beloved family pet. Yes, it's ugly, and a constant reminder of the result of sin on the cosmos.

Disgusting. Sick. Decay. Sin. It killed my dog. It killed those sheep. It will kill us. That's what sin causes, that's the legacy from Adam. It's ugly, and that's the lesson from my dog. We sometimes have a quaint idea of sin, but it took the life of my dog, and that's something never to be forgotten.

Who can have compassion on the ignorant, and on them that are out of the way; for that he himself also is compassed with infirmity. Hebrews 5:2

Compassion on the ignorant doesn't mean people with low IQ. The Law contained provisions for sins you didn't even know existed.

Danger of Dormancy

Some may shout, that's not fair! How can I be held accountable for laws I didn't even know about? Ask the government, as they write tens of thousands of laws; do you know all of them?

In Alabama, it was once (and perhaps still is) illegal to have an ice cream cone in your back pocket. Why you would want to do that, and more, why someone would write a law against it, is unknown. Crazy laws abound — in Portland, Oregon:*

- Shoelaces must be tied while walking down the street.
- You cannot wear roller skates in restrooms.
- It's against the law for a wedding ceremony to be performed at a skating rink.
- People may not whistle underwater.
- Persons may not pass through a "traffic congestion thoroughfare" more than twice per night. (16.70.740)

You can break laws you never even knew existed. That's ignorance. The government isn't so forgiving about breaking laws you didn't know existed — even if the law makes no sense. But we have a high priest who intercedes for us, sometimes when we don't even know we need it.

> *And by reason of this he ought, as for the people, so also for himself, to offer for sins.* Hebrews 5:3

Recall the Day of Atonement as the high priest performed elaborate rituals to deal with his own sin first; if he failed when he entered the Holy of Holies it wouldn't end well. After taking care of himself, he could then offer sacrifices for the sins of the people.

> *And no man taketh this honor unto himself, but he that is called of God, as was Aaron. So also Christ glorified not himself to be made an high priest; but he that said unto him, Thou art my Son, today have I begotten thee.* Hebrews 5:4–5

Ministry isn't so much your choice, as what God appointed you for. You may not be doing what God called you to, but you still have a role. Tragedy arises when people don't step up and do what they should be doing. Contrary to popular belief, it's not only the pastor's job — Christianity is not (supposed to be) a spectator sport.

---

* http://www.dumblaws.com/laws/united-states/oregon?page=20

God calls you to a role, but He won't force you to perform it. You can sit decade after decade and do nothing, and no lightning strike will come. You'll miss out on opportunities and rewards for doing what He empowered you for, but you won't be struck down, lose your salvation, or anything else; no penalty exists for lost opportunities.

> *As he saith also in another place, Thou art a priest for ever after the order of Melchizedek.*   Hebrews 5:6

Melchizedek arrives in Genesis 14, one of those passages you'd probably blip over if not for the mention here in Hebrews. Only a few verses exist about him in Genesis, but he brings bread and wine, and that should cause the serious Bible student to look more closely.

> *Who in the days of his flesh, when he had offered up prayers and supplications with strong crying and tears unto him that was able to save him from death, and was heard in that he feared; Though he were a Son, yet learned he obedience by the things which he suffered; And being made perfect, he became the author of eternal salvation unto all them that obey him, called of God an high priest after the order of Melchizedek.*   Hebrews 5:7–10

The priests for Israel came from the line of Aaron, but notice Melchizedek arrives *before* God changes Abram's name to Abraham in Genesis 17, or if you will the Melchizedek priesthood arrives pre-Judaism.

That's the easy part of the chapter. Everyone fears chapter 6 of Hebrews, but the next section holds greater challenges. Why? Chapter 6 contains theology, and in a way it's abstract. It's something people have argued over for centuries, but in reality holds little bearing on how I live my life. The following section contains concrete application, and it's hard to hear. If it doesn't make you nervous, you're not paying close enough attention. If you're offended by the next verses, take it up with Paul.

> *Of whom we have many things to say, and hard to be uttered, seeing ye are dull of hearing.*   Hebrews 5:11

Paul wants to continue, but considers his audience. They can't handle it. They're not prepared, not because they haven't heard, but because they haven't absorbed and applied what they know.

A difference exists between hearing and applying. It's easy to sit in church year after year and hear the Word, but fail to apply it.

Perhaps you've known someone who attended church for years, but suddenly does something crazy like leave their wife for someone found on the Internet. When I heard of others doing that, I thought it must be a failure of proper teaching and instruction. Perhaps if they attended a church teaching through the Bible chapter by chapter those things wouldn't happen.

However, I've seen people sitting under quality teaching for decades suddenly go sideways. The only reason I can think of is they failed to *apply* what they *know*. It's head knowledge only, and the failure to implement what they hear leads to their downfall.

When Paul says they're dull of hearing, it can also mean they don't have the fundamentals down, thus it's impossible to move on to more mature subjects. Suppose I was teaching Quantum Mechanics, you first require some Calculus, differential equations, wave theory, and so on. Paul doesn't mean you don't understand those, as those are advanced concepts.

Rather, if you don't know $2 + 2 = 4$, we've got problems, exactly as Paul says. We should all have those basics down, ideas forming the foundation on which to build. So Paul has more to say, but we don't get to hear it because he issues the following warning:

> *For when for the time ye ought to be teachers, ye have need that one teach you again the first principles of the oracles of God; and are become such as have need of milk, and not of solid food. For every one that useth milk is unskilful in the word of righteousness; for he is a babe.*   Hebrews 5:12–13

When Paul mentions teachers it doesn't mean everyone should all be leading Bible Study, rather it implies what goes on before and after the service, or during the week. You should be able to apply and repeat what you've already learned. You don't get out of the warning by saying you haven't been called as a teacher. No, in some sense, we're *all* teachers, not only the guy standing in the pulpit Sunday morning.

> *But solid food belongeth to them that are of full age, even those who by reason of use have their senses exercised to discern both good and evil.*   Hebrews 5:14

It's time to get back in the game. Remember Zechariah? The Jews began to build the temple, but quit. Coach Zechariah arrives on the scene and motivates them to keep going. Don't quit, don't give up. Sadly, too many times we hear the cry it's too hard, or I'm too busy, or something else. Anything and everything takes priority over service for God, as God becomes relegated far down the list. Sure, service for God is tough, but Paul reminded the Corinthians to stay in the game, despite the setbacks.

> *Therefore, my beloved brethren, be steadfast, immovable, always abounding in the work of the Lord, knowing that your labor is not in vain in the Lord.* 1 Corinthians 15:58

Zodhiates notes labor isn't the actual work, rather it's the weariness coming *from* that work. You're going to be tired at times, and occasionally require a break. It's okay to take a rest. When that happens, the church should have others ready to step in, as a lesson from the Oregon football teams of the Chip Kelly era illustrate.

> *Chip Kelly's mantra has always been — "next man up." That's how the Ducks practice and that's the philosophy of this team. If a player goes down to injury, the next player in should be prepared — mentally and physically — to play.**

Coach Kelly *never* talks about injuries.

> *"We don't talk about it, ever," said Kelly, whose team improved to 2–0. "We're going next man in, if we have to go next man in."*†

A player gets dinged up, next man up, grab your helmet, you're in. No problem. Sure, the team functions a bit differently, but it's not the end of the team. The church should (no, must) work the same way. Is someone on the disabled list for a while? Grab your helmet and get in the game. Are you prepared to do so? Do you know where to find your helmet when the coach says you're in?

Let's rephrase Paul's words in Chip Kelly terms: You guys aren't ready to be next man up. If a teammate goes down, you must be ready, or the team suffers. It's time to step up — or as I say, it's 2:59 AM — and get back in the game.

---

* http://oregonduckfootballnews.com/uncategorized/alonso-and-jordan-expected-to-return-to-oregon-defense-next-man-up-philosophy-a-valuable-role-in-team-success

† https://web.archive.org/web/20120915060139/http://www.registerguard.com/web/updates/28721464-55/boyett-ducks-saturday-kelly-oregon.html.csp

Danger of Dormancy

Sadly, the difference between football and the church comes down to dedication — while football players prioritize team, working in the weight room, and practice, the church argues over which presents the bigger problem, ignorance or apathy? With the answer being "I don't know, and I don't care."

Apparently it's too much for the church to be at least as dedicated as a football team, as the church can be infested with slackers and pew-warmers. Are you prepared to be next man in? If not, what holds you back? It's easy to expend time and effort on things having little or no eternal value. Yes, you need to work and feed your family, but how many other activities consume time with no benefit? Yes, that means watching MTV probably doesn't make the list of priorities.

We easily become like the Pillsbury dough-boy. Fat and lazy. Oh that message was great, and those worship guys were on today. But make an impact? Get involved? Not me, not right now. The kid has to get to bed, but once he's a bit older, man I'm there. Oh, wait, school starts soon, but when it's over, oh yeah, I'm all about service.

Month after year goes by with nothing but excuses. Face it, service for God is tough. It's a sacrifice, and sometimes you just don't feel like it. That's why they call it sacrifice, you know. If what you hear Sunday and Wednesday doesn't come into play on Monday and Tuesday, what's the point? You're not prepared to be next man in. If you keep eating and feasting, but not exercising, you'll end up worse than the Pillsbury dough-boy, or as Keith Green said "How can you be so dead, when you've been so well fed?"*

This warning appears before what people find challenging in Chapter 6, but keep it in context, when we're done with the difficult part everyone focuses on, Paul returns to the message of next man in.

> *For God is not unrighteous to forget your work and labor of love, which you have shown toward His name, in that you have ministered to the saints, and do minister. And we desire that each one of you show the same diligence to the full assurance of hope until the end; that you be not slothful, but followers of them who through faith and patience inherit the promises.* Hebrews 6:10–12

God uses situations for His purpose. Ministers, elders, and others are only coaches, so what can the coaches do for you?

---

* Keith Green "Asleep in the Light"

Coaches don't play the game, they prepare players. How can you be better prepared? It's time to get off the bench, dust off your helmet, and get in the game, because it's almost 3 AM as Paul continues:

> *Therefore leaving the principles of the doctrine of Christ, let us go on unto perfection; not laying again the foundation of repentance from dead works, and of faith toward God, Of the doctrine of baptisms, and of laying on of hands, and of resurrection of the dead, and of eternal judgment.*
>
> Hebrews 6:1–2

There's nothing wrong with being a baby. It's a normal part of life — you're not born potty-trained after all. Nobody yells at a baby for failure to perform, but if at 16 the kid still isn't potty trained, well, we've got a problem.

The Christian life differs not. You're not born (again) with all the knowledge and skills you require. Nobody says you should be, and nobody will complain if you ask beginner questions. That's a normal part of life. However, as Paul says, if you've been a Christian for some time, and we still need to lay foundations again, that displays the same problem as a 16 year-old failing potty training. It's time to grow up, because you need to be ready when the coach tells you you're next man in.

Chapter 9

Danger of Infancy

PAUL CONCLUDED CHAPTER 5 WITH A PLEA to step up and avoid dull hearing. Don't be the person sitting in a chair year after year and yet never accomplishing anything. Those of dull hearing hear ideas many times, but refuse to act on what they've heard. As Coach Kelly would say, are you ready to be next man in? As we begin chapter 6, Paul moves from the danger of dormancy to the danger of development (or lack thereof) to the danger of infancy, or failure to grow.

> *Therefore leaving the principles of the doctrine of Christ, let us go on unto perfection, not laying again the foundation of repentance from dead works, and of faith toward God, Of the doctrine of baptisms, and of laying on of hands, and of resurrection of the dead, and of eternal judgment. And this will we do, if God permit.* Hebrews 6:1–3

Or in the New Living Translation:

> *So let us stop going over the basic teachings about Christ again and again. Let us go on instead and become mature in our understanding. Surely we don't need to start again with the fundamental importance of repenting from evil deeds and placing our faith in God. You don't need further instruction about baptisms, the laying on of hands, the resurrection of the dead, and eternal judgment. And so, God willing, we will move forward to further understanding.*

Paul says to become mature, or continue to develop. A world waits for you which doesn't necessarily have your best interests at heart. Are you combat-ready? Too many never go beyond the basics, and that's not a recipe for success. Yes, we're back to the question of do you want to be the pig, or Chuck Norris? Choose wisely, because at 3 AM it's too late to change your mind. By then, your success or failure has already been determined by your previous preparation (or lack thereof).

If you're reading this, the politically correct response means you're saved, you're a Christian, and you understand foundational Christian concepts. You understand:

- Salvation

- Reality of hell

- Judgment

- Resurrection

Paul's concerned too many people *never* go beyond those ideas. He's concerned as he desires to continue on to deeper subjects, but can't because while they should stand on a firm foundation, they don't. When crisis arises (as it always will), they can't respond, not because they don't want to, but because they haven't learned anything. To survive trials and bad times in life — yet maintain focus — requires effort, study, and determination.

My uncle could have been a professional golfer. A long time ago we were on the driving range hitting a bit, as a little cart drove around picking up balls. The guy in his little car (surrounded by a cage to avoid getting pummeled) drove around picking up balls. Back and forth, up and down — from 50 yards or so out to 300.

My uncle pulls out a 9-iron, proclaims he's waiting until he's "in range," and plonk! The ball lands right on top of the car. The guy drives out a bit, he pulls out a 5-iron, and plink! He drives out a bit, and 3-iron, plonk! Golf is one of his favorite pastimes. It's been a passion for a long time, but that's only a side story.

He visits people who can't come to church — he's really a pastor, but without the title (okay, he's the minister of visitation as I've discovered). He's logged thousands of visits over the years to people who can't get to church. A few years ago his back went out, requiring surgery to place rods in to stabilize it, so he can't play golf. One of his great past-times is no more. He could ride around in the cart, but can't swing a club.

Life goes on...

Later I'm told he's developed Alzheimer's. As he talks to people, he can't remember their names. So his wife gently prods him with the information required (that's Bobby Sue, or Mary Jean, for some reason in the South you must have two first names), and his ministry continues.

They're doing the job, why would God allow such hardships? Paul says not laying again foundations, go deeper. Don't accept a simple view, to survive you must continue to learn. You discover when Paul talks maturity and growing, he's not worried about Calvinism vs Arminianism, pre-trib this, post-that, Bible Translations (Textus-Receptus vs Westcott-Hort), learning Greek and Hebrew, or being scholarly. It's living where the rubber meets the road. It's *practical*.

Paul certainly understood, and didn't ask anyone to do something he didn't. Every ship he sailed on went down, he was sick, in peril in the country, in the city people wanted to kill him. Paul was no stranger to crisis. He above all knew the importance of not stagnating in the faith.

That's where you find yourself when bad things happen. First finding the *nature* of evil — what is it? If you're in trials and wondering where God is you know it's not an academic exercise. We all know Satan appears as a bad guy wearing a red suit while carrying a pitchfork. Evil. That means since God created everything, God created evil, which contradicts His nature. What do you do with that? God created monsters who shoot up schools?

We *must* deal with these problems, they can't be swept under the rug or ignored. If you do, *when* tough times come or evil strikes, you're left hanging and unprepared. Why would God allow my uncle to be put on the sidelines? After all, he's doing the job.

We'll tackle this thorny issue by considering a side question: does heat exist? Duh, yes it does. But does cold exist? The answer might surprise you, no cold does not exist. Cold only exists as the absence of heat, not as an entity itself, which explains absolute zero (-460 Fahrenheit) — once heat no longer exists, it can't get "colder."

You're familiar with a heat pump in your house, does anyone have a cold pump? Nope. Your heat pump transfers heat. In summer, it transfers heat from inside your house to outside (making the house cooler), while in winter it takes heat from outside and moves it inside (making the house warmer). Either way, only heat moves; a cold pump simply doesn't exist.

The same idea exists with light and dark, you can't add "dark," you remove light. If you've been in a cave or somewhere no light exists, you understand once it's totally dark, it can't get any darker. Why? Dark as an entity doesn't exist. Darkness exists by removing light, not adding dark.

Here's where it gets interesting — the same occurs with good and evil. Evil results when beings choose to cease being good. God didn't create evil, it's a choice of His creation. Satan isn't evil because he adds evil, he's evil because he's chosen to cease being good and rebel against God. Thus, God creating evil isn't really a problem.

You might wonder after a disastrous year, where is God? I've been kicked in the head, with sickness, bad finances, doom and despair. That's what Paul means when he says move beyond the basics. It's time to figure this out for yourself, because if even a fraction of what appears likely in the future comes to reality, you won't have your pastor to fall back on, it's up to you. After all, at 3 AM you've got what you've got.

Our current predicament (moral, financial, etc) can't continue. When something can't go on forever, it *will* end. The question is how, and will you be prepared for it? The plane flies merrily along at 30,000 feet, but the engines have run dry. The plane and the ground will soon meet, only the severity of the impact remains unknown. If people recognize the actual crisis and take action, a chance exists for a controlled landing and most if not all to survive. But if they continue to pour champagne and tell you not to worry, then the plane crashes with a spectacular fireball. Which will it be? I don't know. I'm not a prophet, just a mathematician.

You see, while the basics of Christianity are great (and important), they're just that ... basics. If you want to survive the plane running out of fuel, you'd better be prepared. It matters not what people say (politicians have always lied), only reality matters, and reality requires a black belt in Christianity. Too many stare at their white belt, thinking they're something they're not, and when they find themselves in the proverbial back alley, discover they're woefully unprepared. Slaughtered like a pig, if you recall. Because you *will* have 3 AM moments, when nobody is around, and what you've got is what you've got.

As Yogi Berra said, 90% of the game is half mental — I read many blogs on a wide variety of subjects, one from someone who used to be a professional volleyball player.

> *Having finished 17th at beach volleyball nationals, I can tell you that the difference between the very top and those near the top is not skills — everyone has the skills. The difference*

is mental. Players in the top five or ten are so tough that almost nothing makes them waver, and their belief in their ability to succeed is extreme.*

The only difference between pew-warmers and warriors? Attitude and study. We all have the same resources, the same Bible, the same God. Some take those resources, train, and rise above the situation. Others say pass the Bon-Bons, and why is life so hard? You must be strong in faith — and that comes from going beyond the basics, as Paul pleads.

Tough times happen (sickness, financial, and so on), many times we want to quit. What gets us through when people bring up the problem of evil and ask why your God allows you to suffer in such a situation? Paul pleads to go beyond the basics. If you do, when 3 AM rolls around, you'll look down in your toolbox and find all sorts of tools you can pull out.

It's not a theoretical idea — people have made it through and provide role models. In the Bible, Paul says imitate him as he imitates Christ (1 Corinthians 4:16, 11:1). But I can't do that. First, I can't imitate Jesus — He's perfect. So right away I'm in trouble. We can imitate Paul, you may say. No I can't. Paul (after Jesus revealed Himself) immediately left everything he knew and adopted as his mission the spread of the Gospel. I can't imitate him either.

Perhaps none of these work for you. You can't be like Jesus, Paul is too lofty of a goal, and your parents were alcoholics who abandoned you as a kid. What do you do? Who do you pattern your life after? One guy in the Bible responds exactly as we do; the name may surprise you.

Peter? It's easy to relate to him — he always said the wrong thing at the wrong time. But it's not Peter. How about James and John? When things didn't go their way they wanted to call down fire from heaven! (Luke 9) But it's not them. John became known as the apostle of love. Surely he provides the role model the Bible speaks of? Nope. It's Elijah. The Mount Carmel Elijah? You bet. James specifically calls Elijah a man like us.

Elijah was a man subject to like passions as we are, and he prayed earnestly that it might not rain: and it rained not on the earth by the space of three years and six months.

James 5:17

---

* http://blog.penelopetrunk.com/2004/08/14/learn-goal-setting-from-the-olympics/

Let's take a quick review of the famous Mount Carmel episode.

> *And it came to pass, when Ahab saw Elijah, that Ahab said unto him, Art thou he that troubleth Israel? And he answered, I have not troubled Israel; but thou, and thy father's house, in that ye have forsaken the commandments of the Lord, and thou hast followed Baalim. Now therefore send, and gather to me all Israel unto mount Carmel, and the prophets of Baal four hundred and fifty, and the prophets of the idols four hundred, which eat at Jezebel's table.* 1 Kings 18:17–19

At this point in Israel's history, Ahab reigned as king. Not known as one of Israel's better kings, he was down right wicked, with his queen Jezebel — we'll come back to her a little later. For the Mount Carmel story, suffice it to say a drought existed in the land, and Ahab blamed not the spiritual wickedness of himself and the nation, but Elijah. Elijah presents himself to the king, issuing a challenge between himself and 450 prophets of Baal. Who can have their god call down fire from heaven? Two bulls are selected, and Elijah gives them first choice.

> *And they took the bullock which was given them, and they prepared it, and called on the name of Baal from morning even until noon, saying, O Baal, hear us. But there was no voice, nor any that answered. And they leaped upon the altar which was made.*
>
> *And it came to pass at noon, that Elijah mocked them, and said, Cry aloud; for he is a god. Either he is talking, or he is pursuing, or he is in a journey, or perhaps he sleepeth, and must be awaked. And they cried aloud, and cut themselves after their manner with swords and lances, till the blood gushed out upon them.*
>
> *And it came to pass, when midday was past, and they prophesied until the time of the offering of the evening sacrifice, that there was neither voice, nor any to answer, nor any that regarded.* 1 Kings 18:26–29

They strike out. Nothing. Nobody heard them. Gods made by man's hand can't hear. Isaiah speaks of a craftsman who cuts down a tree and burns part of it in the fire to cook with, but with the rest makes a god and falls down to worship it and ask for deliverance.* In any event, the prophets of Baal accomplish nothing. Their god does not answer, so it's up to Elijah.

---

* Isaiah 44:14–17

Danger of Infancy

> *And it came to pass at the time of the offering of the evening sacrifice, that Elijah the prophet came near, and said, Lord God of Abraham, Isaac, and of Israel, let it be known this day that thou art God in Israel, and that I am thy servant, and that I have done all these things at thy word. Hear me, O Lord, hear me, that this people may know that thou art the Lord God, and that thou hast turned their heart back again.*
>
> *Then the fire of the Lord fell, and consumed the burnt sacrifice, and the wood, and the stones, and the dust, and licked up the water that was in the trench. And when all the people saw it, they fell on their faces: and they said, The Lord, he is the God; the Lord, he is the God.* 1 Kings 18:36–39

The Lord responds. Nothing of the alter remains — even the stones vanish in the fireball.

Back to role models. That's it, you say, I could never be like Elijah. But this is *not* the story we're looking for. Stay with me for a minute; it's not the Mount Carmel episode we're interested in, it's what comes after this great victory that shows importance for us. You can imagine Ahab and Jezebel were not too happy — not only does their god not answer, but their prophets are wiped out as well. In the beginning of 1 Kings chapter 19, Jezebel threatens to kill Elijah. So what does this mighty man of God do? He flees.*

Elijah was afraid. This I can relate to. Most of us experience fear from time to time. *For God hath not given us the spirit of fear; but of power, and of love, and of a sound mind.*† The Lord does not want us to be afraid. He provides power and ability to carry out anything He asks of us. Many men in the Bible experienced fear; many required a special word of encouragement from the Lord Himself — Isaiah in Isaiah 43:1–2, Paul in Acts 18:9–10, and so on. I relate to fear; I'm sure most people do also. But that wasn't Elijah's only problem.

> *But he himself went a day's journey into the wilderness, and came and sat down under a juniper tree. And he requested for himself that he might die, and said, It is enough! Now, O Lord, take away my life; for I am not better than my fathers.*
> 1 Kings 19:4

Now he's depressed! Depression frequently follows fear. After fear does its part to paralyze us, depression sets in and we dwell

---
*   1 Kings 19:3
†   2 Timothy 1:7

on our own resources, becoming depressed at our lack of ability to change the situation. Again, many men of the Bible became depressed. Even Paul.

> *For we would not, brethren, have you ignorant of our trouble which came to us in Asia, that we were pressed out of measure, above strength, insomuch that we despaired even of life.* 2 Corinthians 1:8

Paul got depressed — you can imagine why. He was shipwrecked, stoned, left for dead, beaten, and more. Paul endured depression just as Elijah did. I can relate to depression. But Elijah doesn't stop there.

> *And he said, I have been very jealous for the Lord God of hosts. For the children of Israel have forsaken thy covenant, thrown down thine altars, and slain thy prophets with the sword; and I, even I only, am left; and they seek my life, to take it away.* 1 Kings 19:10

Now he's pouting and prideful. Pride lies at the root of all sin — it caused the fall of Satan originally (Isaiah 14:12–14).

Elijah expresses fear, depression, a desire to end his life, and pride. I can relate to each of those. So what you say? Remember the words of James, Elijah is a man like us! And so we see he is. But wait, remember the Mount Carmel episode? How many of us thought we can't be like that? Let's go back and take another look at the words of James — if Elijah was a man like us, we can turn that around to say we can be like Elijah.

Elijah prayed it wouldn't rain, and it didn't for 3 years. God is not a genie who grants wishes, but I wonder what would happen if we displayed faith when we prayed — would mountains move? Would we obtain similar results as Elijah? Yet we can pray like Elijah, because we are like him.

We need role models — let's try Elijah for a change. When Paul speaks of going beyond the basics, it's not as if we don't have examples to follow. It's not an abstract, academic exercise. We all can be like those guys. When you can't golf, walk, get out of bed, or much of anything else, that's when you discover your faith, and what's in your toolbox. You'll either discover an echo from the steel walls of the box, or lots of tools to work with. Your fate was sealed *long* before you opened the box, however.

If you decide to dig in, you *will* meet opposition. That's tough, for anyone. If you're going to engage, be assured the enemy knows exactly how to best target you. Everyone has their Kryptonite. Something creating weakness. Something requiring help to get through. Don't despair, lots of help exists, if you're willing to ask for it. Remember your labor is not in vain, and you have a job to do.

> *Therefore, my beloved brethren, be ye steadfast, unmovable, always abounding in the work of the Lord, forasmuch as ye know that your labor is not in vain in the Lord.*
> 1 Corinthians 15:58

Christianity isn't a spectator sport. It's time to get back in the game, or for some, to get *in* the game. Once you're in the game, Paul in Hebrews 6 says go beyond the basics of the faith, that means evil exists, it's opposed to you, and it will actively work to harm and destroy you. Don't be surprised when evil happens, as it surely will. But that evil, as we've seen, does *not* mean God abandoned you, or He doesn't exist.

The enemy always seeks your "honorable surrender," where you can live out the rest of the war in captivity in a prison camp, instead of engaging. Staying in the fight remains harder than quitting. Doing the right thing usually is.

As we head into the future, maybe it will be better than the past, maybe not. No matter what, our job hasn't changed: soldier on and never quit. Paul warns about lack of development. It's time to move beyond the basics, and the only person who can do that is you.

Chapter 10

Danger of Departing

CONTINUING PREVIOUS WARNINGS INVOLVING dull hearing and progressing to Christian maturity, this section might cause the most trouble in the Bible, and it's certainly been used and abused for many purposes unrelated to the actual issue at hand — progressing to maturity.

> *Therefore leaving the principles of the doctrine of Christ, let us go on unto perfection, not laying again the foundation of repentance from dead works, and of faith toward God, Of the doctrine of baptisms, and of laying on of hands, and of resurrection of the dead, and of eternal judgment. And this will we do, if God permit.* Hebrews 6:1-3

Paul says we arrive at the tough stuff. What follows might be the toughest passage in the Bible, or at least the most misunderstood. Normally for so-called tough sections, one idea clearly makes more sense than others, and the commentators I turn to generally all agree. Not so with this section.

I've read the warning James gives to teachers, and I certainly lean toward one interpretation for this passage. It would be easy to only expound on that, but I'm not going to be dogmatic about it, and I certainly reserve the right to change my mind as new information appears.

The problem this section presents comes from a logical error called confirmation bias. It means when considering information, people tend to see what confirms their already held ideas. In Hebrews 6, that means we must wade into one of the oldest and most contentious issues in Christianity: Calvinism versus

Arminianism. Calvinism contains five points, usually referred to by the acronym TULIP.

- **T**otal depravity — man is a sinful creature.
- **U**nconditional election — God chose who would (and thus would not) be saved.
- **L**imited atonement — Jesus' death only paid for the sins of the elect.
- **I**rrestiable grace — Since God chose, you have no choice.
- **P**erserverance — Once saved, always saved.

Arminianism *roughly* equates to the opposite of those views. When people enter this debate, one idea dominates the discussion: did God choose those who would be saved (and thus those to be dammed), or is it your responsibility to respond to the Gospel? Do you have free will, or were you chosen by God? This causes the huge debate. Before we delve into that, allow Chuck Smith to explain his position.

Do you believe in eternal security? I say, "Yes, of course I believe in eternal security. As long as I abide in Christ, I'm eternally secure." Now, dispute that.[*]

I agree with Chuck. Who can argue if you're in Christ, nothing can take you away, and your salvation is assured? Both the Calvinist and Arminianist should agree. But if you're *not* in Christ, do you have any reason to believe you're saved? To begin the discussion, we must begin on common ground. I doubt anyone holding any of the many positions on this issue could find a problem with Chuck's statement.

Chuck continues to state both Calvinism and Arminianism are correct, but he can't reconcile the two. I've studied Quantum Physics, and discovered principles of advanced Physics solve or illuminate Bible passages. No, you don't need a PhD to understand the Bible, but I'm amazed how applying modern Physics to problem passages illuminates or solves so-called problems.

Zechariah 4:7 says "Who art thou, O great mountain? Before Zerubbabel thou shalt become a plain." Most people blip right over that. However, if you posses background in Physics, you

---

[*] Smith (2000, page 116)

immediately think of quantum tunneling (yeah, I'm sure that's the *first* thing that came to your mind). In "Get Back in the Game" I wrote about this section, so allow me to quote from that work.

What did God just say? Not by power, nor by might, but by *My* spirit. Do you see a mountain of opposition in your way? If you allow God to use His power (and not rely on yourself) those mountains become a plain. Recall the disciples in the boat with Jesus during the storm. When Jesus woke up, how much effort did He expend? Two words proved sufficient to end the storm, and the same guy from the boat flattens the mountains of opposition as well.

Do mountains exist in our lives? Perhaps you're staring at a mountain, wondering how you'll get past it. Perhaps like Paul and others, you're discouraged. Maybe you see no possible way to overcome and make it to the other side. If so, you're missing a critical example from Physics called Quantum Tunneling. Simply put, a particle lacking in energy somehow finds itself on the other side of a quantum barrier.

Okay, that might not be clear — or even interesting — so let's provide a more familiar example. Suppose a seven month old baby is beginning to play ball (it's never too early to toss the 'ol pigskin around). His mother and father give him a bowling ball (16 pounds), take him to Mount Shasta and say have at it boy, roll the ball up and over the mountain.

If you were placing bets, would you bet he could do it?

Did you ever see the "Back to the Future" movies? You might remember Doc and his plans, but Marty had problems understanding the concepts. Doc said "you're not thinking fourth dimensionally Marty" to which Marty replies, "Yeah, doc, I've got problems with that." You're in the same boat if you would bet against the kid — you're not thinking quantum mechanically.

Somehow (against the odds and what we plainly see) we find the ball on the other side of the mountain ... the mountain became a plain before the Lord. Once again what lays before us isn't what the Lord sees, and what we think of as mountains in life are nothing but plains to God.*

An interesting Bible study is to find all the phrases "but God" in the Bible — it appears over 40 times (Genesis 31:7, 48:21, 50:20, 1 Samuel 23:14, Psalm 73:26, Acts 7:9, Romans 5:8, Ephesians 2:4, Philippians 2:27, etc). You'll quickly discover how we view events frequently looks like a mountain, but to the Lord it's all

---

* In Physics that's called Relativity.

flat land. Those verses may show a situation hopeless and futile, *but God.*

I know what you're thinking. Yeah, that applies to other people, but my situation is different. I've got a *really* big mountain, so this doesn't apply to me. Chuck Missler says never underestimate a person's ability to rationalize, so yes, it *does* apply to you, in your situation. Paul told us in Ephesians to "be strong in the Lord and in the power of His might (Ephesians 6:10)," a verse in the present imperative voice; it's a command to be continuously strong.

Zechariah explains a principle of Quantum Physics. I've said many times if you want to dig deep into the Bible you'll require a bit of Physics. Still not convinced? Try one of the most puzzling passages in the Bible.

> *God is light, and in him is no darkness at all.*   1 John 1:5

Why is that puzzling? Most people don't see a problem, unless you've heard of the wave-particle duality of light. We're all familiar with light acting as a wave, as when you throw a rock in a pool. You see the pattern, and a wave bouncing off a side interfering with other waves as it travels back, creating high and low places in the water. Light can also exist as a particle, like a golf ball. If you've played in those boxes filled with balls at your local pizza parlor, you notice an entirely different set of rules at work.

Light exists with dual properties — both wave *and* particle. Experiments with light can obtain either the wave nature, or the particle nature, but *not both at the same time**; light exists as two-in-one — two natures together, yet distinct. A duality.

Perhaps now you see why this verse can keep you awake at night — God is light — not light-like, not having the characteristics of light. If God exists as a trinity (and He does), and light exists as a duality (and it does), Houston, we've got a problem. It doesn't fit. Yet if the Bible is inerrant (and it is), it *must* fit. Now you understand why this passage keeps people awake at night (okay, maybe just me). Looking at other translations, as well as the original Greek, you'll discover it's translated correctly (God is light), so translation does not cause the problem.

What do we do? How do we solve the apparent contradiction between duality and trinity? As always, the answer appears elsewhere in the Bible.

---

*   For those interested in details, look up the two-slit experiment with light and you'll find plenty to occupy your time.

> *But when the Comforter is come, whom I will send unto you from the Father, even the Spirit of truth, which proceedeth from the Father, he shall testify of me.* John 15:26

The answer comes from the same guy writing the problem passage in the first place: John. The Holy Spirit doesn't speak of Himself, only of Jesus. It will turn out light actually has three properties, but the third will only be observable by indirect means, because under experimental conditions it appears as either a wave or particle — as John wrote the Holy Spirit will testify of Jesus, never of Himself.

Those examples illustrate how applying Physics solves tough Bible interpretation problems. Let's return to Calvinism. How can we use Physics to solve — once and for all — this problem? We discover Relativity solves the Calvinism versus Arminianism debate.*

What is Relativity? Simply stated, time and events are not absolute, they can only be interpreted from a specific point of view. For example, suppose you watched a lightning storm from your window, and you see two lightning strikes hit different points on the ground at the same time. Would it surprise you to learn someone else may not see those as simultaneous events?

Wait a minute, you say. They either did or didn't hit the ground at the same time. As Lee Corso says "not so fast, my friend." You can't answer the question *absolutely*, only by a specific person's *frame of reference* — movement and gravity relative to other objects affects the notion of simultaneous events. The radical notion Einstein proposed — time is not an absolute property, it varies.

When I sat in Physics class we'd perform calculations involving time, and of course arrive at different answers. Inevitably some person would raise their hand and ask "which one is correct?" at which point my professor would grin widely and say, "it's all relative — see, Relativity isn't that hard."

It's a tough concept to wrap your arms around — time and simultaneous events are not absolute. The only thing known for sure is in some reference frame, they were or were not simultaneous. We'll not cover the minute details of Relativity, the important (and difficult) point comes from the fact time itself is not absolute, it only can be interpreted in a specific reference frame.

Okay, you all stuck with us for the big finale, right? What does Relativity imply for the Bible? Let's solve the great debate in

---

* See https://www.dyeager.org/post/frames-of-reference.html or Appendix D for a discussion of Relativity.

the church — God's predestination versus man's free will. Which is "right"? By now you know the answer — they both are! *It all depends on your frame of reference.*

To illustrate, let's consider two extremes. First, suppose man has ultimate free will, in fact, God barely knows what's going on, and certainly can't do much about it. When I jump out of bed in the morning, what eternal question faces me? — Fruit Loops or Corn Flakes? Now consider the other extreme. God pulls your strings, like working a giant puppet. You have no choice in anything, as God controls every aspect of your life. When I jump out of bed in the morning, what eternal question faces me? — Fruit Loops or Corn Flakes?

Obviously, from our point of view, we have free will. Each day as I rise from bed, I'm faced with that eternal question while gazing at the cereal selection. It *appears* as if I choose, whether I actually do or not. I'd also submit a supreme, all-powerful, all-knowing God is in charge, and in His reference frame, everything ultimately goes His way — after all, it's His sandbox.

Ultimately, it matters not if we do or do not have free will, *we must act as if we do*, because that's *our* frame of reference. What happens in other reference frames (God's) does not matter, because we cannot inhabit His reference frame. Calvinists can become jaded and ineffective; why bother, after all, if God chose someone, they'll be saved anyway, so why do I need to witness or do anything? Because God said so. That should be reason enough, and as we've already demonstrated, we must live as if we have free will, even if we don't actually posses it. I hear the heckler in the front row — "Sure, but does that exist in the Bible, or did you just make it up?"

Consider as Jesus says "All that the Father giveth me shall come to me." AH HA! The Calvinist proclaims. You have no choice! It's God's choice all the way. See, I was right all along! But keep reading, as He continues "... and him that cometh to me I will in no wise cast out." AH HA! The Arminianist proclaims. It's up to you. You're responsible. You can't weasel out saying you are or are not chosen, it's your responsibility to respond and come to Christ.

The kicker comes when you discover *both ideas come from a single verse* in John (6:37). So which is "right"? They both are — it all depends on your frame of reference. Once again, knowledge of Physics provides Bible insight; in this case solving once and for all a debate that splits churches and pits Christian against Christian.

When you come to a passage you'll naturally look at it through the lens of your preconceived theology. That's something you don't

Danger of Departing

want to do, as much as possible. Calvinists consider Hebrews 6 one way, while the Arminianist sees something completely different. Unlocking Hebrews 6 only comes if you put aside your ideas, and see what the passage says, not what you hope it says.

> *For it is impossible for those who were once enlightened, and have tasted of the heavenly gift, and were made partakers of the Holy Spirit, And have tasted the good word of God, and the powers of the age to come, If they shall fall away, to renew them again unto repentance, seeing they crucify to themselves the Son of God afresh, and put him to an open shame. For the earth which drinketh in the rain that cometh often upon it, and bringeth forth herbs fit for them by whom it is tilled, receiveth blessing from God; But that which beareth thorns and briers is rejected, and is nigh unto cursing; whose end is to be burned.* Hebrews 6:4-8

I've looked over many commentaries, and it seems each commentator has their own idea, probably agreeing with their ideology. Among the ideas for this passage:

- Professing, but not real, believers.
- Truly saved, then permanently lost.
- "Impossible" means "difficult."
- Repetitive lost and resaved, to a limit.
- Purely hypothetical.

These aren't real Christians — the Calvinist solution. Problem: why would this warning be the *only* one *not* to true believers? The warning of drifting in chapter 2, dull hearing of chapter 5, and then chapter 6 continues with similar themes. Why should this passage — barring an explicit mention from the author — be treated as applying to a different group? That's hard to accept.

The Calvinist could say it's hypothetical, it could never actually happen. Then why talk about it at all? Certainly the other warnings in Hebrews *are* possible, why would this one not be? Neither position staked out by the Calvinist satisfies, and both seem to torture the text.

Perhaps these people are saved, then permanently lost — the Arminianist position. Problem: we've all seen examples of people not living correctly, and then returning like the prodigal son. What about them? It also contradicts eternal life — if you can lose it, it's not really eternal, is it? Since God grants eternal life, it logically follows you can't possibly lose it, as eternal means never ending. Just like the cottage cheese in your refrigerator, an expiration date means it won't last forever.

How about impossible means difficult? — it's thus a miracle of God, but impossible for man. That tortures the clear reading a bit trying to make the passage fit a preconceived theology. Impossible means it's not gonna happen — it's *impossible* to time-travel backward.

None of those seem to completely fit, and if a correct interpretation exists, it *must* fit. Exactly. With no parts left over.

Chuck Smith equates apostasy with falling away. It's a *willful* abandonment (read the book of Jude). This seems to fit with both Calvinism and Arminianism — you're safe if you're in Christ, but you're free to leave if you wish. Personally, I'd say if you're truly in Christ, you'll *never* leave (not because you can't, but because you won't), as Peter said, where will we go? Any reasonable and logical person truly experiencing the love of Christ won't leave because he doesn't *want* to, not because he can't. God doesn't force you to be with Him if you don't want. In fact, He created a place with the exact opposite characteristics of Him, for those who desire it.

We call that place hell — the opposite of heaven. Torment. Dark. Nobody *has* to be there unless they choose it, but if that's what they desire by rejecting God, He gives them exactly what they want.

Chuck's view of apostasy becomes more theoretical, simply because for a Christian who has experienced the goodness and grace of God, why would they go anywhere else? It's walking quite close to the idea this section can't apply to Christians, as a debate exists on whether a Christian can actually walk away from the faith. Calvinists would say no, but that doesn't necessarily make it so.

One final idea comes from Chuck Missler and J. Vernon McGee — it's not actually about salvation at all, but rewards. That is, perhaps, the best idea, as we usually equate repentance and salvation, but the two do not necessarily have the same definition. McGee notes "fell away" in Greek means to stumble, or fall down, the same as in the garden as Jesus *fell* on His face (not apostate!). It can't be given the meaning of apostate.*

---

*   McGee (1982b, page 547)

We've seen pastors and others do things they shouldn't, and thus be disqualified from ministry. They can still be saved, but disqualified from the race Paul speaks of; Paul spoke often of running the race and fearing disqualification, but nothing exists in his writing of a fear of losing his salvation. Quite the opposite — he told Timothy he knew in whom he trusted, and He was able to keep it.

Which of these ideas is right? I turn to a handful of commentators, and it's rare they contradict each other. In this section many commentators I highly respect hold different positions. I lean towards either Chuck Smith's view on apostasy, or J. Vernon McGee's view of rewards, not salvation. But I can't be dogmatic about it. It's an extremely tough section, and one I'll be interested in talking to the author about.

I lean towards J. Vernon McGee's view because the idea you can do something to lose your salvation you sincerely desire runs straight into a contradiction — you can't have eternal life if it's possible to lose it. When Jesus grants eternal life, it must (by definition) be permanent and irrevocable. After all, when you sin tomorrow, does that catch God by surprise? For those troubled by this, for those who think — like the passage on the unpardonable sin — that something they can do can cause them to be forever lost, remember the passage in John 6 we alluded to earlier.

> *All that the Father giveth me shall come to me; and him that cometh to me I will in no wise cast out.* John 6:37

If you come to Christ, you will *never* be rejected. Never ever. Well, you might say, I don't want to come to Christ, I'd rather live by my own rules. Then perhaps you're one of the lost, and you should deal with that. God doesn't sit there tricking people. AH HA! Look at that poor sap, he sincerely came to Me but he doesn't know he doesn't make it. That doesn't happen, so don't be tormented. Anyone sincerely coming to Christ will be accepted, another of those rare ideas both Calvinists and Arminianists agree on.

> *But, beloved, we are persuaded better things of you, and things that accompany salvation, though we thus speak.* Hebrews 6:9

Paul's readers differ. People previously spoken of had problems, but not you. Notice Paul specifically uses the word salvation, in contrast to repentance earlier. Different words, different uses, different meanings. Another clue J. Vernon McGee's position of verses 4–6 proves correct.

> *For God is not unrighteous to forget your work and labor of love, which ye have showed toward his name, in that ye have ministered to the saints, and do minister.* Hebrews 6:10

Look around. Feel beat up? Kicked in the head perhaps? Wonder why you're doing what you're doing? The enemy's strategy remains simple. He knows he can't win the game (he's read the back of the book too), but if you walk off the playing field he wins by forfeit. That's why it's vital to *stay in the game.* It doesn't mean an easy life. It doesn't mean a long life. It doesn't mean a Lexus. It doesn't mean ice cream. It certainly doesn't mean a pony.

It simply means the Christian remains unbeatable. Don't fall in the trap the disciples did, though. When Jesus said let's go to the other side, that's all the information they had. They *heard* we're going on a cruise to the other side. When the storm raged, they shrank in fear because it contradicted their incorrect assumptions. No guarantee of an easy life exists, only ultimate victory. Never quit. Never give in. Never surrender.

> *Therefore, my beloved brethren, be ye steadfast, unmovable, always abounding in the work of the Lord, forasmuch as ye know that your labor is not in vain in the Lord.*
> 1 Corinthians 15:58

That labor means "not so much the actual exertion which a man makes, but the weariness which he experiences from that exertion."* When your head aches, it's not in vain — stepping up to the challenge and getting in the game isn't easy, or sometimes even fun. It's hard, not fun, that's what sacrifice means. Never forget God won't abandon you.

Bad things happen to good people. At the point of breaking, it's common to hear cries of "I'm so under attack right now." That's a wimpy excuse expressing a defensive position. You must transition to offense — being surrounded means you can attack in any direction and exist in a target-rich environment.

I doubt military teachers extol the strategy of folding like a cheap lawn chair. Have you read stories from WWI, WWII, or any other battle where the strategy was fold and quit? Did Washington

---

* Zodhiates (1992b, page 916)

quit at Valley Forge? Did our soldiers quit at Bastogne? Or Iwo Jima?

I love cartoons, and Wile E. Coyote and the Road Runner will always be my favorite. In one episode two kids watch TV and ask "why does the coyote even want the Road Runner?" Wile E. Coyote then stopped (whatever ACME product he was working on) and addressed the boys.

A legitimate question, one that deserves a legitimate answer.

You can analyze the situation and make a tactical response, or perish while doing nothing. Wile E. keeps trying, planning, scheming, and believing *this* time ACME Corporation won't let him down (I think the Road Runner moonlighted as president of ACME Corporation, but that's only my guess).

Wile E. Coyote isn't just smart, he's a *super genius* (it said so on his business cards). If he failed, so will you, if he has problems with ACME Corporation's gizmo, you'll have problems with your cell phone, if he gets crunched by the piano as it falls to the bottom of the canyon ... well, you get the idea.

The Road Runner won't surrender, you must take the fight to *him*, on offense. How? The answer appears back in 1 Samuel 17, with David and Goliath. Everyone knows the story (it's probably the most popular flannel story), but most likely don't remember what killed the giant — it wasn't a stone and sling.

> *Then said David to the Philistine, Thou comest to me with a sword, and with a spear, and with a shield; but I come to thee in the name of the Lord of hosts, the God of the armies of Israel, whom thou hast defied. This day will the Lord deliver thee into mine hand; and I will smite thee, and take thine head from thee; and I will give the carcases of the host of the Philistines this day unto the fowls of the air, and to the wild beasts of the earth; that all the earth may know that there is a God in Israel. And all this assembly shall know that the Lord saveth not with sword and spear; for the battle is the Lord's, and he will give you into our hands.* 1 Samuel 17:45–47

You all know the story, but forget the ending.

> *So David prevailed over the Philistine with a sling and with a stone, and smote the Philistine, and slew him; but there was no sword in the hand of David. Therefore David ran, and stood upon the Philistine, and took his sword, and drew it*

out of the sheath thereof, and slew him, and cut off his head therewith. And when the Philistines saw their champion was dead, they fled. 1 Samuel 17:50–51

David cut off Goliath's head with his own sword. That's our method — take the enemy's resources and use them against him. When you're under attack and wake up in the middle of the night in terror, don't freak out, pray for those in your church. Pray for your pastor. Pray for people who teach and write books. Pray for boldness. Pray for endurance. What happens then? You've slayed the giant with his own sword, turning his attacks into your weapons. When those attacks happen (and they will), despair not, for as always, you face two choices: tap-out or tag-out.

If you've seen MMA bouts, you've seen a fighter work on another and trap them in an arm-bar, choke hold, or some other submission. When he finally realizes he can't win (or he's about to black out), he'll "tap out" by tapping the leg or mat, and the referee stops the match — that differs from the tag-out.

I watched Saturday morning wrestling matches long ago, when they'd have two-on-two tag matches. But only one of each side fought in the ring at a time. If you were in a bad position, you tried to reach the side and tag your friend, who (hopefully) would fly in and whomp your oppressor. Life differs not. Do you tap-out or tag-out?

Times exist to say I'm not making it right now, and I need help. Guys, there's nothing unmanly about that. Women *generally* don't have a problem asking for help (we make generalizations because they're *generally* true). Yet men have issues asking for help — it's why we don't read directions (unless all else fails). You hear the phrase "man-up," but none of the ladies ever say "gee, Helen, why don't you just woman-up."

Why? Man-up implies taking care of it yourself. Guys have the base nature to never ask for help, never admit fault, and handle everything themselves. But men, it's *not* a sign of weakness. Even Superman had his Kryptonite. You do also. When you come across your Kryptonite, it's time to put your big-boy pants on and ask for help.

Tap-out and tag-out only differ by one letter. Notice a "P" and "G" are almost mirrors of each other? Look in the mirror, it's time to turn the tables. It's when you decide to start using the enemy's own sword against him you'll move from tap-out (defense) to tag-out (offense). The gates of hell shall not prevail, and what do armies use gates for? It's a *defensive* fortification. It's something we (on offense) power through.

We *all* have situations when we're struggling and tired and too proud to ask for help. That's not a Biblical position — see Nehemiah 4:10–20 as the Jews continue building the wall, but under duress. A man with a trumpet stood by Nehemiah's side, and if the battle became too fierce, he blew the trumpet and allowed everyone to rally around. You are no different. If you're going through tough times, blow the stinking trumpet!

Never, ever, *never* believe you're all alone, or going on offense means never being tired, or discouraged, or frustrated. Wile E. Coyote *never* gives up. For most people, falling off a thousand foot high cliff or getting pummeled by a train would quench their desire quite a bit. But not Wile E. Coyote (naturally, being able to walk away from such disasters, even if looking like a Slinky, helped a bit I'm sure).

Be ye steadfast, unmovable, always abounding in the work of the Lord. It's not easy, if it was, everyone would do it. Too many sit on the bench in today's church, and won't get in the game. That must change.

> *These are the times that try men's souls. The summer soldier and the sunshine patriot will, in this crisis, shrink from the service of their country; but he that stands by it now, deserves the love and thanks of man and woman. Tyranny, like hell, is not easily conquered; yet we have this consolation with us, that the harder the conflict, the more glorious the triumph.**

It's tough to stay on offense, but the best defense comes from a daily offense keeping the enemy off balance.

> *And we desire that every one of you do show the same diligence to the full assurance of hope unto the end;*
> Hebrews 6:11

Stick with the game plan. It's hard. The enemy uses strategies with many names: depression, despair, desperation, discouragement. You posses one: diligence. Never quit, never give in, never surrender. Fight back with diligence — I won't quit, ever. You can throw whatever you want, but I won't back down.

> *That ye be not slothful, but followers of them who through faith and patience inherit the promises.*   Hebrews 6:12

---
*   Thomas Paine, "The Crisis"

Slothful means unfit for activity. We return to the Jews leaving the promised land. They didn't inherit because they didn't believe what God said, and thus failed to follow. In other words, slothful.

For when God made promise to Abraham, because he could swear by no greater, he swore by himself,   Hebrews 6:13

We swear on the Bible because you swear by something greater, but nothing exists greater than God, so He swore by Himself.

Saying, Surely blessing I will bless thee, and multiplying I will multiply thee.   Hebrews 6:14

Return to study Genesis 15 and 22. Notice the promises given to Abraham and the Jews were unconditional and unilateral. A strange idea blows through the church called replacement theology, proposing the church in some way replaced Israel. Once they lay that foundation, various proponents of replacement theology differ in how far they'll go.

The milder versions claim Israel existing today isn't actually the Israel of God's plan, and the church now enjoys the promises God made to the Jews, while the "real" Jews will make an appearance later. More extreme views declare God cast off the Jews, and Israel no longer holds special treatment from God; the church is now Israel, and when the New Testament refers to the Jews (Revelation), you can allegorize that to the church.

It could be popular to use replacement theology to meld the church with the world (not a good idea), since if Israel isn't really God's people you can join the popular notion Israel lies at the source of all problems, and if they would disappear, the Middle East (and the world) would live happily ever after.

Of course, replacement theology promotes nothing but nonsense, whether it's the mild form, or the extreme anti-Semite form. God gave Abraham an unconditional and unilateral covenant in Genesis 15 ("In the same day the LORD made a covenant with Abram, saying, Unto thy seed have I given this land, from the river of Egypt unto the great river, the river Euphrates"). If you study Genesis 15 carefully and note the historical background, you'll quickly discover the covenant with Abraham was by God alone, and only He can break it. Recall Daniel's famous 70 week prophecy for clarification.

Seventy weeks are determined upon thy people and upon thy holy city, to finish the transgression, and to make an end of sins, and to make reconciliation for iniquity, and to bring in everlasting righteousness, and to seal up the vision and prophecy, and to anoint the most Holy. Daniel 9:24

Who are Daniel's people? The Jews. Has the end of sin come? Everlasting righteousness? Not if you read the morning paper. Thus, two things become clear: the prophecy involves the Jews, and it hasn't happened yet. The Jews, therefore, *must* have a future in God's plan. Only allegorizing the Bible allows you to opt out of that conclusion, and that's right back to the heresy of liberal theology we've already discussed.

The more you study, the more problems replacement theology causes. At best it's misleading and wrong, causing problems in prophetic studies, while at worst it's heretical and anti-Semitic. Don't be deceived.

And so, after he had patiently endured, he obtained the promise. Hebrews 6:15

Abraham didn't see it right away. Remember the events with Hagar in Genesis 16? They tired of waiting for God's promise, and tried to "help" God out a bit. It didn't turn out to be a good strategy. Times exist when you have no idea what's going on. Even when God gives a clear indication of the end point, you still wonder why you're going the way you are.

For men verily swear by the greater, and an oath for confirmation is to them an end of all strife. Hebrews 6:16

When people argue about something and someone says "I swear" that ends it.

Wherein God, willing more abundantly to show unto the heirs of promise the immutability of his counsel, confirmed it by an oath, That by two immutable things, in which it was impossible for God to lie, we might have a strong consolation, who have fled for refuge to lay hold upon the hope set before us Hebrews 6:17–18

God can't lie. One of the things God *can't* do. Some people might be shocked, but don't make the mistake being all-powerful provides the ability to do anything. Some things God can't do — He can't lie. He can't learn. He can't make you love Him.

Chapter 11

A High Priest After Melchizedek

PAUL SPOKE OF BEING DULL, ENCOURAGING his readers to press on and dive deeper. Paul presents a difficult idea, not so for us as we're familiar with it, but for the Jewish group he writes to Paul presents radical new ideas they may never have considered before, as Paul concluded chapter 6 introducing Melchizedek.

Whither the forerunner is for us entered, even Jesus, made an high priest for ever after the order of Melchizedek.

Chapter 7 expands on Melchizedek — a rather obscure injection in chapter 14 of Genesis, and appearing to have little to do with the main subject of that chapter, appearing in only three verses. Chapter 14 of Genesis relates the story of Abraham rescuing Lot with men from his own house.

Many claim the Bible teaches to be pacifist (turn the other cheek), and Christians should never be involved in war or defense. Those ideas appear easy in academic settings, but when your family lies in harm's way, do you think God tells you to ignore their plight and let them be slaughtered? Me neither.

Abraham certainly didn't. He had 300 trained men in his camp, and when the capture of Lot occurred, he set out to rescue his family using all his resources. Yes, you should trust in the Lord, but remember the proverb — the horse is prepared for the day of battle, but safety is of the Lord. That means you *should* do what you can (as Abraham did) to insure the safety of your family, but realize ultimately it's the Lord who saves.

Melchizedek only appears in a few verses in Genesis, and Psalm 110. That's about it. So for Paul to take a chapter to discuss this guy, it must be a big deal; Paul doesn't waste his time on small issues.

> *For this Melchizedek, king of Salem, priest of the most high God, who met Abraham returning from the slaughter of the kings, and blessed him;* Hebrews 7:1

A summary of what we already know from Genesis 14. Abraham rescued Lot from harm, meeting Melchizedek upon his return from battle.

> *To whom also Abraham gave a tenth part of all; first being by interpretation King of righteousness, and after that also King of Salem, which is, King of peace;* Hebrews 7:2

King of peace and righteousness, which should be a clue to who this guy represents. Notice Abraham gives Melchizedek tithes, which Paul will return to in a few verses.

> *Without father, without mother, without descent, having neither beginning of days, nor end of life, but made like unto the Son of God, abideth a priest continually.* Hebrews 7:3

As a type of Christ, he appears for a few verses, then disappears into history. No lineage is recorded (what the Bible *doesn't* record can be significant as well). Notice *when* he shows up — just before Abraham encounters the king of Sodom.

> *And the king of Sodom said unto Abram, Give me the persons, and take the goods to thyself. And Abram said to the king of Sodom, I have lift up mine hand unto the Lord, the most high God, the possessor of heaven and earth, That I will not take from a thread even to a shoelatchet, and that I will not take any thing that is thine, lest thou shouldest say, I have made Abram rich.* Genesis 14:21-23

Abraham will be tempted twice. First, taking spoil from his adversaries. According to code, as the victor it *was* his. But Abraham held to the promise of God, and chapter 15 opens "Fear not, Abram: I am thy shield, and thy exceeding great reward." Temptation to help God out doesn't usually work well; it's best to stick to God's plan and let it work its course.

Genesis 16 records what happens when Abraham and Sarah decide it's taking too long for God's plan to work out, so they try to help God along, and the handmaid Hagar bears Abraham a son, Ishmael. Read the next few chapters and see how Abraham helping God's plan along worked out (hint: not so well).

The second test occurs as the King of Sodom says give me the souls, and take the stuff for yourself. The enemy will always trade stuff for souls. If you saw the movie "Damn Yankees" it involves a common sports theme. The poor guy sits on his couch and continues to see his team lose to the Yankees. If we could just have a long-ball hitter, I know we could beat them, he laments. I'd sell my soul for a long-ball hitter. Poof! Here's comes the red dude holding a pitchfork, and offers such a deal.

Make a deal with the devil, and you can have stuff, in trade for your soul. Stuff is temporary and has no real value. It does reveal what the enemy thinks important, and what isn't. Of course, Satan doesn't appear in a form you'll recognize him in. If he said hey, I'm the devil and I'm here to entrap you to hell for eternal torment, in exchange for a few brief moments, we all would immediately reject him.

But that's not the way it usually works. He's more subtle. More cunning. More easily missed. Nevertheless, many people trade their soul for fame and fortune. It never ends well. Never. We forget what we're here for. It's not to have an easy life. It's not to get a pony. Or a Lexus. It's to do the job. Service for God is tough, and it's easier to give up and sit on the couch eating Bon-Bons. As Walter Martin said:

> *We're suffering from an endemic disease. This disease in the Christian world is known by its Latin name, non-rock-a-boatus. What it really means is, "Whatever you do, don't rock the boat." The cure for this disease is a baptism of boldness.*
>
> *... You may be thinking, "You seem pretty uptight about this, Dr. Martin." And I am, because we need to get rid of this non-rock-a-boatus mentality that is so prevalent in this country*
> *...*
> *Do you know there are Christians running around today waiting for a convenient moment to "preach the word" that never comes? And the reason it never comes is because God doesn't care about convenience; God cares about obedience.**

The church worries more about being friendly instead of speaking the truth as politeness replaces God's Word. Modernizing

---

*   https://web.archive.org/web/20150724044249/http://www.iclnet.org/pub/resources/text/cri/cri-nwsl/web/crn0030a.html

softens the message and waters it down so much it can hardly be recognized. We need to return to the truth — all have sinned and fallen short. Your sin disqualifies you from heaven. Hell is real *and you're going there unless you do something about it.* Offensive? Maybe to some. When someone stands on the train tracks and a train barrels down, you don't worry if you'll hurt their feelings. It might be popular to talk more about personal relationships than the gospel. It might be friendly to tread lightly on sin. It might be non-offensive to be seeker-friendly. It might be, but it most definitely is wrong. Truth needs to be spoken, it matters not if people like it or not. After all, if someone doesn't like 2+2=4 that changes not reality.

It's time for the church to return to truth, discarding feel-good correctness. How many churches can you attend where you don't need a Bible? If a church isn't teaching line by line through the entire Bible you're being ripped off. Yep, those are strong words, but true. Church messages should prepare troops for battle, and that can't happen if the pastor spends time on puppy dogs and kittens, ignoring reality.

Before this interaction with the King of Sodom, a guy appears out of the pages with bread and wine. Communion. It's fellowship. It's encouragement. Stay in the game, tough times may lie ahead. Abraham recognized this guy as something special from the Lord. How many times do we miss such an opportunity? Even sickness and crisis can be an opportunity to hear clearly. When you're flat on your back with a migraine headache and can't even listen to the radio or open your eyes, you have nothing to do except wait to hear a word from the Lord. Sometimes it takes such extreme measures for us to pause a bit and see what He has to say.

He won't always speak when we want, or the way we want, but it will arrive at the right time. Moses fled Egypt after killing the Egyptian, and then spent 40 years in the outback. 40 *years*. One day he sees a bush burning (not uncommon in the desert), but for some reason not consumed by the fire. The Lord says, after 40 years, I think I can work with this guy now. Earlier in life Moses was brash and impulsive. After 40 years in the desert, those attitudes mellowed a bit.

Just because you're not hearing the Lord *right now* doesn't mean He's forgotten you, or hasn't heard your cry. It could be it's simply not the right time. It could be you're not listening. Take the time to listen, and discover what you've missed. When we frantically try to take action before we've waited, the results

A High Priest After Melchizedek

can be less than satisfactory. As the saying goes, don't just do something, stand there.

I love dogs. When my dog has problems it makes life hard — few things are more special than a man and his dog. When my dog was a puppy, he contracted Parvovirus.* I stayed up with him at night, cleaned up after him, and tried to get him to drink. We finally had to take him to the vet, where he stayed for a week. No matter how sick he was, when I'd visit him each day, as soon as he saw me his tail would wag. We bonded fast. About a week later the hospital called and said he felt better — he had chewed through his IV tube.† We brought him home the next day, and he's had a good life since.

That week was a real bummer. He's been sick a few more times, and while I lay in bed *not* sleeping, I thought about *why* it's so hard when animals or babies are sick. It's because we can't effectively communicate with them. With an adult, it's easy to talk. How do you tell a dog? Sure, they have some communication, but you can't really explain all this is for *their* benefit. It's tough.

Once again the Lord says ... you're the dog.

That's the problem God faces. Me trying to communicate with my dog is much easier than God trying to deal with us. Sometimes it requires extreme measures for us to slow down and listen for a change — when the horse you turn to for relief can no longer walk. Those are the times we need special encouragement from the Lord, but we're missing it because we're so busy with other things. In Abraham's case, Melchizedek shows up just before he needed strength dealing with the king of Sodom. Don't miss Melchizedek moments in your life. They might not appear with bread and wine, but they're easy to miss, and then you miss the strength you *will* need soon after.

> *Now consider how great this man was, unto whom even the patriarch Abraham gave the tenth of the spoils.* Hebrews 7:4

Paul begins his legal argument. The Jews place Abraham and Moses as pinnacles of faith and leadership, yet Abraham gives Melchizedek a tithe. That means Melchizedek supersedes Abraham — Abraham was the patriarch of the Jews. The best of the best. If *he* gave a tithe to Melchizedek, it means he was above Abraham.

---

* Parvo can be likened to severe stomach flu, usually killing the dog.
† Dog IV's are a bit funny. They put the IV in the paw, and then make a sort of cast around the paw so the dog can't get to the needle.

> *And verily they that are of the sons of Levi, who receive the office of the priesthood, have a commandment to take tithes of the people according to the law, that is, of their brethren, though they come out of the loins of Abraham; But he whose descent is not counted from them received tithes of Abraham, and blessed him that had the promises. And without all contradiction the less is blessed of the better.* Hebrews 7:5–7

If the Levities came from Abraham, this means Melchizedek rises above the Jewish priesthood as well. Notice Paul isn't appealing to emotion, his argument comes from Mosaic Law the Jews already accepted, and simple deductive logic. It's irrefutable and not open for debate.

> *And here men that die receive tithes; but there he receiveth them, of whom it is witnessed that he liveth. And as I may so say, Levi also, who receiveth tithes, payed tithes in Abraham. For he was yet in the loins of his father, when Melchizedek met him.* Hebrews 7:8–10

Paul presents a detailed case. If Levi and the priesthood came later from Abraham, in a way all priests paid a tithe to Melchizedek as well, thus Melchizedek supersedes Levi also.

> *If therefore, perfection were by the Levitical priesthood, (for under it the people received the law), what further need was there that another priest should rise after the order of Melchizedek, and not be called after the order of Aaron?* Hebrews 7:11

Paul tells us in Romans the Mosaic Law provides the knowledge of sin.* That's it. If the Law could save you, why would another priest be required? He wouldn't. Before continuing let's take a sidebar to consider the LAW, Law, and law. They're not the same, and definitely not interchangeable.

- law — Normal human law. Taxes, etc.

- Law — Mosaic Law.

- LAW — God's universal law.

---

* Romans 3:20

With Cain and Able, pre-Moses, God's universal LAW proclaims murder is wrong. That also appears in the Mosaic Law, and it's part of (most) human law. Murder is more or less universally understood as wrong and bad.

However, the dietary regulations in Mosaic Law Christians don't have to follow. It's okay to have a ham sandwich. That's the Law Jesus came to free us from. Of course, society as well doesn't normally prohibit ham either.

Some overlap occurs between the three (murder), but all three are distinct and may or may not overlap. When Peter faced a contradiction between man's law and God's LAW (Acts 5), he correctly discerned to follow God's LAW. He understood he likely would face penalties from the government, but in a choice between God and man, God must win out.

A similar situation exists in Daniel 6, as a decree went forth anyone petitioning anything from anyone but the King will be cast into the lions' den. What did Daniel do? He continued on as he always had. In the choice between following the King and God, God wins. Daniel still faced the penalty for disobeying the King's decree, and he certainly had no idea if he would survive or not, but doing what's right overrode personal comfort.

Daniel's three buddies faced the choice as well. Bow or burn, the King said. Their response? We don't need to answer the King in this matter. Our God can deliver us from the fiery furnace, and even if He doesn't, we *will* be delivered from thee, O King. Doing what's right, instead of what's popular or politically correct.

> *For the priesthood being changed, there is made of necessity a change also of the law.*   Hebrews 7:12

The Mosaic Law links with the Aaronic priesthood as priests performed sacrifices for breaking the Law. If another priest supersedes Aaron, so to will another law. That law is grace; Christians are *not* obligated to Mosaic Law.

> *For he of whom these things are spoken pertaineth to another tribe, of which no man gave attendance at the altar. For it is evident that our Lord sprang out of Judah; of which tribe Moses spoke nothing concerning priesthood.*   Hebrews 7:13-14

The Old Testament priests came from the tribe of Levi, while Jesus came from the tribe of Judah. That should tell you something different is going on. It's a new system.

> *And it is yet far more evident; for that after the similitude of Melchizedek there ariseth another priest, Who is made, not after the law of a carnal commandment, but after the power of an endless life. For he testifieth, Thou art a priest for ever after the order of Melchizedek.*
> Hebrews 7:15-17

Back to Psalm 110, that Jesus would be a priest after the order of Melchizedek.

> *For there is verily an annulling of the commandment going before for the weakness and unprofitableness thereof. For the law made nothing perfect, but the bringing in of a better hope did; by the which we draw nigh unto God.*
> Hebrews 7:18-19

All through the gospels we notice the Pharisees believed following the Law made them righteous. The sermon on the mount uncovered they had no hope of following the Law, as it was spiritual, and can't be followed simply outwardly. The Law came so you would know how short you come, not to make you righteous, which is why it had to be replaced.

> *And inasmuch as not without an oath he was made priest (For those priests were made without an oath; but this with an oath by him that said unto him, The Lord sware and will not repent, Thou art a priest for ever after the order of Melchizedek), By so much was Jesus made a surety of a better testament.*
> Hebrews 7:20-22

The priesthood was superseded, thus so was Law. Notice the logical progression laid out in this chapter regarding Melchizedek. By deducing each step, you arrive at the inescapable conclusion grace trumps Law. Had Paul only made the statement without providing the logical analysis, many Jews would recoil in horror at the abandonment of the Law. But Paul creates a precise logical argument, and explains from the Old Testament exactly how and why the Law was superseded.

> *And they truly were many priests, because they were not allowed to continue by reason of death;*
> Hebrews 7:23

Another clue the Law can't save. It ends in death. 100 out of 100 people die. Thus following the Law won't save you.

A High Priest After Melchizedek

> *But this man, because he continueth ever, hath an unchangeable priesthood.* — Hebrews 7:24

In contrast Melchizedek had no beginning and no end, with no oath to begin, and no end. Melchizedek represents a permanent priesthood.

> *Wherefore he is able also to save them to the uttermost that come unto God by him, seeing he ever liveth to make intercession for them.* — Hebrews 7:25

Because his priesthood has no beginning and no end, He can continue to serve as our intercessor. Aaron can't do much when he's dead.

> *For such an high priest was fitting for us, who is holy, harmless, undefiled, separate from sinners, and made higher than the heavens; Who needeth not daily, as those high priests, to offer up sacrifice, first for his own sins, and then for the people's; for this he did once, when he offered up himself. For the law maketh men high priests which have infirmity; but the word of the oath, which was since the law, maketh the Son, who is consecrated for evermore.* — Hebrews 7:26–28

Priests had to make offering for their sin first. Only then could they offer for the people, as they were imperfect. Since priests were sinful, and the wages of sin is death, they could not provide a permanent solution.

Chapter *12*

The Work is Done

IT'S HARD TO STAY IN THE GAME. IF YOU use your own effort you'll find it tough going. While Paul writes to Jewish Christians, the lesson remains for us. To stay in the game you must understand who did the work, how it's completed, and why it's superior to the Mosaic system.

> *Now of the things which we have spoken this is the sum: We have such an high priest, who is seated on the right hand of the throne of the Majesty in the heavens;*   Hebrews 8:1

After laying groundwork and qualifications, Paul makes the argument we have a high priest meeting those qualifications. Notice Jesus sits, something easy to skip over. But the priests in the temple never sat down, in fact, no chairs existed in the temple. Why the difference? Mosaic priests continually worked, while Jesus performed the work once and for all. Nothing remained to do — another subtle clue of the superiority of Jesus over the Old Testament priesthood and Law.

Would you rather work or rest? To stay in the game, you must rest in completed work — not your own, but Jesus'. Why continually attempt to re-do what's already been done? The failure of works-based salvation rears its ugly head as many Christians simply fail to rest in a completed work, always seeking to re-do what has been finished.

> *A minister of the sanctuary, and of the true tabernacle, which the Lord pitched, and not man.*   Hebrews 8:2

In Numbers 20 Moses displayed weariness with the people as they continually complained regarding lack of water. God heard their cry, and provided instructions for Moses to obtain water for the people. But Moses didn't exactly follow God's direction with the rock, striking it instead of speaking to it as God directed. For that, God denies Moses entry into the promised land.

A minor point? Nope. God plans His models extremely carefully and exactly. We'll see this more in the next few verses, but notice the tabernacle existed as a model of the real tabernacle. You wonder why the Lord concerns Himself with details and specifics? They model the real thing. We should be able to learn about God from the models He provides — He's trying to use models as learning tools.

> *For every high priest is ordained to offer gifts and sacrifices; wherefore it is of necessity that this man have somewhat also to offer. For if he were on earth, he should not be a priest, seeing that there are priests that offer gifts according to the law*
>
> Hebrews 8:3-4

A priest represents man to God. If Jesus is high priest, He must offer something. He's not of the tribe of Levi, so can't offer sacrifice according to Mosaic Law (another clue of a new priesthood). Second, he's priest of new order, not old law.

> *Who serve unto the example and shadow of heavenly things, as Moses was admonished of God when he was about to make the tabernacle; for, See, saith he, that thou make all things according to the pattern showed to thee in the mount.*
>
> Hebrews 8:5

The Old Testament priests to some extent modeled the real tabernacle; God is specific about His models. It's to teach us something we can't relate to by showing something we can.

One math instructor I had in college used this method, when trying to explain something in calculus. When people didn't get it, she said ignore what's going on there, come over here, and she'd boil it down to 2+2 or something, then when you understood that, apply your new-found knowledge to what you didn't understand, making the complex understandable. That's the reason God models things for us. We have no ability to understand multi-dimensional spiritual realms, so He provides simpler ideas we can understand.

> *But now hath he obtained a more excellent ministry, by how much also he is the mediator of a better covenant, which was established upon better promises.*   Hebrews 8:6

Models aren't perfect, however. The New Covenant demonstrated superiority over the old in several ways we'll discover later in the chapter. The idea the Old Law would be superseded appeared in Jeremiah 31:31–34; the Old Testament Prophets understood a new covenant would someday eclipse the old.

The Law was never intended to save. By the time Jesus walked the earth, the Pharisees mistakenly believed they could keep the Law and be righteous before God. They missed the idea sacrifices continued because the Law failed to create righteousness. It covered sin, but could never put it away. In contrast, later in verse 12 God says He will remember your sin no more. Not because it's covered from the sacrifice of animals, but because the price is paid in full. No debt remains.

> *For if that first covenant had been faultless, then should no place have been sought for the second.*   Hebrews 8:7

If you own a Lexus, you don't go looking for a Pinto. You don't replace superior with inferior, thus if a new covenant replaces the old, it must be superior to the old. If Law and works could make you righteous, Jesus died in vain, and when Jesus prayed in the garden to the Father if any other way existed, it means the Father lied to Him. Most Christians understand salvation comes from faith alone (not works), but miss the logical conclusion — if works *could* save, Jesus died in vain. I don't think that's a place many people want to be in.

> *For finding fault with them, he saith, Behold, the days come, saith the Lord, when I will make a new covenant with the house of Israel and with the house of Judah;*   Hebrews 8:8

You can't keep the Law, therefore the Lord created a new covenant. Recall the sermon on the mount. Jesus states you can't keep the Law as it's spiritual, not an outward appearance.

> *Not according to the covenant that I made with their fathers in the day when I took them by the hand to lead them out of the land of Egypt; because they continued not in my covenant, and I regarded them not, saith the Lord.*   Hebrews 8:9

In Exodus 32:1–8 while Moses met with God on the mountain, the people constructed a golden calf in his absence. They couldn't even receive the Law before corrupting it. No chance exists to keep the Law, no chance by yourself to make yourself acceptable to God. None. Zero.

> *For this is the covenant that I will make with the house of Israel after those days, saith the Lord: I will put my laws into their mind, and write them in their hearts: and I will be to them a God, and they shall be to me a people.* Hebrews 8:10

The priesthood required each person to use an intermediary — no direct access to God existed. Post-Law God speaks directly to man, and everyone holds equal access to God.

> *And they shall not teach every man his neighbor, and every man his brother, saying, Know the Lord; for all shall know me, from the least to the greatest.* Hebrews 8:11

Jon Courson presents an interesting point Christians can treat the New Testament almost like new Law — here's a list of to-do items, and a list not to do, and you better not get out of line. Remember, the early church didn't posses all we have. How did they get by? Each person knew the Lord for themselves.

We've almost replaced the outdated priesthood with pastors and churches. Want to know what God thinks? Run to the pastor and he'll be the intercessor. That's not what God intended, and not the way it should be. God gave you a brain and a mouth, use 'em both. It returns to Paul's warning about slothfulness, drifting, and immaturity. You don't need the equivalent of a priest, you should be able to learn and grow for yourself.

As we've been saying, the pastor won't always be around. Know the Lord for yourself. That doesn't mean teachers and pastors aren't important, but at 3 AM when you need to stay in the game, you've got what you've got. Don't look down in your toolbox and be like Charlie Brown on Valentines day looking in his mailbox — greeted only by a hollow echo. Don't go back is the message of Hebrews — stay in the game.

> *For I will be merciful to their unrighteousness, and their sins and their iniquities will I remember no more.* Hebrews 8:12

Mercy is not getting what you deserve. If you exceed the speed limit and receive a ticket, when you arrive in court if the judge

The Work is Done

says you don't need to pay a fine you've received mercy — you deserve a fine, but don't get it. The Lord provides a way to be forgiven for sin — mercy. That's the new covenant, as the old one only covered sin, but could never forgive it or provide mercy.

> *In that he saith, A new covenant, he hath made the first old. Now that which decayeth and groweth old is ready to vanish away. Then verily the first covenant had also ordinances of divine service, and an earthly sanctuary.* Hebrews 8:13–9:1

My last car came with voice commands. It's easy to get directions, change radio stations, and put a thumb drive in the USB slot and ask it to play specific artists or tracks. It also provides navigation, providing the new phrase we've all discovered — "recalculating" — as the GPS notices you missed your turn and attempts to plot a new route. With all that new technology, the old Pinto from the 70's doesn't look so good anymore. The same with the new covenant versus the old. Once you discover the new covenant, why would you return to the old?

> *For there was a tabernacle made; the first, wherein was the lampstand, and the table, and the showbread; which is called the sanctuary. And after the second veil, the tabernacle which is called the Holiest of all; Which had the golden censer, and the ark of the covenant overlaid round about with gold, wherein was the golden pot that had manna, and Aaron's rod that budded, and the tables of the covenant; And over it the cherubims of glory shadowing the mercy seat; of which we cannot now speak particularly.* Hebrews 9:2–5

The tabernacle wasn't much to look at. Not much in it.

> *Now when these things were thus prepared, the priests went always into the first tabernacle, accomplishing the service of God.* Hebrews 9:6

They never sat down and always had something to do. Even if they wanted a break, the sparsely decorated tabernacle failed to provide any place to sit. Like other models, it illustrated the lack of rest provided by the Law, and should have been a not so subtle hint something would replace it. Among their duties keeping them busy were:

- Twice daily, burn incense (Exodus 30:7–8).

- Twice daily, tend the Menorah (Exodus 27:20–21).

- Weekly, change showbread (Leviticus 24:5–8).

These were repetitive and offered over and over again. Notice Jesus offered once and for all, then sat down. Once again, it's quite easy to see a contrast, and why the new rises above the old. The priests worked alone. Others were stopped at the entrance. All the ritual and sacrifice failed to bring people to the presence of God.

> *But into the second went the high priest alone once every year, not without blood, which he offered for himself, and for the errors of the people,*   Hebrews 9:7

Only once a year, and only after elaborate ritual cleansing could the high priest enter the presence of God. If he didn't complete all the cleansing required, he wouldn't survive the experience. It wasn't something to take lightly. The average person didn't have access to God, and even the high priest only once a year. It's easy to forget the advantage we have as Christians over the Old Testament Jews.

> *The Holy Spirit this signifying, that the way into the holiest of all was not yet made manifest, while as the first tabernacle was yet standing; Which was a figure for the time then present, in which were offered both gifts and sacrifices, that could not make him that did the service perfect, as pertaining to the conscience; Which stood only in foods and drinks, and various washings, and carnal ordinances, imposed on them until the time of reformation.*   Hebrews 9:8–10

Contrast our high priest with the Old Testament priesthood.

- Only once instead of repetitive.

- Permanent, not temporary.

- Heavenly, not earthly.

- Accessible.

> *But Christ being come an high priest of good things to come, by a greater and more perfect tabernacle, not made with hands, that is to say, not of this building;*   Hebrews 9:11

The Work is Done

The earthly tabernacle only modeled the heavenly one not made with hands as a shadow of the real one. It's designed to illustrate.

> *Neither by the blood of goats and calves, but by his own blood he entered in once into the holy place, having obtained eternal redemption for us.* — Hebrews 9:12

In most Bibles, "for us" appears in italics — it's not in the original text. Why does it matter? Redemption covers more than us, as Romans 8 says the whole creation groans and will be delivered from bondage of corruption.

How did Jesus obtain eternal redemption for us? By the blood sacrifice. Today, many churches and groups talk about following Jesus, or working to make heaven on earth, or some other diversions, while forgetting *how* redemption comes. It's not by following or works. The Gospel is Jesus died for our sins, was buried, and rose again the third day, as Paul says in 1 Corinthians 15. How some groups (like the social justice crowd or liberal theology adherents) miss such a critical and obviously stated idea will always be bizarre.

> *For if the blood of bulls and of goats, and the ashes of an heifer sprinkling the unclean, sanctifieth to the purifying of the flesh, How much more shall the blood of Christ, who through the eternal Spirit offered himself without spot to God, purge your conscience from dead works to serve the living God?* — Hebrews 9:13-14

Let's summarize Paul's arguments of the last few chapters.

- The Law was intended to be temporary.

- The Law can't provide righteousness.

- A superior priesthood comes after the order of Melchizedek.

- Jesus is after the order of Melchizedek.

- With a new priesthood comes a new Law (grace).

- The earthly tabernacle modeled the heavenly tabernacle.

- Jesus *sits*, while Levitical priests didn't. The Work is done.

All these points crush the discussion of salvation by any kind of works. We can't be any better than the Old Testament priesthood, so nothing we can do saves us either. Purge the dead works. You can't earn it, only accept the *completed* work. If you want to stay in the game, don't rehash what's already been accomplished. You can't add to it or improve it, so rest in it.

Chapter *13*

The New Covenant in Force

THIS SECTION MIGHT BE THE MOST CRITICAL for Christians. We've covered rest, and how that does not mean cessation of activity, rather it means to stay in the game, but understand your role. Too many people labor instead of rest. It's an inward situation, not an outward one. Some can rest while performing considerable work, others labor while doing nothing.

The question Paul answers: Jesus has superiority over all the Old Testament priesthood and Law, but how do we know it applies? For Christians, it's an important issue, because rest will forever elude you until the realization occurs you do nothing, He did all the work. Sure, you know that now, but it might only be head knowledge. Until that knowledge makes an impact on your daily life, rest won't come easy.

> *And for this cause he is the mediator of the new testament, that by means of death, for the redemption of the transgressions that were under the first testament, they which are called might receive the promise of eternal inheritance.*
> Hebrews 9:15

When Paul says this cause, he refers back to what we've discussed in previous chapters covering in detail the superiority of Jesus over the old priesthood, how it was insufficient to solve the base problem: sin and transgression requires a penalty be paid. The old sacrificial system couldn't do it, and it's not one you could pay either, so Christ did that for you.

> *For where a testament is, there must also of necessity be the death of the testator. For a testament is of force after men are*

> *dead; otherwise it is of no strength at all while the testator liveth.*
>
> Hebrews 9:16–17

You can (and should) have a will. If your will says your kids receive $100,000, what do they have now? Zip. While you're living, it's of no use as it doesn't come in to force until you die. We'll deal with a few not so politically correct concepts in this section, ones that aren't popular with even the mainstream church, and here's the first one: Jesus' life can't save you.

Shock! Horror! The modern church easily looks away from sin and salvation; you'll find many books and talks about helping the poor, social works, and the common good, mixed in with Jesus as a good teacher. But *none* of that saves you. None of that represents the gospel; run far and fast from anyone peddling such false ideas.

What saves you is what those groups don't like to talk about — the death of Christ. It's not popular anymore. Yet what did Paul tell you? The will applies only *after* death. It's Christ's death that saves, that's the penalty I couldn't pay. The testament isn't in force unless the person dies. It may not be popular, and it may offend people, but that's too bad.

Of course, that does *not* mean Jesus wasn't a good teacher, and we should not follow what He said, only if you never get to the death and resurrection, you're missing the foundation of Christianity. Sadly, even atheists have a better grasp of this sometimes than "pastors," as atheist Christopher Hitchens said:

> *I would say that if you don't believe that Jesus of Nazareth was the Christ and Messiah, and that he rose again from the dead and by his sacrifice our sins are forgiven, you're really not in any meaningful sense a Christian.*[*]

For many people this may be obvious, but so-called pastors deny it. The testament isn't in force without the death. It doesn't mean Jesus wasn't a good teacher, but the Gospel is not anything but the death and resurrection. It's not good works, social justice, or common good. The Gospel could be one of the most clearly stated ideas in the entire Bible. Nobody can argue about it (though they might ignore it), since Paul wrote exactly what the Gospel is.

> *Moreover, brethren, I declare unto you the gospel which I preached unto you, which also ye have received ... For I*

---

* Sewell (2009)

> *delivered unto you first of all that which I also received, how that Christ died for our sins according to the scriptures; And that he was buried, and that he rose again the third day according to the scriptures.* 1 Corinthians 15:1–4

Liberal theology proponents might claim Paul wasn't complete, or left something out like social justice (a popular, but deceptive, fad). That's not a good place to go, but as Chuck Missler says, the Bible anticipates every heresy. Paul destroyed that idea in his letter to the Galatians, including a warning against anyone trying to change the Gospel.

> *I marvel that ye are so soon removed from him that called you into the grace of Christ unto another gospel; Which is not another; but there be some that trouble you, and would pervert the gospel of Christ. But though we, or an angel from heaven, preach any other gospel unto you than that which we have preached unto you, let him be accursed. As we said before, so say I now again, If any man preach any other gospel unto you than that ye have received, let him be accursed.* Galatians 1:6–9

Strong language from Paul, illustrating the seriousness of modern perversions like social justice being the essence of the Gospel. It can't be, unless Paul is wrong. Paul defines the Gospel, and warns some would try to pervert or change it. As said earlier, run far and fast from people trying to change the Gospel. Paul says called unto another gospel, which is not another. That's a strange construction in English, but Greek supplies two different words for another.

> *The King James Version translates this passage like this: unto another gospel: Which is not another. Actually, the New King James Version translation is much better, because it makes a distinction between different and another, because there are two distinct Greek words used. Different has the idea of "another of different kind" and another has the idea of "another of the same kind." It is as if Paul writes, "They brought you a completely different gospel. They claim it is just an alternative gospel of the same kind, but it isn't at all. It is all together different."*[*]

---

[*] Guzik, David. "Study Guide for Galatians 1." Enduring Word. Blue Letter Bible. 7 Jul 2006. 2013. Retrieved 23 Mar 2013.

The first another in verse 6 is Strongs 2087, meaning other but different — I want another car, meaning not my current Ford but a Lexus. The second another in verse 7 is Strongs 243, meaning another of the same kind — I want another car, a Ford exactly like the one I have. If that sounds a bit murky, consider the passage in the New Living Translation.

> *I am shocked that you are turning away so soon from God, who called you to himself through the loving mercy of Christ. You are following a different way that pretends to be the Good News but is not the Good News at all. You are being fooled by those who deliberately twist the truth concerning Christ.*

That's clearer than the King James. Peddlers of substitute gospels want you to swallow their poison, wrapping it in a thin veneer of truth, but like replacing an M&M chocolate inside with Drano, it may *look* the same, but if you swallow it you'll die. Don't fall for poison wrapped in candy. Peddlers of alternate gospels may or may not know the truth, but it doesn't matter — if you swallow what they're shoveling, you'll end up far away from truth.

For those groups minimizing the death of Christ or substituting strange ideas like social justice, common good, and good works for the real Gospel, they're missing the Gospel and the power of salvation. Either they're right, or Paul is. Your choice, *but they can't both be right* because Paul defined the gospel. People subtly or not-so subtly use a different gospel because they're offended by blood, death, and sin, or they want to use their own gospel for political or other purposes.

If you think you're being conned by a peddler of alternative gospels, *get them to define their terms.* That may sound absurd, but terms like sin, salvation, and even Jesus aren't always used the way you think they should be. If two people aren't using the same definitions of sin and salvation, they can't communicate at all. Using phony perversions means someone can sound completely acceptable, all while selling snake oil. Get people to define terms to discover if you're talking about the same thing — definitions of words are important.

> *The problem of semantics has always played an important part in human affairs, for by its use or abuse, whichever the case may be, entire churches, thrones, and even governments, for that matter, have been erected, sustained, or overthrown.*

> *The late George Orwell's stirring novel 1984, in which he points out that the redefinition of common political terms can lead to slavery when it is allowed to pass unchallenged by a lethargic populace, is a classic illustration of the dangers of perverted semantics. It should be of no particular surprise to any student of world history that trick terminology is a powerful propaganda weapon.**

The preceding may be a distasteful shock to some people. It may be uncomfortable. It may offend some people. However, if you have experience in liberal theology, you'll quickly notice how often these bizarre ideas pop up — they can be quite trendy. The issue remains what the Bible says and what is *true*, not what bothers people, and certainly what may be popular will not always be true.

> *Whereupon neither the first testament was dedicated without blood.*
> Hebrews 9:18

We're returning to the Old Testament. The point will be reinforced this isn't a new idea, it was long ago established, in fact, back in the garden of Eden.

> *For when Moses had spoken every precept to all the people according to the law, he took the blood of calves and of goats, with water, and scarlet wool, and hyssop, and sprinkled both the book, and all the people, Saying, This is the blood of the testament which God hath enjoined unto you. Moreover he sprinkled with blood both the tabernacle, and all the vessels of the ministry. And almost all things are by the law purged with blood; and without shedding of blood is no remission.*
> Hebrews 9:19–22

Second non politically correct point: the blood. Oh, some say, that's offensive and we don't like to talk about it. Let's be seeker-friendly and talk about potlucks. Then you're going to have a tough time with forgiveness of sin, for without shedding of blood there is no remission. Groups avoiding sacrifice and blood find themselves in the peculiar spot of having no good news to offer — people remain trapped in their sin.

This began back in the Garden of Eden. After Adam blew it, God provided skins to cover them. Why? First, they can't clothe themselves, second, only by the shedding of innocent blood could

---

* Martin (2003, page 28–29)

their sin be covered. This isn't a new point Paul brings up in Hebrews, rather it's the application of an old one to Jesus.

Careful reading of the Old Testament reveals the temple functioned like a slaughterhouse. Think of the passover. The family brings home a lamb, keeps it for a while, then cuts the throat and butchers it. It's messy, it's personal, it's a reminder of what sin does, and the principle God laid out — sin requires a sacrifice and penalty to be paid. Sin causes death. In contrast, Jesus at the last supper said do this in remembrance of *me*, not as a reminder of sin. The new covenant reminds us of life and peace, while the old, sin and death. Different covenant, different reminders.

> *It was therefore necessary that the patterns of things in the heavens should be purified with these; but the heavenly things themselves with better sacrifices than these. For Christ is not entered into the holy places made with hands, which are the figures of the true; but into heaven itself, now to appear in the presence of God for us; Nor yet that he should offer himself often, as the high priest entereth into the holy place every year with blood of others; For then must he often have suffered since the foundation of the world. But now once in the end of the ages hath he appeared to put away sin by the sacrifice of himself.* Hebrews 9:23-26

As the priests entered the holy place, Christ entered the holy place in heaven, as our high priest. The difference between the old priesthood and Jesus was the priests couldn't offer the perfect sacrifice. It covered sin, that's all. It couldn't do away with it or pay the required penalty, which is why those sacrifices were continually offered. Jesus, being the perfect sacrifice, *could* do that, so His sacrifice only required a single offering.

> *And as it is appointed unto men once to die, but after this the judgment,* Hebrews 9:27

Only one opportunity exists. Proponents of the strange idea of universal salvation — the idea God allows everyone, no matter how they conducted their life, to live in heaven — must cut this verse out of their Bible. You have one life, and then be judged based on your acceptance or rejection of Jesus. Toss universal salvation on the scrap heap of failed un-Biblical ideas along with the gospel of social justice. You only get one chance in life. You're not going to go somewhere else (purgatory), or come back for another chance (reincarnation). This is it. Choose wisely.

> *So Christ was once offered to bear the sins of many; and unto them that look for him shall he appear the second time without sin unto salvation.* Hebrews 9:28

He's coming back again. One question people ponder is why did He come the way He did? Pastor Ken Graves noted at His first coming He rides on not even a donkey, but a junior donkey. No pyrotechnics, no 100,000 watts of music. No big show. Nothing. If you're wanting the big show, just wait a bit, it's coming. He'll do the big show soon. Remember, the answers are always in the back of the book.

> *For the law having a shadow of good things to come, and not the very image of the things, can never with those sacrifices which they offered year by year continually make those who come to it perfect.* Hebrews 10:1

The Law can't save you. Sure you know that, when it's the Old Testament Law. But for Christians, they don't place themselves under the Mosaic Law, but maybe Mosaic-Lite Law. It's the one saying if you don't pray right, or often enough, go to church enough, or do xyz you're in trouble. What did Paul just say? The sacrifice is done, dude (and dudettes). If you're not resting, perhaps it's because you're trying to live under your own law. No matter what you do, it can *not* make you acceptable to God. That's why it's frustrating.

> *For then would they not have ceased to be offered? Because that the worshipers once purged should have had no more consciousness of sins.* Hebrews 10:2

If any law *did* work, why continue sacrifices? If it worked, there's no need to continue. It's interesting to note soon after Jesus' death, the Romans destroyed the temple and it hasn't existed since. That provides a subtle clue of what Paul says: sacrifices aren't required anymore.

> *But in those sacrifices there is a remembrance again made of sins every year.* Hebrews 10:3

Those sacrifices didn't put away sin, they were a reminder of how far the mark was missed. Why didn't they work?

> *For it is not possible that the blood of bulls and of goats should take away sins.* Hebrews 10:4

The principle that began in Genesis explicitly stated, in case we missed all the hints throughout the Old Testament. The Law was never meant to save, it was meant to point out your sin so you would understand your position and need for a savior.

> *Wherefore when he cometh into the world, he saith, Sacrifice and offering thou wouldest not, but a body hast thou prepared me; In burnt offerings and sacrifices for sin thou hast had no pleasure. Then said I, Lo, I come (in the volume of the book it is written of me) to do thy will, O God. Above when he said, Sacrifice and offering and burnt offerings and offering for sin thou wouldest not, neither hadst pleasure therein; which are offered by the law, Then said he, Lo, I come to do thy will, O God. He taketh away the first, that he may establish the second. By the which will we are sanctified through the offering of the body of Jesus Christ once for all.*
> Hebrews 10:5–10

Those quotes come from Psalm 40, and remind us of a hidden bit: the volume of the book is about Christ. There aren't two different Gods, a mean, vengeful God of the Old Testament, and a nice, forgiving God of the New. Same God — justice, mercy, love, compassion. It's *all* about Him, but you can't have justice and look the other way and ignore transgression. When God judges, it's justice — you can't have mercy without justice, and without justice no possibility for mercy exists.

> *And every priest standeth daily ministering and offering oftentimes the same sacrifices, which can never take away sins.*
> Hebrews 10:11

They weren't intended to. Paul said in Romans the Law was a schoolmaster to drive us to Christ. It wasn't meant to save, it was meant to show how bad you are. By the time Jesus arrives, the Pharisees believed you could be made righteous by observing the Law. Jesus illustrates in the sermon on the mount you have no chance of keeping the Law — it's a matter of the heart, not outward actions.

> *But this man, after he had offered one sacrifice for sins for ever, sat down on the right hand of God, From henceforth expecting till his enemies be made his footstool.*
> Hebrews 10:12–13

Was He tired? Nope. The work was done. Nothing else to do. Don't worry when you look around at the mess the world is in. All in good time the enemies of God *will* meet justice.

> *For by one offering he hath perfected for ever them that are sanctified.*   Hebrews 10:14

Forever. It's not what *you* do. One debate the church engaged in for centuries involves the possibility of losing your salvation. Can you lose it? Not if it's for ever. Forever and eternal are permanent conditions. If even a possibility exists of losing it, it can't be eternal.

> *Whereof the Holy Spirit also is a witness to us; for after that he had said before, This is the covenant that I will make with them after those days, saith the Lord, I will put my laws into their hearts, and in their minds will I write them; And their sins and iniquities will I remember no more.*   Hebrews 10:15-17

First, no priest is required between you and God. Second, your sin is remembered no more. Why? Because the perfect sacrifice was offered. The old sacrifices continued because they weren't perfect.

> *Now where remission of these is, there is no more offering for sin.*   Hebrews 10:18

No more, the work is complete. To stay in the game, you need to rest, not stop working, but understand and ask the questions any good reporter asks: WHO did WHAT work WHEN and WHY. Jesus wrote the testament, died so it will be in force, and rose to be the executor of the testament. Does *any* of that involve you? Nope. So to stay in the game, you must realize that. Once you do, you can continue the work without being sidetracked. Simple, yes. Easy, no.

Chapter *14*

Danger of Despising

WE'VE DISCUSSED THE NEW COVENANT IN FORCE as Paul laid out detailed arguments discussing the superiority of Jesus over the old priesthood, implying the question: why would anyone desire to return to the old system? In this section, Paul moves to the next problem — what about people who don't want to believe in the Gospel? What about people claiming to be Christians, yet appearing to deny foundational principles?

Those people could exist in a worse condition than atheists who openly reject the Gospel, as they know truth and want to appear spiritual, all while denying the truth of the Gospel. We'll lump all those ideas under one banner — liberal theology. However, before continuing, it's critical to remember we're concerned with their *theology*, and that theology does not necessarily indicate anything about their character. They could be the nicest people you want living next door, or axe murderers.

Don't make any assumptions about how nice or evil a person is; correct theology concerns us (and Paul as well). Remember, everyone has the right to believe whatever they want. That doesn't make it true, however. It's tragic we need to state such ideas, but the probability of having civil discourse without name-calling and insults decreases daily. Be concerned with correct theology — what people do with that remains entirely up to them. Your job is to be the watcher on the wall warning about danger, whether people choose to listen and heed is up to them.

Having therefore, brethren, boldness to enter into the holiest by the blood of Jesus,   Hebrews 10:19

Because of the perfect sacrifice, we can be bold, meaning freedom. It's not arrogance, but more like you see in the military "permission to speak freely." Boldness comes from the new covenant in force, meaning freedom from works. In the Old Testament, you could not come freely. The priest wondered, did I perform all the ceremony right? Will it be accepted? But under the new covenant, that's all behind us.

> *By a new and living way, which he hath consecrated for us, through the veil, that is to say, his flesh, And having an high priest over the house of God, Let us draw near with a true heart in full assurance of faith, having our hearts sprinkled from an evil conscience, and our bodies washed with pure water.* Hebrews 10:20–22

You come boldly not by the old way, but by a new high priest offering the perfect sacrifice once and for all. Because you're no longer required to offer sacrifices, your ability to come before God comes from Jesus' completed work, not insufficient levitical sacrifices. A true heart differs from a pure heart. True meaning real, genuine. You don't have to be perfect.

Due to Jesus' work (and not ours), we can have full assurance of faith. The difference between those making it in tough times and those struggling is the full assurance of faith. Faith isn't blind belief, it's a reasonable understanding of something you can't know based on facts and events you *do* know. We'll get to faith in the next chapter so we'll move on.

> *Let us hold fast the profession of our faith without wavering; (for he is faithful that promised)* Hebrews 10:23

Notice Paul includes himself — let *us* hold fast; without wavering means steady, without inclining or giving way.* Notice it's not holding to *our* faith, rather it's the *profession* of it. All through the Bible not-so-subtle hints tell us our righteousness comes not from anything we do. All this prefaces the next chapter called the hall of faith where we'll find many examples.

Simply put, Paul says stay in the game. Don't quit for the simple reason it's nothing *we* do or say, or as Paul said to Timothy I know who I believed, and am convinced *He* is able to keep it. He that promised is faithful to guarantee His promises work exactly as He said. Even the super-saint apostle Paul doesn't say to hold

---

* Zodhiates (1992a, page 111)

Danger of Despising

fast to faith in him, or his teaching. If you're holding fast to faith in me, or your pastor, you've got trouble. Too many people have misplaced faith. We're returning to the Old Testament Law, only substituting pastors for priests.

If you put your faith in people, prepare to be disappointed. Nobody *wants* to let you down, but sometimes circumstances arise making keeping commitments impossible. One Sunday when I was supposed to teach, I ended up in the emergency room the night before. Finally, at 9 o'clock, I was forced to call in and say I couldn't make it. No matter how hard I tried, I simply could not respond, and was out of the game that day. If you relied on me that day, you were sorely disappointed.

You might say, gee, that's not your fault, there's no way you could have known. Doesn't matter. I failed to perform, and let people down because of it. Something I'm not very happy about for sure. If you're counting on people — even reliable people — sometimes it's not going to work out well. People don't know what the future holds, and occasionally those sorts of things happen. I certainly didn't *want* to end up in the hospital, but that's what happened. James warned about presuppositions on the future also.

> *Come now, ye that say, Today or tomorrow we will go into such a city, and continue there a year, and buy and sell, and get gain; Whereas ye know not what shall be on the next day. For what is your life? It is even a vapor, that appeareth for a little time, and then vanisheth away. For that ye ought to say, If the Lord will, we shall live, and do this, or that.*
> James 4:13–15

Saturday night I certainly *planned* on teaching the next day, but was unable to. It's time to do your own homework and learn for yourself, because Paul tells you to hold fast, and you can't do that without knowing what you believe, and why. Someday at 3 AM you're going to be alone, or the person you would call will be unavailable. Imagine how you would handle situations if you knew nobody would be around to bail you out. Would you prepare a bit more today?

> *And let us consider one another to provoke unto love and to good works,*
> Hebrews 10:24

Paul says motivate others to love and good works. For you Bible students, which Greek word do you suppose Paul used for love? Agape. Lot's of confusion about love exists. It's not what you see on TV; realize love is a commitment, not an emotion. In Greek, it's a *verb*, not a noun. It means commitment. It says until I draw my last breath, I'm committed. In the marriage realm, in sickness or health, richer or poorer, till death do us part. In marriage, times will occur when your spouse doesn't like you very much. But if love truly exists, commitment never wavers. In Biblical terms you can't stop loving someone, or it means you never actually did — commitment means non-terminating or it's not really a commitment.

Paul also answers a question causing much confusion in today's church — what is the purpose of the church? Is it social justice, building homes, radical political ideology, helping the common good, and good works? Well, once again we don't have to guess, as Paul explains for us.

Those things aren't wrong, but saying since the church *isn't* doing the job well enough we should lobby the government to forcefully redistribute everything until we get heaven on earth run into a problem with Paul. What does Paul say? It's an *individual* duty. The good Samaritan didn't lobby the government for more funding for road patrols, *he* did the job. Pastors spending time on radical politics (social justice, etc) are out of line. It's our individual responsibility, and the function of the pastor and church must be to spur each person on, exactly as Paul says. Jesus didn't say to lobby Rome to spread the gospel and help others. It's *your* job.

> *Not forsaking the assembling of ourselves together, as the manner of some is, but exhorting one another, and so much the more, as ye see the day approaching.* Hebrews 10:25

Every now and then a movement pops up encouraging dropping out of church. The church contains hypocrites and so on, so I'll stay home. After all, I can fully worship God and admire His creation on the 15th tee, or while catching salmon. Why should I bother with such incorrect people? Paul's specific warning: do *not* drop out of church.

> *For if we sin willfully after that we have received the knowledge of the truth, there remaineth no more sacrifice for sins, But a certain fearful looking for of judgment and fiery indignation, which shall devour the adversaries.* Hebrews 10:26-27

Another part of Hebrews causing a lot of problems. By now, you should see this has nothing to do with losing your salvation, but

Danger of Despising

a warning about abandoning or despising what you *know* to be true. If you trade the new covenant for works, you're helpless. No acceptable sacrifice exists, and worse, you're saying the death of Jesus was both insufficient and unnecessary to salvation. That's not a good place to be in.

Nothing else will arrive to solve the problem, either. As we've seen through the chapters, Paul presents a precise argument about the death of Jesus providing salvation, and how the new covenant trumps the old. So don't despise it or try it your own way, because nothing else will be accepted, or required. Jesus' death was both a necessary *and* sufficient event for salvation. Those two words aren't the same. Necessary means it was *required*, sufficient means nothing else is *needed*.

- Necessary — it was required as the blood of bulls and goats could never put away sin, only cover it.
- Sufficient — nothing else is needed. It's not Jesus+.

He that despised Moses' law died without mercy under two or three witnesses; (Hebrews 10:28)

Paul makes a comparison of those who despised Mosaic law, and those who despise Jesus' death or call it insufficient. If you know the truth, and reject or despise it, no mercy is available. It's a willful abandonment of what you know to be true. Every person is free to accept or reject Jesus as they wish, but understand each person will also be held accountable for that choice.

Of how much sorer punishment, suppose ye, shall he be thought worthy, who hath trodden under foot the Son of God, and hath counted the blood of the covenant, wherewith he was sanctified, an unholy thing, and hath done despite unto the Spirit of grace? Hebrews 10:29

A sobering thought for those trampling on truth, if under the Mosaic law those died without mercy, how much more those who deny Christ? As previously mentioned, it's not popular to talk about the blood of the new covenant anymore. Those dismissing the foundation of salvation trample on Christ. Movements today exist under many names — liberal theology, social justice, progressive, modern, and others — that frequently abandon Biblical truth. Generally, I lump all those together for discussion purposes and simply call them *liberal theology*. Liberal theology originates from post-modern philosophy (see Appendix 22). As representative of liberal theology, consider Bishop Spong and his 12 theses. While we won't cover every one,* you'll quickly understand how post-modern philosophy and liberal theology fundamentally transforms the Bible into a bag of mush.

1. Theism, as a way of defining God, is dead. So most theological God-talk is today meaningless. A new way to speak of God must be found.

2. Since God can no longer be conceived in theistic terms, it becomes nonsensical to seek to understand Jesus as the incarnation of the theistic deity. So the Christology of the ages is bankrupt.

3. The biblical story of the perfect and finished creation from which human beings fell into sin is pre-Darwinian mythology and post-Darwinian nonsense.

4. The virgin birth, understood as literal biology, makes Christ's divinity, as traditionally understood, impossible.

5. The miracle stories of the New Testament can no longer be interpreted in a post-Newtonian world as supernatural events performed by an incarnate deity.

6. The view of the cross as the sacrifice for the sins of the world is a barbarian idea based on primitive concepts of God and must be dismissed.

7. Resurrection is an action of God. Jesus was raised into the meaning of God. It therefore cannot be a physical resuscitation occurring inside human history.

Let's look at what some of the twelve points imply; Spong's "Christianity":

- Denies the deity of Christ. (#2)

- Denies the virgin birth. (#4)

- Denies the creation. (#3)

- Denies the inerrancy of the Bible. (#2, #3, #4)

---

* http://web.archive.org/web/20070203143306/http://www.dioceseofnewark.org/jsspong/reform.html

- Denies the atonement of the cross. (#6, #7)

What's left? Church potlucks? No deity of Christ. No creation. No atonement. And finally, you can't accept the entire Bible as the Word of God. That truly expresses a form of religion but denying the power thereof. Recall atheist Christopher Hitchers words:

I would say that if you don't believe that Jesus of Nazareth was the Christ and Messiah, and that he rose again from the dead and by his sacrifice our sins are forgiven, you're really not in any meaningful sense a Christian.*

It's popular today — in spite of Paul's warning — to trample on Jesus, the cross, and God's Word. You must be careful, they may use the same terms, read the same Bible, but what they profess is not Christianity in any reasonable form. We're not concerned over minor disagreements about pre-trib verses post-trib, which Bible translation to use, or to worship on Sunday or Saturday. No, liberal theology denies the foundations of Christianity and rejects Paul's warning in Hebrews concerning alternate gospels. It's not unreasonable to state they exist as Christians in name only.

For we know him that hath said, Vengeance belongeth unto me, I will recompense, saith the Lord. And again, The Lord shall judge his people. Hebrews 10:30

A strange idea floats around called universal salvation, or the idea *everyone* will be saved, because God is a God of love, and He wouldn't condemn people to hell, would He? Three obvious problems with that heresy.

- From a Biblical standpoint, the Bible *does* speak of hell and judgment.

- Logically, justice requires judgment. You can't be just without judging sin and evil.

- It's not God sending you to hell, it's your choice. If you don't want to go, you don't have to.

But, if you ignore all that and want to go it your own way, the next verse destroys that as being a good idea.

---

*   Sewell (2009)

> *It is a fearful thing to fall into the hands of the living God.*
> Hebrews 10:31

For those so-called Christians who despise the Gospel so much they substitute another (which Paul warned the Galatians about), and those who reject the offer of salvation, they'll both fall into God's judgment. Justice *requires* judgment.

> *But call to remembrance the former days, in which, after ye were illuminated, ye endured a great fight of afflictions, Partly, while ye were made a gazingstock both by reproaches and afflictions; and partly, while ye became companions of them that were so used.* Hebrews 10:32–33

The enemy doesn't like what you're doing. Period. This isn't some paranoid devil-behind-every-door delusion (like the Church Lady on SNL), it's a realistic understanding of good and evil. Paul told Timothy to be watchful in everything, endure affliction, work as an evangelist, and fulfill your ministry.

Phases of persecution exist. First, identify the target group, and marginalize them. Try to shut them up and prevent them from speaking, ridicule them and so forth. That's becoming a gazingstock of reproach.

> *For ye had compassion of me in my bonds, and took joyfully the spoiling of your goods, knowing in yourselves that ye have in heaven a better and an enduring substance.*
> Hebrews 10:34

Next phase of persecution creates laws against the target group, and then enforces the law. Throughout history, persecuted groups had their possessions plundered. That's nothing new as thieves always exist. The great tragedy occurs when that plundering occurs under the full force of law, when it's legal. The Jews had their goods stolen by the Nazis, and it was all legal (and generally popular as well).

Today forfeiture laws combine with so-called hate speech to create a similar situation. What is hate speech? Something a certain group doesn't like. We've moved from whether something is true, to whether it offends people. If it's true, but offends a person, it's "hate speech." Whatever happened to tolerance? Reasonable people understand tolerance to mean we each believe what we wish, and I can try to convince you I'm right, and you can do the same to me. Modern politically correct thought replaces

Danger of Despising

that definition to mean only tolerating what a group (usually the government) defines as worthy of acceptance. That's Newspeak,* not tolerance. Sounds crazy, does it not?

Under those laws, your goods can be plundered for speaking the truth. Those laws, similar to what happened to Daniel in chapter 6, are designed to keep the target group from speaking or expressing themselves. For those who believe such actions could not happen, it's important to realize it *already* happens.

Tolerance and freedom of speech means the right to say what's on your mind, it does *not* mean you won't hear anything you don't agree with. Never forget legal does not make it right. Moves today exist to take from certain groups, and just because someone may get a law passed does *not* make it right. What's right is not always legal, and what's legal isn't always right. Paul says for those it happened to, they took it well, even knowing it was an unjust, if legal, event.

People mistake courts for justice. Not so, courts exist for law. We hope law and justice match, for example thou shalt not murder. It's illegal, and also wrong. Rights are *never* given by government, rather government should acknowledge and protect God-given rights. After all, where does morality come from?

> *We hold these truths to be self-evident, that all men are created equal, that they are endowed by their Creator with certain unalienable Rights, that among these are Life, Liberty and the pursuit of Happiness — that to secure these rights, Governments are instituted among Men ...*

Notice without standards from God, morality becomes whatever the majority wish it to be. No standard exists. Rights and justice are unchangeable, no matter what laws man may make. Making a law against God-given rights does *not* make it correct, only legal. For those Paul speaks to, he reminds them they have a better situation coming, so if something immoral—though legal—happens, look to the future. There are hills to fight on, and some that aren't worth it. Knowing the difference is wisdom. Right and

---

* Newspeak comes from Orewell's "1984," a language twisting what words actually mean. Phrases like "slavery is freedom" are classic Newspeak. If you think that might never happen, simply read Congressional legislation, and compare it with titles. You'll discover Newspeak has been in use for a long time, as titles of legislation normally are the opposite of what they actually do. "Affordable" means sky-high prices, "Freedom Act" means restriction, "deficit-reducing" means more debt.

wrong will never be found via political means, it can't be voted on, and it never changes.

> *Cast not away therefore your confidence, which hath great recompense of reward.*   Hebrews 10:35

Sure, it might be tough, with persecution and the government moving in the wrong direction trying to take away God-given rights (remember, rights and liberty come from God; government's job must be to protect those rights). But stay in the game, I peeked at the end, and the good guys win. John Wayne said "courage is being scared to death but saddling up anyway." A time comes — usually at 3 AM — when you face a choice. Stick with what's right, or give in and quit. What's right may not be legal, and if you choose to stand up for what's right, you'll face the consequences of an immoral law, exactly as Daniel did, the same as Daniel's three friends did, just as the apostles did.

Daniel faced that when they made a law — not just — against praying. As usual, for Daniel it was simply mind over matter. Their stupid unjust law didn't matter, so he didn't mind. Of course, he faced the consequences, but maintained his normal routine anyway. The secret isn't found in chapter 6, but way back in chapter 1, as it records Daniel purposed in his heart not to defile himself. Staying in the game means deciding beforehand how you'll react. When the situation comes, you'll respond like you've thought. Did you ever wonder why the band on the Titanic played while the ship sank?

> *Since writing my book, "The Band That Played On: The Extraordinary Story of the 8 Musicians Who Went Down with the Titanic," the most frequent question I've been asked is why the Titanic's eight musicians continued to play on the deck even as the ship was going down. Were they told to do so by the Captain? Was it part of their job description? Did they think they would be saved?*
>
> *I believe the band took the courageous decision to play because of the moral character of their leader, the violinist Wallace Hartley. ... By all accounts Hartley was a highly principled person and a devout Christian.*
>
> *... a musician on the Mauretania, who had served under Hartley. He told a British newspaper; "I remember one day I asked him what he would do if he were ever on a sinking*

Danger of Despising

ship and he replied I don't think I would do better than play 'Oh God Our Help in Ages Past' or 'Nearer, My God, to Thee'."

So it appears almost certain that Wallace Hartley had contemplated being on a sinking ship and had already decided how he would respond. He believed that music could prevent panic and create calm. He had also chosen his final piece of music.*

You respond in a crisis how you've been trained, and how you've prepared beforehand. Contrary to popular belief, you won't rise to the occasion, you'll regress to the level of your preparedness. If history provides any guide, we're heading towards dark times. You may wake up one day and discover nobody around to bail you out. What gets you through is what you've been trained to do. If you're trained and committed to Biblical truth, you'll make it.

But for pew-warmers always looking for a bailout, maybe not so much. I know that's not popular or politically correct, but that's the truth, and we ignore it at our peril. If you want to go along with political correctness, lots of dead churches exist who won't need new pastors after the rapture. Don't cast aside or ignore your confidence in the truth. The difference between what we consider super-saints like what we'll find in the next chapter and pew-warmers is the super-saint *acts on what he knows*.

For ye have need of patience, that, after ye have done the will of God, ye might receive the promise. Hebrews 10:36

Patience in Greek is Strongs 5281; endurance might be a better translation. Endurance means never quitting. Sure, we all get discouraged sometimes. Service for God is tough. Doing the right thing is tough. Standing for truth is tough. People don't like to hear truth, those living in a world of deception.

Romans 8:28 says all things work together for good. It does *not* say you'll understand, or even see the good in your lifetime. To continue on when things look dark requires endurance and the c-word nobody likes to talk about anymore: c-c-c-c-character.

I've been a fan of Zig Ziglar for a long time. Zig was a motivational speaker, usually for sales groups. Zig said "it was character that got us out of bed, commitment that moved us into action and discipline that enabled us to follow through." We're always

---

*   http://www.foxnews.com/opinion/2013/04/27/what-made-titanic-band-keep-playing-even-as-ship-sank/

looking for that special encouragement or inspirational words. I've discovered the secret: there aren't any (well, not very many). Only character and an unwavering refusal to yield exists, and that decision must come before you face the situation. We have need of endurance, as Paul says. Notice he doesn't say look to your pastor for it, he says *we* need it. It's 2:59 AM folks. The promise will come, but that doesn't mean between here and there will be easy. Or you'll get a Lexus. Or an ice cream. You might get a pony though, if you're lucky (just kidding). Stay in the game.

> *For yet a little while, and he that shall come will come, and will not tarry.* Hebrews 10:37

The second coming will appear right on schedule. Through history, periods existed with people believing the return must be close; we're in another as we can't see how events can continue on this path. It's truly a dark time, but don't make the mistake the end is soon. It could be, or it could be decades away.

> *Now the just shall live by faith; but if any man draw back, my soul shall have no pleasure in him.* Hebrews 10:38

Faith is misunderstood a lot, and we'll deal with that in the next chapter. This is the danger if you draw back, it's Paul's way of saying stay in the game. It's tough, it's hard, it's frustrating at times. Retreat isn't an option, it's not on the table, it must not exist in your vocabulary. The only way is forward; being surrounded means you can attack in any direction. Some people quit when the situation gets tough; don't be in that group.

> *But we are not of them who draw back unto perdition; but of them that believe to the saving of the soul.* Hebrews 10:39

In contrast, another group exists who refuse to quit. That's the group you want to be in. Old commentaries are not so politically correct and state the truth without worrying about how people think about it; J. Vernon McGee certainly wasn't worried about what people might think.

> *There is a lot of boo-hooing today among Christians. There is a lot of complaining and criticizing. There are a bunch of crybabies and babies that need to be burped. Oh, my Christian friend, the whole tenor of this marvelous epistle is "Let us go on." So let us go on for God.**

---

* McGee (1982b, page 579)

Danger of Despising

I've said martial arts relates to your Christian life and it does. When you're in a trial, or praying for your child who's gone sideways, or imploring God for a healing, you'll definitely come to the point when every fiber of your being screams give in and quit.

I'm quite sure Job felt that way, and his problems had nothing to do with him at all. Paul definitely did, telling the church at Corinth he despaired even of life, while Elijah became afraid after defeating the prophets of Baal at Mount Carmel.

Think you're all alone when you feel that way? Think again.

We've failed as a church to prepare people for the events we *know* will occur. Thus, when people face trials and can't figure out why, or they get smacked in the face by the enemy for the first time they fold like a cheap lawn chair. Why? Pastors and teachers gave a phony happy-land view of Christianity where everyone gets a pony.

Don't draw back. Retreat only leads to destruction. It's time to stay in the game. It's hard. It's tough. It's discouraging at times. Never forget as a soldier for Christ the retirement package is out of this world. Maintain focus. Move forward. You *can* do it — be stubborn and never give in. Never surrender.

Chapter 15

The Hall of Faith

I'M NOT A VERY GOOD FARMER. FARMERS IN OUR church get a good laugh at my feeble attempts to grow things. On more than one occasion I've planted vegetables, and then — out of a clear blue sky — a massive hailstorm appears destroying my plants. As a mathematician, I'm far too analytical for farming. Farmers have the uncommon knack to figure out this year we'll plant June 20, in spite of last year planting in May, because gosh darn it, the sky looks a bit bluer than last year. My spreadsheets never get it right, while our farmers look up at the sky and say, today we plant, based on little more than a gut feeling.

We built our raised garden using concrete cinder blocks. Being the physicist and mathematician I am (and more than a little OCD), I created a drawing showing where each block would go, and how many I needed. Driving down to the store, I found the blocks, and discovered they weighed about 38 pounds each (about is not a good word for OCD people). I required 72 of them, so you quickly discover that's 2,736 pounds.

In a half-ton truck with a capacity of 1,000 pounds (as you note from watching commercials) includes "occupants and cargo," we'll subtract 200 pounds for me and stuff (okay, maybe 225), and calculate 2,736 divided by 800 equals 3.42 trips. Nuts. Four trips? I'll be at this all day, as the lumber yard requires a 20 mile drive each way. After the first trip, we had some friends visit us, a married couple who actually volunteered to help move bricks and set up the garden. And the peasants rejoiced (that's Peggy and me). What great people to stop by for a visit and say sure, we'll help do all that hard work!

After we're done, we're talking about how long it took, and he said he finished it all in a few hours. How could you do that, I asked, since it requires four trips. Four trips? Nah, he only took one. Did he get a big truck? Farm vehicle? Nope, just a regular Nissan truck. What about the weight? You can't (shouldn't) put that much in a compact truck (not that he or I knew the actual weight involved).

Man spouts lots of stuff that actually are only recommendations, since we don't really know everything. Some you should pay attention to, other times you'll notice the best of man's wisdom changes day by day. As we arrive at one of the most famous chapters in the Bible, you'll find this chapter isn't really a recommendation, it's something you *have* to do (God didn't call them the 10 suggestions, after all).

Paul frequently splits his letters in two parts, the first deals with theology and doctrine, the last practical applications — in Hebrews, the last three chapters are faith, hope, and love. What is the theme of Hebrews? Stay in the game. It's easy to get discouraged, and at times we all want to quit; it's then we must re-double our efforts. Sometimes at 3 AM all you've got is faith, the reasonable belief in truth. It might not be scientific truth, but don't let that make you believe it's not valid.

> *Now faith is the substance of things hoped for, the evidence of things not seen.* Hebrews 11:1

It's not wishful thinking. As you drive over bridges, you have faith and hope you'll make it to the other side. You understand engineers designed it for specific loads, and built it with steel and concrete. Yet have any of us examined the structural calculations? You trust the creators, engineers, and builders because of what you *do* know. I don't just drive off the bank and say I'll have faith I'll fly to the other side. No, my faith in that bridge I've crossed thousands of times comes from what I do know. God is no different, you have faith in what you haven't seen because of what you *have* seen.

What faith is *not* can be just as important. It's not a magic genie where you can get your pony, or a Lexus. It's not gab-it-and-grab-it or name-it-and-claim-it. I think most of us have at one point or another seen "pastors" claim such ideas. But that's a perversion of faith. God is not a genie so you can get a pony and three wishes — and the first wish is for more wishes.

> *For by it the elders received witness.* Hebrews 11:2

The Hall of Faith

Most of the chapter will be examples of people having a reasonable expectation of what they hadn't seen from what they had seen. It's not I'll believe it when I see it, but I'll see it when I believe it. Faith comes from reasonable deductions from what you do know, not blind hope.

> *Through faith we understand that the worlds were framed by the word of God, so that things which are seen were not made of things which do appear.* Hebrews 11:3

This refers way back to page one, Genesis. Similar to the Hebrew in Genesis, the Greek in Hebrews implies made from nothing. Things seen are made of things which do not appear — atoms and the laws of Quantum Physics. Notice Paul conflicts with Darwin. People say how are you going to prove Paul right? I don't need to, at least by their standards. Science should use something called the scientific method, where you make a guess, perform experiments to prove or disprove the guess, then modify your guess. Lather, rinse, repeat.

That's the way it *should* work, and the way all science works except for one field — evolution. I've asked these questions for years, and nobody provides scientific answers: show me peer-reviewed, repeatable, experimental evidence for a few foundational ideas of evolution.

1. Matter comes from nothing (first there was nothing...).

2. Explosions produce order (...and then it exploded).

3. Non-life becomes life (abiogenesis).

4. New species suddenly appear.

The idea explosions produce order makes no sense, as anybody who has watched Mythbusters knows. Their motto is "when in doubt, C-4." If you watch the show, they use ... you know ... actual *science*. They make a guess, design an experiment (which somehow always includes explosives), and after performing the experiment, determine if their original idea matches reality. That's science, and I've yet to see any of their explosions produce an ordered system.

Evolution can be summarized as from the goo to the zoo to you. And they say *I* don't follow science? I don't claim to prove God from the scientific method, rather it's faith — a similar faith I have in the bridge I drive over. I may not know *how* it works, but I reasonably conclude when I drive over the bridge it will get my car to the other side. But their so-called evolution? It doesn't follow their own methods. If it did they could easily supply experimental data to answer my questions. Every time I ask, I get personal attacks and religion, instead of science.

> *Observation, reason, and experiment make up what we call the scientific method.**

You'll hear things like "scientists overwhelmingly agree." So what? It's about experimental data. Remember their agreement on Piltdown man? Decades passed before they discovered the "missing link" a fraud. Why were scientists so easily duped? They *wanted* to believe anything proving evolution, so they failed to follow proper investigative methods. Never fall for the mistake that if everyone believes it, somehow it must be true. Actual science follows the scientific method with experimental data agreeing with reality, pseudo-science does not, and falls for deceptions like Piltdown man.

> *The principle of science, the definition, almost, is the following: The test of all knowledge is experiment. Experiment is the sole judge of scientific "truth."*†

Without it? No science. As another author wrote:

> *These aren't gaps in a scientific theory — there is no scientific theory. There is only a story about how a bear might have fallen into the ocean and become a whale ...*
>
> *In the end, evolutionists' only argument is contempt. The cultists know that if people were allowed to hear the arguments against evolution for just sixty seconds, all would be lost. So they demonize the people making those arguments. You're just saying that because you believe in God! You probably believe in a flat Earth, too! You sound like a Holocaust revisionist! That's all you ever get.*‡
>
> *You will begin to notice that the Darwiniacs' answer to everything is to accuse their opponents of believing in God — and*

---

* Feynman (1964, page 2-1)
† Feynman (1964, page 1-1)
‡ Coulter (2006, page 244)

The Hall of Faith

a flat Earth for good measure — even when responding to an argument based on biochemistry, physics or mathematics.*

I continue to ask for scientific, experimental data for foundational ideas of evolution, and continue to hear nothing. That means evolution is unscientific by definition. It's philosophy. Contrast with verse 1, as faith is the substance and evidence of things not seen, as J. Vernon McGee explains what Paul's Greek means.

The Greek word for "substance" is hupostasis. It is a scientific term, the opposite of hypothesis or theory. It is that which rests on facts.†

While evidence is...

In the Greek the word is elegchos. It is a legal term meaning "evidence that is accepted for conviction."‡

Faith is the opposite of scientific theory or guesses. It's evidence used in court. McGee thus concludes:

Faith is not a leap in the dark. Faith is not a hope-so. Faith is substance and evidence — substance for a scientific mind, and evidence for a legal mind.§

It's important to keep the definition of faith in mind. So with that brief introduction, Paul moves on to specifics.

By faith Abel offered unto God a more excellent sacrifice than Cain, by which he obtained witness that he was righteous, God testifying of his gifts; and by it he being dead yet speaketh. Hebrews 11:4

What's the difference? Abel followed God's instructions, while Cain used the Frank Sinatra plan — he did it his way. Abel offered part of his flock, while Cain offered the works of his hands. Paul informs us of something else: Abel had faith, Cain did not (Genesis 4). Abel had a reasonable expectation of God — even if he never saw Him — because of what he heard from his parents, who did have first-hand experience. That's faith — a reasonable belief in the truth.

---

* ibid, page 205
† McGee (1982b, page 580)
‡ McGee (1982b, page 581)
§ McGee (1982b, page 581)

> *By faith Enoch was translated that he should not see death; and was not found, because God had translated him; for before his translation he had this testimony, that he pleased God.* Hebrews 11:5

Genesis 5 says Enoch walked with God. Enoch provides a type of the church that will be removed before the tribulation. The flood illustrates it — some people died in the flood, some were preserved through it, and one was removed prior to it. The one represents the bride of Christ. As Chuck Missler says, Enoch was not post-flood, or mid-flood, but pre-flood.

> *But without faith it is impossible to please him; for he that cometh to God must believe that he is, and that he is a rewarder of them that diligently seek him.* Hebrews 11:6

Impossible. Not hard. This is not "only a recommendation," it's an unchangeable rule. Do you want to please God? No shortcut exists, the path runs through faith, and that frequently comes from trials and tribulation. Those trials aren't usually fun, but they provide skills we normally can't acquire any other way. No pain, no gain might be an old weight lifting motto, but it provides a flavor of how we should view trials.

> *By faith Noah, being warned of God of things not seen as yet, moved with fear, prepared an ark to the saving of his house; by the which he condemned the world, and became heir of the righteousness which is by faith.* Hebrews 11:7

It never rained before, and he worked on the boat for decades. That takes considerable faith — reasonable belief in what you know to be true. I've said many times Noah is the biggest failure in the Bible. He preached for decades and how many did he reach? Zero. Zip. But that's not quite true. His *family* was saved, and as any father will tell you, that's enough.

> *By faith Abraham, when he was called to go out into a place which he should after receive for an inheritance, obeyed; and he went out, not knowing whither he went.* Hebrews 11:8

Faith isn't blind trust, it's a reasonable conclusion. Thus by faith Abraham left not knowing where he was going, because he did know who was leading him. We don't always see the complete picture. Sometimes it's get up and get moving, and then God will reveal the rest, after all you can't steer a parked car.

The Hall of Faith

> *By faith he sojourned in the land of promise, as in a strange country, dwelling in tents with Isaac and Jacob, the heirs with him of the same promise; For he looked for a city which hath foundations, whose builder and maker is God.*
>
> Hebrews 11:9-10

That's called priority. Abraham refused to become bogged down in the cares of this world. His focus remained on God, not worldly stuff.

> *Through faith also Sarah herself received strength to conceive seed, and was delivered of a child when she was past age, because she judged him faithful who had promised. Therefore sprang there even of one, and him as good as dead, so many as the stars of the sky in multitude, and as the sand which is by the sea shore innumerable.* Hebrews 11:11-12

Of course, the story of Sarah is a bit funny. She didn't quite accept it the first time around. However, in Hebrews her faults aren't recorded, only her faith.

> *These all died in faith, not having received the promises, but having seen them afar off, and were persuaded of them, and embraced them, and confessed that they were strangers and pilgrims on the earth. For they that say such things declare plainly that they seek a country. And truly, if they had been mindful of that country from which they came out, they might have had opportunity to return.* Hebrews 11:13-15

Notice the critical point — they died not seeing the promise. Does that make their faith void? Of course not. The same with you — you've prayed for years and decades for something, and nothing happens. Everyone says why do you trust in God when He's not listening. He *is* listening, but God is not a Genie giving everyone a pony (or a Lexus, but you get the point).

> *But now they desire a better country, that is, an heavenly; wherefore God is not ashamed to be called their God; for he hath prepared for them a city.* Hebrews 11:16

It's a good thing this world isn't what God had in mind, because it's pretty messed up. Perhaps you recall the guy in Cleveland who kidnapped girls and kept them for 10 years. What possible defense could exist for such heinous actions? Philosophy presents an interesting theory called determinism, which means you don't actually have free will. Someone sent me an article about Dr. Jerry Coyne from the University of Chicago who argued:

> *Our brains are simply meat computers that, like real computers, are programmed by our genes and experiences to convert an array of inputs into a predetermined output.*

No free will. No choices. No morality. No responsibility. Coyne concludes his article:

> *Further, by losing free will we gain empathy, for we realize that in the end all of us, whether Bernie Madoffs or Nelson Mandelas, are victims of circumstance — of the genes we're bequeathed and the environments we encounter. With that under our belts, we can go about building a kinder world.**

Notice the logical error? His article states you have no control over your actions, and then states if you follow his advice and abandon free will, we can build a kinder world, which is a choice. Tilt. He's running in circles. You can't argue your life is predetermined, and then say if you follow my advice you can change. Can't have it both ways. Yes, the world is messed up. We're waiting for the world God prepared, which won't be so confused.

> *By faith Abraham, when he was tested, offered up Isaac; and he that had received the promises offered up his only begotten son, Of whom it was said, That in Isaac shall thy seed be called; Accounting that God was able to raise him up, even from the dead; from whence also he received him in a figure.* Hebrews 11:17-19

Paul refers to Issac as Abraham's only son. What about Ishmael? God doesn't acknowledge works of the flesh. Without faith it's impossible to please God. Don't go off on your own. Sure God, you said this, but that's not really practical, so I'll just move things along. Not a good idea.

Abraham didn't worry about it; he had the promise Isaac would be his heir, so if he dies, God would have to resurrect him, as God made a promise. Of course, every time this comes up, we

---

* https://web.archive.org/web/20130918032821/http://usatoday30.usatoday.com/news/opinion/forum/story/2012-01-01/free-will-science-religion/52317624/1

must state the disclaimer God doesn't promote child sacrifice. Why then did he tell Abraham to do this? Did God not know Abraham's character? Yes, he did. But *Abraham* needed to know his character. God had no plans to allow child sacrifice, it was so Abraham would know his character. You don't go through trials so God will know your character, you go through trials so *you* know your character. And there's one other reason.

> *But now thus saith the Lord that created thee, O Jacob, and he that formed thee, O Israel, Fear not; for I have redeemed thee, I have called thee by thy name; thou art mine. When thou passest through the waters, I will be with thee; and through the rivers, they shall not overflow thee; when thou walkest through the fire, thou shalt not be burned, neither shall the flame kindle upon thee.* Isaiah 43:1–2

Notice it says *when*, not *if*. As we learn in Zechariah about the potter, we're familiar with the image of the potter and the clay, and how the maker can choose what to make of the clay. But clay has an interesting characteristic — you can take a lump of clay, make a pot, and what happens when you put water in it? It turns back to clay. It's useless for work.

How do you make clay useful? By putting it through fire. The fire causes changes in the clay to make it useful for work, and those changes are irreversible. When you go through the fire, it makes you useful for work. You certainly won't be the same after the fire as before, and those differences make you useful later. What allows you to stay in the game through the fire? Two things.

1. Faith. That's what Hebrews 11 is all about.

2. Figuring out before how you'll handle it. Daniel's three buddies before the king.

Is any of this process fun? Maybe not. But it's required to be useful, and don't we want to be useful? Earlier we discovered without faith it is impossible to please God. It's not just a recommendation. The politically correct idea is you *want* to please God, thus it follows you must understand what faith is, in the Biblical sense. Thus, chapter 11 of Hebrews. So we're about halfway through, and the end supplies a surprise twist.

> *By faith Isaac blessed Jacob and Esau concerning things to come.* Hebrews 11:20

Isaac didn't know the future, but he did understand the nature of God.

> *By faith Jacob, when he was dying, blessed both the sons of Joseph; and worshiped, leaning upon the top of his staff.*
>
> Hebrews 11:21

If God can save Jacob, He can save anyone. Jacob was a conniver and a cheat. Some people don't like to believe in reality — God saves bad people, and those rejecting His offer end up in a place they'd rather not be. I read a lot of blogs and articles, and once I discovered somebody talking about a new Christianity, and on their "what they believe" area, said this:

> *There is no support in the Bible for the morally repugnant idea that hell is an actual place to which God sentences people to spend eternity in mortal agony.**

I don't really understand that, because God doesn't send anyone to hell. God gives each person a choice — you can live with Him, or not. If you don't want God and His characteristics of love, light, and peace, God provides an environment *exactly* without those characteristics, in a place called hell. Nobody has to go there unless they want to. Sin and transgression requires a penalty to be paid, and more important a just God can't exist without it.

J. Vernon McGee says you have to wait until the end of a man's life before you can say he's a man of faith. McGee is right — people on their deathbed focus a bit more about their life. Jacob certainly didn't live what you would call a model life, yet he appears in the hall of faith, as we find out at the end. If God can accept Jacob, He can accept anyone. Nobody exists beyond the grace of God, and it's never too late to repent. At the end of his life, Jacob finally got it right, and that's why he's in the hall of faith.

> *By faith Joseph, when he died, made mention of the departing of the children of Israel; and gave commandment concerning his bones.*
>
> Hebrews 11:22

Strange Paul chooses this to include. What about the rest of Joseph's life? Nothing about his life in Egypt. Why? In Genesis 50, Joseph tells them to take his bones with them when they

---

* https://www.patheos.com/blogs/johnshore/2013/05/christian-without-a-christianity/

leave Egypt. He knew they would leave, and considered himself only a visitor in the foreign land he lived in.

> *By faith Moses, when he was born, was hidden three months of his parents, because they saw he was a beautiful child; and they were not afraid of the king's commandment.*
> Hebrews 11:23

This involves Moses' parents, not him. They took a stand against what the law said. Everyone seems to know when it comes to a conflict between God's law and man's, you have to choose God. Yet don't forget, you'll suffer consequences for that. Daniel's three buddies didn't follow the King's decree, and were willing to accept the consequences. As we'll find out later, not everyone gets a happy ending.

> *By faith Moses, when he was come to years, refused to be called the son of Pharaoh's daughter; Choosing rather to suffer affliction with the people of God, than to enjoy the pleasures of sin for a season;*
> Hebrews 11:24–25

If Moses had given in, his life would have been easy. He could have been in line to be Pharaoh himself. But it's more important to be right than have an easy life.

> *Esteeming the reproach of Christ greater riches than the treasures in Egypt; for he had respect unto the recompence of the reward. By faith he forsook Egypt, not fearing the wrath of the king; for he endured, as seeing him who is invisible.*
> Hebrews 11:26–27

Notice Moses' faith resulted in *action*. Yes, he gave up a lot, and could have been in a lot of trouble, but if you don't act on faith and what you know is right, what good is it? That doesn't mean to be reckless, but a time likely will come when you'll face the same choice Moses did. Usually at 3 AM. You need to figure out how you'll respond, because at the time it's too late. As Chuck Missler says, never underestimate a person's ability to rationalize.

Remember Daniel's three buddies — it's only an idol, who cares? We know it's really nothing, and surely God wants us to stick around to witness to this pagan culture, right? We can't do that if we're dead. Don't be reckless, but it's time to figure out what you stand for. Not just in an abstract way, but where the rubber meets the road.

> *Through faith he kept the passover, and the sprinkling of blood, lest he that destroyed the firstborn should touch them.*
> Hebrews 11:28

He didn't question, though the whole passover thing is a bit odd. Take blood and sprinkle it, and then the angel will pass over our house? Doesn't make much sense, can't God just give the angel a list of addresses? Sure, He could, but that wouldn't help with the next situation.

> *By faith they passed through the Red sea as by dry land, which the Egyptians attempting to do were drowned.*
> Hebrews 11:29

You all know the story. Charlton Heston led the people out of Egypt in Exodus 14. The people leave, but upon seeing the army behind them, begin to complain about it, with their popular refrain — why did you bring us out here to die? Moses says "Fear ye not, stand still, and see the salvation of the Lord, which he will show to you today; for the Egyptians whom ye have seen today, ye shall see them again no more for ever. The Lord shall fight for you, and ye shall hold your peace." The Lord responds as Moses cries out "Wherefore criest thou unto me? Speak unto the children of Israel, that they go forward." The sea parts, they cross over, and the Egyptian army drowns. Would Moses have had that much faith without the earlier part of his life?

> *By faith the walls of Jericho fell down, after they were compassed about seven days.*
> Hebrews 11:30

Perhaps the most bizarre plan in the Bible. March around the city but make no noise, then on the last day, blow trumpets and make noise and the walls fall down. If you're a general in the army, how would you respond? Give up the Apache helicopters and cruise missiles for this?

> *By faith the harlot Rahab perished not with them that believed not, when she had received the spies with peace.*
> Hebrews 11:31

As the Jews took the land, word certainly traveled before them. Rahab must have heard and knew they had no chance against the Lord's people, so instead of fighting, she makes a deal. I'll protect you spies, if you'll spare my family.

The Hall of Faith

> *And what shall I more say? For the time would fail me to tell of Gideon, and of Barak, and of Samson, and of Jephthah; of David also, and Samuel, and of the prophets,*   Hebrews 11:32

Interesting David gets small billing here. The giant killer? Not much about him here. But Paul continues.

> *Who through faith subdued kingdoms, wrought righteousness, obtained promises, stopped the mouths of lions, Quenched the violence of fire, escaped the edge of the sword, out of weakness were made strong, waxed valiant in fight, turned to flight the armies of the aliens. Women received their dead raised to life again...*   Hebrews 11:33–35

This all sounds great! I see why it's the hall of faith. Where do I sign up for this program? But you need to continue...

> *...and others were tortured, not accepting deliverance; that they might obtain a better resurrection. And others had trial of cruel mockings and scourgings, yea, moreover of bonds and imprisonment; They were stoned, they were sawn asunder, were tested, were slain with the sword; they wandered about in sheepskins and goatskins; being destitute, afflicted, tormented;*   Hebrews 11:35–37

These others were of the same kind as the rest of the chapter, but didn't get the good stuff. They had the same faith as Moses and David, but a different end, from our perspective anyway. The sawn asunder according to tradition refers to Isaiah, who was sawn in two. If that's true, it's a vision of what heretics attempt to do with his book, the so-called deutero-Isaiah hypothesis (see Appendix F for why the theory doesn't make sense).

Why are some healed, others not? A heresy slithers around saying if you're not healed, if you don't have a big house, a Lexus, and a pony in the backyard, you don't have faith. This chapter should shatter that heresy. It's laughably absurd.

My uncles have had a tough few years. One uncle lost his wife when she was traveling in Israel. She sat on a bench, had a heart attack and died. Why? My other uncle was a great golfer. Could perhaps have been a pro. A few years ago had back problems, and with surgery can no longer play golf. Why? Does my family lack faith? If they just had faith, they'd be healed with a big Lexus and a pony, right? Not according to Paul. Not only here in Hebrews, but recall Paul's thorn in the flesh. Did he lack faith when he prayed? I doubt it. Yet he wasn't healed. Why?

I've discovered the secret — I have no idea, and nobody else does either. I think sometimes God doesn't heal or deliver because He knows those people can handle it. Raise your hand if you think Paul lacked faith or devotion to be healed. Yeah, me neither. So we have at least *one* situation where a giant of faith wasn't healed, and the Lord specifically informed Paul it wasn't going to happen.

If you're in trials, sure, you should ask the Lord for intervention. But if nothing happens, consider the *possibility* the Lord considers your shoulders broad enough to handle the burden. An old Jewish proverb says "I ask not for a lighter burden, but for broader shoulders." Maybe you're exactly such a person — and the Lord *knows* you can handle it. I'm reminded of what the late great Earnhardt said after one race in Daytona about another driver.

> *Early in the qualifier, Dale got into the back of me and got me all sideways up through the middle of Turns 3 and 4, Houston said. I thought I was gonna crash. I mean, I was way out of control. Well, when we got down there for pre-race for the 500, he come up and grabbed me around the neck like he always does and kinda squeezes you half to death.*
>
> *He said, "You were bad out of shape in that qualifying race, wasn't you?!?" I said, "Yeah, because you had my back wheels off the ground." He kind of snickered a little bit, and said, "Yeah ...I knew you could handle it."**

Perhaps, just perhaps, you're stuck in a trial because while you think you're sideways and bad out of shape the Master says "I know you can handle it."

> *Content. That's the word. A state of heart in which you would be at peace if God gave you nothing more than he already has. Test yourself with this question: What if God's only gift to you were his grace to save you. Would you be content? You beg him to save the life of your child. You plead with him to keep your business afloat. You implore him to remove the cancer from your body. What if his answer is, "My grace is enough." Would you be content?*

---

*   http://web.archive.org/web/20110213170058/http://www.nascar.com/news/110210/2001-daytona-500-memories-10/index.html

The Hall of Faith

> *You see, from heavens' perspective, grace is enough. If God did nothing more than save us from hell, could anyone complain? If God saved our souls and then left us to spend our lives leprosy-struck on a deserted island, would he be unjust? Having been given eternal life, dare we grumble at an aching body? Having been given heavenly riches, dare we bemoan earthly poverty?*
>
> *But there are those times when God, having given us his grace, hears our appeals and says, "My grace is sufficient for you." Is he being unfair?**

Our job is to be content. Life may be good, or bad. You may be healed, or not. You may have a Lexus, or not. But does any of that change God's character? The one who says "For I know the thoughts that I think toward you, saith the Lord, thoughts of peace, and not of evil, to give you an expected end." When things work out, you're healed, and you've got a Lexus, it's *easy* to have faith. I've never struggled with it when life goes my way. But when it doesn't? I've got to re-read Lucado's book again. After all that, Paul slips something in.

> *(Of whom the world was not worthy);*   Hebrews 11:38

Right in the middle we find a pause, of whom the world was not worthy. It doesn't say that about Moses, or Jacob, or Abraham, or anybody in the first half, but only about those appearing in the second half — those *not* delivered. Another clue the second group that wasn't delivered might have more faith than those which are delivered. Maybe you're experiencing trials right now because the Lord knows you can handle it, and you will help someone else — who might not have as much faith as you do — by the experience.

> *they wandered in deserts, and in mountains, and in dens and caves of the earth.*   Hebrews 11:38

Not a good life. I'll take the Lexus and pony, God, thank you.

> *And these all, having received witness through faith, received not the promise, God having provided some better thing for us, that they without us should not be made perfect.*
>   Hebrews 11:39–40

---

*   Lucado (2005, page 131)

You may not see the results. That does *not* mean there won't *be* results. So Paul concludes:

> *Therefore we also, since we are surrounded by so great a cloud of witnesses, let us lay aside every weight, and the sin which so easily ensnares us, and let us run with endurance the race that is set before us.*   Hebrews 12:1 NKJV

It's time to get in the game, or if you're already in, time to be encouraged to *stay* in the game. Nobody said it was easy (except for TV preachers). Christianity isn't a spectator sport.

Chapter *16*

Stay in the Race

Wherefore seeing we also are compassed about with so great a cloud of witnesses, let us lay aside every weight, and the sin which doth so easily beset us, and let us run with patience the race that is set before us,   Hebrews 12:1

Wherefore means a conclusion is coming, and refers back to the hall of faith in chapter 11. Because those guys provide examples, it's not something impossible for us — they provide role models we can (and should) follow. It takes work, but can be done. Because of that, Paul encourages us to have faith like them. How do we do that? Paul's three-step program:

1. Lay aside weight.

2. Put aside sin.

3. Stay in the race.

First, lay aside weight. Paul told Timothy "No man that warreth entangleth himself with the affairs of this life; that he may please him who hath chosen him to be a soldier." How often do we engage in activities holding no eternal value? Probably more than we think. That's not to say we should not have a job, or ever watch sports, but it's a question of priorities. What are your priorities right now?

Some take this idea to extremes. Obviously work is vital to feeding your family and should not be avoided. In our church when summer arrives, the farmers don't show up for weeks while they do their tractor stuff. That's not a big deal, as we don't operate on the points system. You don't receive points for being here on Sunday, so for those guys who have considerable work to perform in a short time, they're doing what they should, and it's entirely appropriate.

That's *not* the problem. However, if a person's attitude continually shows slackness, that's a problem. So many people think of church as a low priority. How hard is it to get volunteers to do *anything*? It's the 80/20 rule where 20% of the people perform 80% of the work. Church isn't a spectator sport. Everyone has a role, everyone should be pitching in. Many in the church struggle with what their gifting is. How can you know? It's simple — ask the Lord to give you something to do, and wait for Him to do so.

Suddenly you'll find yourself doing work, and won't even realize it. After some time, someone will notice you have ability others don't. Of course, when that comes up the response usually is "what this? It's really nothing, it's no trouble at all." Bingo. Gifts of the spirit are *not* burdensome, and should more or less come naturally. That does not mean pastors don't study, musicians don't practice, and writers don't spend hours agonizing over a single word. No, gifting simply means it's what comes natural. Too many struggle and strive over what they think is their gift. If it truly comes from the Lord, it ignites a fire deep in your soul, and you can't help but do it.

That weight Paul refers to can also be petty disagreements about minor doctrine that divide the church. Pre-trib this, post-trib that, which Bible translation to use, which songs to sing, and other non-essential issues. The church wastes time fighting over nothing, while Satan and his minions laugh.

Second in Paul's plan: put aside sin. If you're involved in something you shouldn't be, it will be a weight and hinder your efforts. You don't show up for a race wearing boots. Same with your life — you need freedom and flexibility. Nobody says you have to be perfect.

Finally, stay in the race. Patience is better translated endurance, as Zodhiates says it means "endurance as to things or circumstances ... refers to the quality that does not surrender to circumstances or succumb under trial."[*] The race is long, and hard. If it was easy, everyone would do it. God isn't a genie granting wishes, and a long and easy life. If that were true, the entire world would be Christian, would it not? Because the life isn't easy many forgo it. Even in the church, many simply don't want to

---

[*] Zodhiates (1992b, page 943)

Stay in the Race

make an effort. The quality of a soldier says to put aside their own safety to accomplish the mission. This is Paul's Lou Holtz speech — it's not something you can't do, many examples exist, so no matter where you are, stay in the game!

- Coach Daniel says I know what it's like to be fed to the lions.
- Coach Moses says I know what it's like to have your back against the wall.
- Coach Jeremiah says I know what it's like to want to quit speaking.
- Coach Ezekiel says I know what it's like to have people ignore the message.
- Coach Paul says I know what it's like to despair of life.
- Coach Elijah says I know what it's like to feel all alone.

We find many examples of people having problems. Because all those made it through, that means you can too, if you stay in the game and don't quit. It's not easy though, so don't think it is.

Looking unto Jesus the author and finisher of our faith; who for the joy that was set before him endured the cross, despising the shame, and is set down at the right hand of the throne of God. Hebrews 12:2

Remember back in the garden, what was Jesus' prayer? Father, if there be any other way to save man, let's take it. He didn't look with joy about the events, but did about the results — completing the mission. We spend too much time worrying about comfort, instead of the mission. A soldier doesn't do that.

That doesn't mean having a Lexus is bad, but it should not be the focal point of your life. I think it was Raul Reis who said the first thing you should do when you get a new car is run your key down the side. After that, you won't worry about it much anymore. Perhaps that's an extreme idea, but it certainly is true after the door gets re-arranged a bit you no longer park in the space farthest away from the entrance.

For consider him that endured such contradiction of sinners against himself, lest ye be wearied and faint in your minds. Hebrews 12:3

If they hated Him, why are we surprised when the world hates us? That doesn't mean to go out of your way to be a jerk, but if you live a godly life and follow Him, the world won't like it, and you'll be the victim of attacks. When that happens, be sure it's because of your example, not some sandwich-board evangelism — you know the type, those holding boards on the street corner proclaiming the end is near.

> *For this is commendable, if because of conscience toward God one endures grief, suffering wrongfully. For what credit is it if, when you are beaten for your faults, you take it patiently? But when you do good and suffer, if you take it patiently, this is commendable before God.* 1 Peter 2:19–20 NKJV

If you suffer because of your witness, fine. But if it's because you're a jerk, you can't walk around and say oh, look how much persecution I'm under.

> *Ye have not yet resisted unto blood, striving against sin.*
> Hebrews 12:4

You haven't resisted as much as others, some paid with their lives. It's a serious issue. The church in the United States has become a bit soft. We don't realize what we're experiencing hasn't existed much in the world, for most of the last 2,000 years. Church history contains persecution and struggle, not easy living. Consider the apostles, as well as Paul himself.

> *Of the Jews five times received I forty stripes save one. Thrice was I beaten with rods, once was I stoned, thrice I suffered shipwreck, a night and a day I have been in the deep; In journeyings often, in perils of waters, in perils of robbers, in perils by mine own countrymen, in perils by the heathen, in perils in the city, in perils in the wilderness, in perils in the sea, in perils among false brethren;* 2 Corinthians 11:24-26

Many of the early church — and many elsewhere today — know what it's like to resist unto blood, while we get upset when zoning laws aren't favorable. That doesn't mean small injustices are okay, just keep perspective. Paul called it "light affliction." Instead of complaining over the small stuff, we should understand and use the ability we have that doesn't exist much in the rest of the world. That door will slowly close as Christians become more and more unpopular.

> *And ye have forgotten the exhortation which speaketh unto you as unto children, My son, despise not thou the chastening of the Lord, nor faint when thou art rebuked of him; For whom the Lord loveth he chasteneth, and scourgeth every son whom he receiveth. If ye endure chastening, God dealeth with you as with sons; for what son is he whom the father chasteneth not? But if ye be without chastisement, whereof all are partakers, then are ye bastards, and not sons.*
>
> Hebrews 12:5–8

Paul notes the Lord corrects His children, just as parents should correct their children. Think of the proverbs discussing discipline of children. You want to instill attitudes they need later in life — integrity, honor, commitment, dedication, honesty. If you don't care about your kids, you don't do that. If enough people fail their children, a society dissolves.

It might surprise you to discover groups exist working to eliminate the traditional family for *exactly* that reason. Once the family unit disappears, control of people becomes easier, as children only obtain their values from whatever nonsense the government promotes. Yes, it really happens: Pravda in 2011 wrote under the headline "Europe to destroy traditional family and sexual identity."

> *Traditional words 'father' and 'mother' will be replaced with official terms Parent 1 and Parent 2 in Britain. The terms will be used in official documents. The authorities decided to make such a "politically correct" move to accommodate same-sex couples. Experts are sure, though, that the matter is not about the requirements of certain social groups. The decision is another step towards the destruction of traditional families.**

Vladimir Lenin reportedly said "Destroy the family, destroy the country." Many people attribute that to him, but I can't find a source.† Regardless of who said it, the principle remains true. Once the family disappears, the country will as well. So be non-politically correct. Install proper godly attitudes in your children. When they need correction, issue it. No, it won't be popular, but would you rather be popular, or raise children correctly?

---

* http://english.pravda.ru/society/stories/10-10-2011/119281-family_europe-0/

† I'm always reminded what Abraham Lincoln said in 1863 when asked about reports the Union wasn't doing well in the war and he replied, "I don't believe everything I read on the Internet."

When God deals with you, don't take it like He hates you, no, discipline displays love. God's discipline isn't always punitive — it's not punishment. God remembers your sin no more, and the penalty has been paid. God's discipline provides course correction. It's motivation to stay on the right track. As we wander off the correct course, God's steady hand nudges us back on the right track, if you're listening. God doesn't force Himself on people, so if you want to ignore God's hand, you certainly can.

> *Furthermore we have had fathers of our flesh which corrected us, and we gave them reverence. Shall we not much rather be in subjection unto the Father of spirits, and live? For they verily for a few days chastened us after their own pleasure; but he for our profit, that we might be partakers of his holiness.* Hebrews 12:9–10

You should respect your father. He's not perfect, but if you do respect your father, how much more should you respect the Lord, the one who says "I know the thoughts I think toward you, thoughts of peace." As imperfect people, sometimes parents don't get discipline right. The Lord, of course, doesn't have that problem. So the example of parents and kids applies to the Lord and Christians, with one difference: the Lord never makes mistakes.

> *Now no chastening for the present seemeth to be joyous, but grievous; nevertheless afterward it yieldeth the peaceable fruit of righteousness unto them which are exercised by it.* Hebrews 12:11

Discipline isn't fun, but it's not supposed to be. It's a course correction to stay in the game. It's amazing how much smarter your parents get from your teen years to when you're older. All those things you thought were stupid make sense.

Raising a child, sometimes I say stuff in the hope he'll remember it later when I'm dead and buried and think that crazy old guy might not have been so crazy after all. I know it won't do much good right now, but I'm trying to fill up the memory bank with stuff he can pull out later — long after I've returned to the ground. You see, I won't always be around to help, but what I can do is provide an appropriate education so when he faces situations, he'll posses the proper foundation and logic to come to the right decision. Discipline is the same — the kid doesn't think much of it, but decades later when the parents are gone, he realizes it was for his benefit, and created the character he needs.

> *Wherefore lift up the hands which hang down, and the feeble knees;*   Hebrews 12:12

Don't be grumpy. Circumstances that appear to be a problem sometimes aren't. That's where trust comes in. Sometimes we *need* correction, so don't be in a bad mood. Some people are just always in a bad mood. Zig Ziglar relates a story about a flying experience he had. As a public speaker, he flew a lot. One day he arrived early and went to the counter to check in, and was told his flight had been canceled.

Some people immediately become grumpy, and take their displeasure out on the poor person behind the counter. But not Zig, he replied "fantastic." When the lady told him he'd have several hours before the next flight, he again replied "fantastic." Now she simply had to know, why are you saying everything is fantastic? Zig replied, ma'am, it's quite easy, since only three reasons exist why anybody would cancel my flight;

1. Something must be wrong with that airplane.

2. Something must be wrong with the pilot who will fly that plane.

3. Something must be wrong with the weather he'll fly that plane in.

Ma'am, if *any* of those exist, I don't want to be up there, I want to be right down here, so I say fantastic. Zig certainly was a positive person — I heard him say he'd spend his last two dollars on a money belt. That kind of attitude doesn't come easy. Most of us are pessimists of some sort. You know the difference between and optimist and pessimist, don't you? The pessimist is just the optimist with better information.

Seriously, when things are tough, it's hard not to complain, rationalizing you should have better; after all, you deserve a break today. When discipline comes along, it's hard to say I need to learn something. When trials come, it's hard not to ask why they get a Lexus, and I'm driving a Pinto. Maybe it's time to stop pouting and learn the lesson.

And make straight paths for your feet, lest that which is lame be turned out of the way; but let it rather be healed. Follow peace with all men, and holiness, without which no man shall see the Lord;   Hebrews 12:13-14

People do see your response. When they see you having terrible problems, but remaining calm, it's time to explain why it's no big deal, since the Lord will deliver you either from it, or through it. I know I will make it to the other side, because that's what the Lord said. He didn't say the *condition* I'd be in, however. But that attitude provides a witness for others. It's not easy though. Stay in the game. Don't quit.

Looking diligently lest any man fail of the grace of God; lest any root of bitterness springing up trouble you, and thereby many be defiled;   Hebrews 12:15

Bitterness comes when you doubt God's plan, or you think you deserve better (pride). It eats like cancer. If you haven't heard of Zig Ziglar, I'd encourage you to obtain some of his tapes or books. Remember, no matter how you react to the situation, the situation hasn't changed, and still might be out of your control. How *you* respond, of course, remains entirely under your control. People panicking when crisis arrives never fare as well as someone remaining cool under pressure. Don't let bitterness overtake you — the Lord has it all under control, even if it doesn't feel like it.

Lest there be any fornicator, or profane person, as Esau, who for one morsel of meat sold his birthright.   Hebrews 12:16

Sure, you wouldn't sell your birthright for a bowl of stew. That's bad, right? When I was growing up, mom and dad liked going to the theater. We used to go to a little live theater in San Juan Capistrano. One of the plays was about a Washington Senators baseball fan, who tired of losing to the Yankees. He says "I'd sell my soul for a long-ball hitter," and poof, Mr. Applegate appears, better known as the devil. I can arrange that, he says.

Maybe not for a bowl of stew, but how many trade their birthright for sports? Or fame? Or fortune? Many *have* sold their soul to obtain those things, and it doesn't end well. Maybe that's an extreme example, but Christians trade spiritual gold for temporary lead. That's back to the theme — stay in the game. To do that requires priorities, understanding what's important, and what's not.

> *For ye know how that afterward, when he would have inherited the blessing, he was rejected; for he found no place of repentance, though he sought it carefully with tears.*
>
> Hebrews 12:17

Esau was bummed about what he did, but it's too late. Your actions — good or bad — have permanent consequences. The time to figure that out is *before* you do something you may later regret. Hasty actions are usually bad. You can't change what you've done, you'll have to live with it. Yes, you have forgiveness, that's never the issue, but that doesn't mean no consequences. If you get drunk and then drive, wrapping your car around a telephone pole, sure God provides forgiveness, but you may live with paralysis from the broken back the rest of your life.

We all make mistakes. We all mess up. We all take actions later we regret. That can't be stopped; what you *can* do is learn from your mistakes, and don't make them again. That's the sign of maturity.

> *For ye are not come unto the mount that might be touched, and that burned with fire, nor unto blackness, and darkness, and tempest, And the sound of a trumpet, and the voice of words; which voice they that heard entreated that the word should not be spoken to them any more. For they could not endure that which was commanded, And if so much as a beast touch the mountain, it shall be stoned, or thrust through with a spear. And so terrible was the sight, that Moses said, I exceedingly fear and quake.*
>
> Hebrews 12:18-21

In Exodus when God gave the Law, the people didn't want to talk to God. Moses, you do that, and we'll listen to you. But God wants a relationship. The Law can't provide that. Most important, when God talks, don't refuse to listen.

This was written for the Jews, and for the Jews who became Christians finding themselves tossed out of the temple. All they knew was gone. But the Law can't save. This reminds them the giving of the Law as not something pleasant. The Law reminds them of their shortfalls, how they can never be acceptable to God.

> *But ye are come unto mount Zion, and unto the city of the living God, the heavenly Jerusalem, and to an innumerable company of angels,*
>
> Hebrews 12:22

In contrast, you can come to mount Zion and no penalty of death awaits; rather, eternal life. For those Jews who missed the old way, compare what you have now. It's superior.

To the general assembly and church of the firstborn, which are written in heaven, and to God the Judge of all, and to the spirits of just men made perfect, And to Jesus the mediator of the new covenant, and to the blood of sprinkling, that speaketh better things than that of Abel.   Hebrews 12:23–24

Think of the difference between the blood of Jesus and the blood of Abel.

- Abel — vengeance, sin.

- Jesus — mercy.

See that ye refuse not him that speaketh. For if they escaped not who refused him that spoke on earth, much more shall not we escape, if we turn away from him that speaketh from heaven,   Hebrews 12:25

You don't *have* to listen. You're free to reject. God doesn't force Himself on anyone, even though He could. It's up to you to choose to listen, and follow God's leading. Nothing will force you to do so, so if you want to be bull-headed and do it your own way, you have that choice. Realize, however, ignoring God's prompting will always—always—result in less than optimum outcomes.

Whose voice then shook the earth; but now he hath promised, saying, Yet once more I shake not the earth only, but also heaven. And this word, Yet once more, signifieth the removing of those things that are shaken, as of things that are made, that those things which cannot be shaken may remain.
    Hebrews 12:26–27

The eternal contrasted with the temporary. Never forget the world we inhabit is neither permanent, nor what God intended. It's been corrupted by sin, so at some future point God will provide a perfect habitat.

Wherefore we receiving a kingdom which cannot be moved, let us have grace, whereby we may serve God acceptably with reverence and godly fear: Hebrews 12:28

God's kingdom can't be moved. It may seem despairing right now as we look around and find nothing but corruption, but that's not the future. We will see a kingdom that can't be corrupted, so don't put your effort in trying to create heaven on earth. That's just not going to work.

Two mistakes can be made coming to God:

1. Timidy.

2. Lack of reverence.

Both mistakes prove fatal to having the proper relationship with God. The first example came from the Jews while Moses was on the mountain with God. We don't want to see God, they said, you Moses go talk to God, and then tell us what He said. It also comes from people who don't want to pray about so-called small issues. You know, the ones we don't like to bother God with. Yet what did He say? In everything, make your requests to God. Nothing is too small or trivial. Bring everything to Him, and allow Him to figure it out.

On the other side exist some showing a lack of respect with "the man upstairs." Recall Moses and the burning bush, God reminded Moses to take off his shoes, he stood on holy ground.

For our God is a consuming fire.   Hebrews 12:29

God is a God of grace, but also judgment. You can't have love and justice without judgment and penalty.

Chapter 17

Stay True

Let brotherly love continue. Hebrews 13:1

This assumes you already have it. While disagreements will happen in the body of Christ, it's how you handle them that counts. Common divisions occur over doctrine (and usually minor points), with groups claiming they hold the only true position. It's true we should hold to correct doctrine, but the list containing hills to fight on will be small.

- Deity of Christ.
- Man is sinful, in need of a redeemer.
- Christ died for our sins, and rose again (the Gospel).
- Inerrancy of the Bible.

People may argue what should—or should not—appear on that list, but we should all agree which Bible translation used isn't on that list,* or how you're baptized, or Calvinism. We have a hard time with balance. Some churches swallow any heresy coming down the road, others split fellowship over minor points. Either way is wrong, and either error Satan loves. Anything but the truth is his motto. We'll get into this more later in this chapter,

---

* Certainly some translations prove superior over others, and the modern Westcott-Hort text demonstrates many problems, but dividing a fellowship over use of the NIV isn't a good idea. We certainly hold Textus-Receptus as used in the King James and New King James superior to "modern" translations, but don't split fellowship over it.

but you've probably noticed the Christian life is a battle. Aren't we all on the same team? Chuck Missler asks why Christians organize their firing squads in circles.

The church frequently fights over minor points, yet willingly accepts redefinitions of the Gospel to good works or social justice — in direct contradiction to Paul in 1 Corinthians 15. Brotherly love does not mean accepting everything, but simply not fighting over minor points.

> *Be not forgetful to entertain strangers; for thereby some have entertained angels unawares.* Hebrews 13:2

Visits by supernatural beings appears several times in the Bible. Abraham in Genesis 18, Joshua 5, etc. Those involved may or may not understand the supernatural characteristics of their visitors, so Paul mentions you could have encountered an angel and not been aware of it. However, this doesn't mean to pick up hitchhikers on the road. You'll notice both Abraham and Joshua seemed to understand what they were dealing with was supernatural — God never tells you to check your brain at the door. He gave it to you for a reason.

> *Remember them that are in bonds, as bound with them; and them which suffer adversity, as being yourselves also in the body.* Hebrews 13:3

Paul knew what it was like to be a prisoner and persecuted. Don't forget them. It's easy to forget about people when life sails peacefully along, as we have a tendency to identify with people going through similar situations as we are.

> *Marriage is honorable in all, and the bed undefiled; but fornicators and adulterers God will judge.* Hebrews 13:4

Marriage is God's plan. Societies generally don't do well when the traditional family unit dissolves. Yet there are those today whose *plan* involves destroying the family; we noted previously Europe's attempt to redefine and destroy traditional families. Remember, what occurs in Europe usually lies only a few decades away from appearing in the United States.

Note the garbage appearing today on TV and such God doesn't approve of. God doesn't change, and His rules haven't either. What was sin and corruption when the apostles wrote remains sin and unacceptable today. In Genesis 15 when God talks to Abraham and Abraham worries about not having an heir, God talks about his inheritance, but that chapter contains a strange verse:

> *But in the fourth generation they shall come here again; for the iniquity of the Amorites is not yet full.* Genesis 15:16

What does that mean? God gives you time to repent. Don't mistake that time for acceptance. Too many today mistake God's providing time to change course for acceptance. God has been clear on what is acceptable and what isn't. He allows you time to correct your actions, but if that doesn't occur, His judgment will come.

> *Let your manner of life be without covetousness; and be content with such things as ye have; for he hath said, I will never leave thee, nor forsake thee.* Hebrews 13:5

Be content. You might have a little, or a lot. Paul said in Philippians he learned whatever state he was in to be content. He *learned* it. It's not something you're born with. We're born selfish creatures. Greed and jealousy are wanting more of what you already have enough of, and notice greed isn't limited to "rich" people, or the so-called 1%.

In the old days, you went to college, worked hard for four years, then took a job in the mail room and slowly worked your way up the ladder. Not any more, a few years ago the attitude started right after graduation — where's my corner office? And today, it's not even that, it's I don't want to be educated, I *deserve* money and a Lexus simply because I'm breathing. And it's okay to forcefully take it from someone else. That's greed.

> *So that we may boldly say, The Lord is my helper, and I will not fear what man shall do unto me.* Hebrews 13:6

Ultimately man can cause you a lot of pain, but can't beat you. It's a matter of perspective. We actually had a national discussion regarding the government's legal right to use drones to kill US citizens on our own soil, without a trial. As the Snowden story broke in 2013, we discovered government spying on everyone, the NSA monitoring almost everything, while the administration lies about it. What do they do with all that information? Supporters say if you're not hiding anything, you've got nothing to worry about.

John Loeffler says we have so many laws and regulations on the books, with all that information it's so anyone can be guilty of something *when they need to be.* Need to get rid of a problem person? Search the archive, and you'll eventually find something to convict them of. Why worry about it? The Lord is my helper, and I won't fear what the NSA can do. We know prophetically where the world heads, and eventually one guy will control it all. It's quite likely the surveillance state will get worse and worse, as the world must be set up for one-man control. We know where it's going, but don't forget the Lord is your helper.

> *Remember them which have the rule over you, who have spoken unto you the word of God, whose faith follow, considering the end of their manner of life:* Hebrews 13:7

The pastor is worthy of his labor. Certainly some have abused their position, and used the position for their own benefit, which causes a lot of people problems, as they think the church is only out for money.

> *Jesus Christ, the same yesterday, and today, and forever.* Hebrews 13:8

We do not need bizarre modernizations of the Bible, social justice, seeker friendly, or anything else. He doesn't change, why would His message? It doesn't. All those tossing out centuries of understanding offer nothing more than excuses for their rebellion against God. Want to cheat on your wife? Easy, just modernize those passages speaking of adultery. Don't like rules for leadership? Those don't actually apply today, those only existed for that culture.

Obvious problems exist for the modernizers, one they never provide an answer for. Who gets to decide what is—and is not—applicable for today? Why should their method be taken over others? Once rejecting Bible sections begins, nothing remains but potlucks and arguments over what should be applied today, and what shouldn't. Paul told Timothy "Preach the word; be ready in season, out of season; reprove, rebuke, exhort with all longsuffering and doctrine." That means whether it's convenient or inconvenient. It's not convenient to tell people they're ignoring and replacing the Bible, but it's true.

As a corollary, the idea the Old Testament records a mean and vengeful God, while the New Testament displays a loving God doesn't pass the smell test. He changes not, so anyone pushing such ideas hasn't read Hebrews. God remains the same. We might see different characteristics of Him at different times, but He changes not.

> *Be not carried about with various and strange doctrines. For it is a good thing that the heart be established with grace; not with foods, which have not profited them that have been occupied with them.* Hebrews 13:9

Much strange doctrine floats around, and those taking their Bible seriously notice all of it contradicts the Bible in some way. A choice must be made — are liberal modernists correct, or the apostles? It's a choice everyone must make, but no way exists for contradictory ideas to both be true at the same time. At least one is wrong; the Bible anticipates strange ideas floating around, and provides a clear response negating liberal theology.

- Social Justice — 1 Corinthians 15.
- God of the OT vs God of the NT — verse 8.
- Replacement theology — Daniel's 70 weeks.
- Deutero-Isaiah hypothesis — John 12:39.

All those contradict what the Bible says, so either they're right, or the Bible is. Don't bother with scholarly stuff, take the Bible as it reads. Yes, figures of speech and idioms exist, but if you begin with taking the text as it reads and seeing what happens, you'll find fewer problems.

Paul mentions the heart with grace, not foods. It's back to what the Jews had problems with — returning to the Mosaic Law. It's grace, not Law. The Law can't make you righteous. If you're living by the Law, you won't find rest. Hopefully we've figured that out by the end of the book.

> *We have an altar, whereof they have no right to eat which serve the tabernacle. For the bodies of those beasts, whose blood is brought into the sanctuary by the high priest for sin, are burned outside the camp. Wherefore Jesus also, that he might sanctify the people with his own blood, suffered outside the gate.* Hebrews 13:10-12

Some of the old sacrifices were performed outside the camp. Note as well, Jesus died on Calvary, outside the city.

> *Let us go forth therefore unto him outside the camp, bearing his reproach. For here have we no continuing city, but we seek one to come.* Hebrews 13:13–14

What's in the city? Rules, religion, tradition, Law. Get away from that. You'll find no rest there.

> *By him therefore let us offer the sacrifice of praise to God continually, that is, the fruit of our lips giving thanks to his name. But to do good and to share forget not; for with such sacrifices God is well pleased.* Hebrews 13:15–16

Some things are easy to praise God for. But it says continually, and that means when things don't go our way. That's when it's hard. Sure, it's easy to be thankful when the test comes back negative, but what about when it's incurable? Praise isn't easy then, but remember God's nature never changes. Just as when Paul prayed for his healing, the answer might come back no.

> *Obey them that have the rule over you, and submit yourselves; for they watch for your souls, as they that must give account, that they may do it with joy, and not with grief; for that is unprofitable for you.* Hebrews 13:17

A strange idea floats around called shepherding, in which the pastor tells you what to do. Should I buy a Ford or Chevy? This idea of rule and submission causes many people problems. Before we tackle that, note these guys (like pastors) have to give an account of how they performed. They're responsible for how they run the church. It's easy to be the guy criticizing what goes on, it's quite different to be the one responsible for it.

Okay, now the tough stuff. The idea of submission, rule, and so on has caused, and will continue to cause, many problems. People write books about why it's wrong, or why we shouldn't follow what the Bible says. I've read a bunch of those, and besides the fact they all try to ignore what the Bible says they don't make much sense. Why is the pastor in charge? I'm just as good as he is.

That attitude came up in the Bible. In Numbers 16 Korah and his buddies come to Moses and ask why are you in charge, is not the whole congregation holy? They challenged God's leaders, and well, it didn't end well for them. All these people denying God's structure miss an obvious point: the Christian life is a battle, and any army requires organization. It doesn't mean somebody is better than another. Much can be learned from the Marines and how they organize, what the Marines call the rule of threes.

- Fire Team — a rifleman (M16), grenadier (M203), machine gunner (M249).
- Squad — three fire teams.
- Platoon — three squads.
- Company — three platoons (and support).
- Battalion — three companies (and support).
- Regiment — three battalions.
- Division — three regiments.
- Marines — three or more divisions make up the Marines.

The fire team forms the smallest unit. Notice each man carries different weaponry for different tactical situations. Yet the machine gunner with the M249 can't complain he's not carrying the M203 ... or the unit is dysfunctional and can't perform. Each person has unique qualifications for the job and adds value to the team. Each group has a leader who bears responsibility. Let's put this in perspective of the soldier of God.

- Fire Team — house and family.
- Squad — multiple houses, with elder as leader (local Bible study). Elder doesn't mean elder of the church, but a mature Christian guy.
- Platoon — squads join to form a local church, with a pastor as leader.
- Company — local churches, usually with a pastor as the committee leader.
- Battalion — Regional churches.
- Regiment — church denomination.
- Division — all denominations.
- Church — with Christ in charge.

Some people continue to have a hard time with this. If people have problems with Godly submission to whom He's put in command, they need to take it up with Him. Paul was clear elsewhere on requirements for leaders, and just because people ignore it today does not make it less true.

We always want to be something we're not; God doesn't say to be like someone else. I can do things you can't, that's why I'm here. You can do things I can't, that's why you're here. You are uniquely equipped. Problems arrive if you're not in the game, and thus fail your team.

I believe if you're willing to get in the game you'll meet opposition. I've seen over and over the most engaged, the hardest working, and the most devoted experience the most problems. That makes sense, after all, enemies don't bother to engage non-threats. If you want an easy life, be a pew-warmer and the enemy will (more or less) leave you alone.

I think it's time to stop worrying about what you can't do and start doing what you can do. We must stop wondering why I can't be the boss, or why can't I do this or that, and start focusing on using the weaponry God provides us as part of the fire team. This is not an academic exercise or theoretical idea, as a group ignoring or fighting over leadership is dysfunctional and unfit for combat.

> *Pray for us; for we trust we have a good conscience, in all things willing to live honestly. But I beseech you the rather to do this, that I may be restored to you the sooner.*
> Hebrews 13:18–19

Paul always asked for prayer. He's the guy who wrote most of the New Testament, and yet he asked for prayer and boldness. He didn't say to live honestly, but be willing to. The action follows the decision. Living honestly comes from Psalm 15, look it up for yourself.

> *Now the God of peace, that brought again from the dead our Lord Jesus, that great shepherd of the sheep, through the blood of the everlasting covenant, Make you perfect in every good work to do his will, working in you that which is well-pleasing in his sight, through Jesus Christ; to whom be glory for ever and ever. Amen.*
> Hebrews 13:20–21

The shepherd keeps the sheep, not the sheep themselves. We just covered Biblical order, if you're not at rest perhaps it's because you're trying to be the shepherd, instead of the sheep. You'll never find rest if you strive over your role or attempt to take authority not yours by ignoring God's clear structure and requirements for leadership.

As a small point, perfect is Olde English for complete. It's one of those times Olde English words changed meaning since 1611. Don't think perfect means never making a mistake, rather perfect in the sense nothing needs to be added.

> *And I beseech you, brethren, bear with the word of exhortation; for I have written a letter unto you in few words.*
> Hebrews 13:22

Now I know it's Paul. Only Paul would pen some of the most difficult passages in existence, and claim he wrote in few words. That's Paul.

> *Know ye that our brother Timothy is set at liberty; with whom, if he come shortly, I will see you. Greet all them that have the rule over you, and all the saints. They of Italy greet you. Grace be with you all. Amen.*
> Hebrews 13:23–25

Appendix A

Fluff

WHEN DAD PASSED IT REMINDED me of the great teachers we've lost. Dad remains a giant of Christianity (though like many of the giants toiled in relative obscurity) and the more you knew him, the more you'll understand while he'll enjoy his promotion, we're deprived of more leadership than you can imagine. Besides dad passing, consider Walter Martin, the Chucks (Smith and Missler), and what each taught and warned about.

- Walter Martin — earnestly contend for the faith.
- Chuck Smith — teach the Word and reach the lost.
- Chuck Missler — science agrees with the God of the Bible.
- Dad — Don't divide over (his word) "fluff" issues.

You might not have heard dad's message, but I'd lost count of the times he said about something that's a fluff issue, it's not important (which doesn't mean a right or wrong answer doesn't exist though). We grew up in a Presbyterian church, attending others as well — some non-denominational, but over the decades everything from Baptist to charismatic.

I recall when Chuck Smith set up the tent in Costa Mesa dad wanted to know what was going on; he certainly had disagreement with Chuck on *at least* one area (those who know dad know *exactly* what that is), but in the end said Chuck was a good guy because what they didn't agree on was, well, fluff.

I always wondered how we could attend so many doctrinally different groups. It wasn't until years later dad related his "fluff" principal and I understood. Character, integrity, and accepting Jesus as savior mattered to dad, and frankly not much else. I could relate stories about dad's interaction with people he disagreed with (*strongly* if you know dad), but always considered friends.

Reading the problems existing in the Corinthian (and today's) church, too much focus exists on non-important issues, choosing division over minor (sometimes non-doctrinal) issues instead of agreeing on the majors.

I've noticed each of our giants passed when what they were trying to teach the church desperately needed, but tried to ignore, and later openly rejected.

- Walter Martin — Walter's voice remains a stern warning against "modernizing" the church.
- Chuck Smith — Nobody wants to teach the Bible, and those that do ... frequently ignore the lessons therein. Since Chuck's passing, Calvary Chapel unquestionably morphed from what he founded.
- Chuck Missler — Open hostility to science exists today, yet a stunning creation exists just waiting to be discovered.
- Dad — Fluff? That's now *most* important, even over the Gospel.

Examples abound for stupid, silly, and trivial ideas to divide over instead of focusing on the Gospel:

- At the dawn of the pandemic age (2020–2021) COVID and when/how the church meets (remote meeting via Internet doesn't count, it *must* be in person no matter what), basic sanitization, and protecting the flock from a pandemic (and banishing people not agreeing with certain political views).
- A friend related a story upon her first visit to a church they asked at the door if she was a Calvinist ... for only Calvinists could fellowship there.
- Dad related a guy told him when he read the Bible, he would toss it back on the coffee table, but when he read the KJV, he reverently gently placed it down.

For myself, you wouldn't believe some of the hatred I've received over the years (most of it from "Christians" ... atheists generally show more respect, at least to me) on many so-called vital issues Christians divide over — baptism, Calvinism vs free will, pre-trib, COVID, science, math, and other nonsense (i.e. "fluff"). It seems the church and its leadership forgot (or willfully cast aside) what Paul taught:

> *Moreover, brethren, I declare unto you the gospel which I preached unto you, which also ye have received, and wherein ye stand; ... For I delivered unto you first of all that which I also received, how that Christ died for our sins according to the scriptures; And that he was buried, and that he rose again the third day according to the scriptures ...*

That's it. That's the Gospel. That's *the* definition of Christian. All else has (and always will be) ... fluff. If you agree on that (and the Bible is the inspired inerrant Word of God), we're together. Sadly, often in the church today you must be of political party "D" or "R", a Calvinist (or not), reject health protections in a pandemic, and other silly side issues having nothing to do with foundational doctrine — let's focus on the Gospel, not idiotic side issues.

A theory exists called Strauss–Howe generational theory, where societies traverse through four stages — the last being a crisis, as people forget the concepts and ideas from previous generations. At that point society either fixes the problems or sinks down in quagmire.

The church differs not. As great leaders of the church pass, the church faces its own fourth turning crisis, as lessons from those leaders are forgotten, or worse, willfully abandoned. At the dawn of the pandemic age (2020—2021) many pastors willfully and proudly abandoned rock-solid principles as the church enters its fourth-turning crisis.

The question: will the church and its pastors repent and return to foundational principles, or proudly continue down the path of hypocrisy, destroying their witness in the process?

Dad tried to warn us about the church dividing over stupid issues. I've seen that warning be both heeded, and sadly, ignored. We're repeating the mistakes of Judges as the great church leaders pass on.

> *In those days there was no king in Israel: every man did that which was right in his own eyes.*   Judges 21:25

Putting that in today's terms:

> *In those days Christ was not king in the church: every pastor did that which was right in his own eyes.*

The only thing we learn from church history is the church fails to learn from history.

After someone passes, frequently discussion turns to how can we honor and respect them? What to put on the headstone, flowery words at the funeral, notices in the newspaper — all miss the mark. No, true honor is none of those. It's do you maintain their example, or ignore it? I'm with Elisha, I'd like a double-portion of what dad had.

> ...Elijah said unto Elisha, Ask what I shall do for thee, before I be taken away from thee.
> And Elisha said, I pray thee, let a double portion of thy spirit be upon me. 2 Kings 2:9

I've chosen to pick up dad's mantle, though it's likely as the church continues to focus on stupid and silly stuff few will choose ministry, fellowship, and friendship over politics. People simply don't want to listen and replaced fellowship with politics and litmus tests of fluff you *must* accept or be banished.

> ...we need to remember that we deal with individual people, not a class of students... people who have joy and sorrow, who hurt, who can be lonely, who can be happy, who can be involved or who can turn us off or tune us out.
> So what?
> Well, this means that we can not simply deliver material from the Bible, but that we must relate that material to Christ, to life ... and this must be done with real people in mind, with real life situations. ~ James J Yeager, November 22 1971

I'll try dad to follow your example — hypocrisy is saying we're going to honor someone's legacy ... while ignoring his teaching and example. Why can't people just be honest?

- We want to take our church in a different direction; anyone not agreeing with new political positions will be asked to leave.
- We don't want to contend for the faith *once for all delivered to the saints* so we'll ignore warnings regarding "modernizing" the church.
- Science? We're anti-science so reject math, rational thinking, and logic.
- And we'll specifically focus (and divide over) fluff issues like politics and pandemics, and banish anyone holding different views, after all politics must have priority over ministry, the Gospel, and Paul's teaching.

Fluff

It would be refreshing to see people be honest and admit they reject what they *claim* to follow. Dad's most important lesson? It's all fluff ... focus on 1 Corinthians 15. If you get that right, other minor points are just that. Minor.
...at 3 AM or any other time.

Appendix B

The Scientific Method

WHILE NOT A MAJOR TOPIC IN logic or philosophy classes, failure to understand (and use) the scientific method causes problems in logic, critical thinking, and even theology, ultimately denying foundational characteristics of God.

Scientific Method Defined

A method of research in which a problem is identified, relevant data gathered, a hypothesis formulated from data, and the hypothesis empirically tested. A rather obvious idea — examine data and reality and determine if it matches what you predict or expect, then update your ideas to match results; while steps may be added, the scientific method boils down to a few simple principals:

1. Make a guess (idea)
2. Test it (collect data, experiment, etc.)
3. Modify idea based on results (reality)
4. Lather, rinse, repeat

Not difficult, and it's hard to imagine disputing the common sense of it. After all, only members of the tin-foil-hat brigade fail to update ideas based on reality.

Sadly, that's *exactly* what some do, clutching bizarre delusional ideas in spite of reality (i.e. flat-earthers, etc.). As John Loeffler says, eventually reality becomes reality, and delusional ideas represent the precise opposite of the scientific method.

However, step one often throws people off. Science does *not* require step one to be correct. Any wild guess begins the process; matching with experiment counts, and if not, modifying the original idea until it does.

Christians can become anti-science due to one person: Darwin. Darwin wasn't Satan, he noticed something he couldn't explain, created a theory (guess, hypothesis) to explain it, and stated predictions which would support his idea if true (i.e. innumerable fossilized transitional forms should be found).

Later data doesn't support his theory, and evolution (biology) remains a field not following the scientific method. It matters not how brilliant an idea appears to be, if it doesn't match with reality (data, experiment), it's wrong.

> *The principle of science, the definition, almost, is the following: The test of all knowledge is experiment. Experiment is the sole judge of scientific "truth"** ~ Richard Feynman

Why Does It Work?

The scientific method works for *one* reason — the God of the universe created it and created order and consistent rules for the universe to follow. When you drop an apple, nobody ponders the direction it will travel, it drops to the ground. Always.

Why? God is a god of order. Reason. Logic. The scientific method, properly used, provides a method to discover *how* God designed the universe and the principals governing its existence.

Biblical Examples

For those believing religion is (or should be) anti-science, God Himself provides examples of the scientific method. Man didn't invent the scientific method, he only discovered what God created.

Daniel

> Daniel spoke with the attendant who had been appointed by the chief of staff to look after Daniel, Hananiah, Mishael, and Azariah. "Please test us for ten days on a diet of vegetables and water," Daniel said. "At the end of the ten days, see how we look compared to the other young men who are eating the king's food. Then make your decision in light of what you see." The attendant agreed to Daniel's suggestion and tested

---

* "The Feynman Lectures on Physics", Volume I page 1-1

> *them for ten days. At the end of the ten days, Daniel and his three friends looked healthier and better nourished than the young men who had been eating the food assigned by the king.* Daniel 1:11–15 NLT

As a kosher Jew, Daniel didn't want to eat non-kosher food, even if the best the King could offer. Instead he proposed an idea — let's follow the scientific method and test what happens if we eat only kosher food, not the King's menu.

1. Make a guess — we'll be in better shape if we stay kosher and eat only vegetables.
2. Experiment — feed us for 10 days and see what happens.
3. Modify based on results — after 10 days, they were in better shape; the attendant thereafter fed them only vegetables.

A perfect example of the scientific method, used by one of the pillars of the Bible. Never forget, Paul reminds us in Romans 15:4 what was written before was for *our* learning, so people ignoring the scientific method not only contradict God, but ignore Paul's teaching as well.

God Himself Uses The Method

In Malachi, the Lord lays out problems of His people. They respond "we didn't do that, how did we do that?" And the Lord provides the proof.

One area involved the tithe, or giving 10%. For our purposes, don't become distracted whether this applies today or not, or if poor people should tithe, or anything else (we're focused on science, not the religious aspect).

> *"Bring all the tithes into the storehouse so there will be enough food in my Temple. If you do," says the Lord of Heaven's Armies, "I will open the windows of heaven for you. I will pour out a blessing so great you won't have enough room to take it in! Try it! Put me to the test!"* Malachi 3:10 NLT

What does the Lord do? Propose a test — try Me and see (do an experiment and examine the results). When the creator of the universe validates an idea, it's something we should listen to; those rejecting the scientific method reject God's nature, and thus, God Himself.

One branch of science denies the scientific method. Evolution (recall Piltdown man?). A question to the reader — do you (or your pastor) want to align with the foolishness of evolution? Evolution has *no* experimental evidence for its foundations:

1. First there was nothing (matter comes from nothing).
2. And then it exploded (explosions produce order).
3. From the goo to the zoo (abiogenesis — life comes from non-life).
4. To you (new species evolve from mutations).

If you don't have all four, evolution doesn't work. Period. Yet where are peer-reviewed reproducible scientific experiments for those four items? Lacking that, evolution is un-scientific *by definition.*

In contrast, the Bible and God demonstrate the scientific method. God gave you a brain, and provided examples on how to use it.

The scientific method works.
People in the Bible used it.
God Himself validates it.
That should be enough.

Don't be Anti-Science

The dawn of the pandemic era (2020–2021) saw many pastors willfully reject God as they rejected science. They probably didn't stand in the pulpit on Sunday and proclaim they're rebelling against God, but by denying science they reject God, whether they admit it or not. As the pandemic raged, pastors and others made foolish statements like:

- It's only a few cases, it won't affect us here.
- It's no worse than flu.*
- We don't need to filter the air, create distance, sanitize, or take any precautions.

All those are wrong, as the scientific method (and reality) proves. The data exists for them, and sadly many "Christians" willfully rebelled against God and His designed order to deny

---

* Final data will take years to analyze, but covid turned out to considerably worse than "just the flu", no matter the metric used (deaths, length of illness, severity of symptoms, etc.)

reality, science, and common sense at the dawn of the pandemic age. Don't be anti-science — anti-science is anti-God.

The scientific method, properly used, might be God's greatest natural gift to us. Follow God's example, when you have an idea, create an experiment (or look at actual data) and then *modify your idea based on results (reality)*.

The last part remains key. Don't be stubborn and cling to ideas data and reality prove incorrect. Yes, it's difficult to be humble and admit you're wrong, but everyone makes mistakes; it's silly (and stupid) firmly clutching ideas reality proves completely incorrect.

Do Your Homework

As Chuck Missler says, don't believe anything I (or anyone else) told you — you're called to be a skeptic (Acts 17:11). Do your own work and use logic, thinking skills, and methods God provided you. If you blindly accept ideas without checking them out for yourself you've failed the course. Follow the scientific method, it's one of the best tools God provided us.

Appendix C

Trust the Math

IF YOU'VE BEEN A CHRISTIAN for a long time, you've likely encountered someone asking a question similar to "can you provide a few verses on salvation," or eternal security, or where you go when you die, or something else.

Why are those difficult questions to answer? In math, if a student must review the quadratic formula it's trivial to locate the section explaining it. Not so with the Bible; it's unique by design (and intention), which explains why those questions persist.

The Bible must hold one quality math books need not concern themselves with — the intent of attack by enemies to jam and prevent its message from going forth. Nobody dissects an algebra text and rips out sections on quadratic formulas. Yet many desire to rip-out sections of the Bible:

- Peter didn't author that book, so don't consider what he wrote as authoritative.
- Modern translations using the "critical" text (i.e. Westcott and Hort's magic deletions).
- Daniel was written later by a forger, after the so-called "prophecy" of events.

Scholars debate and discuss (perhaps voting) on what Jesus said, which books of the Bible are written by the author, and when it was written. Ridiculous theories like the documentary hypothesis (Moses didn't write the books bearing his name), the equally laughable deutero-Isaiah theory, Daniel didn't write when he did (but his book appears in the Septuagint so no matter the page count on their thesis, it can't post-date the Septuagint).

Scholars attack the *entire* Bible, as God anticipated pseudo-scholarship and the bogus theories it spawns. Thus, no single chapter in the Bible exists as the "salvation" chapter; the message spreads across the entire book, as revealed in Isaiah.

> *But the word of the LORD was unto them precept upon precept, precept upon precept; line upon line, line upon line; here a little, and there a little;*   Isaiah 28:13

To understand doctrine, the complete Bible must be studied as an integrated system, not picking and choosing favorite parts.

On the spectrum's other end of the science-deniers rest the feeling people, reducing Christianity to feelings and opinion. I *think* Jesus wouldn't have done xyz, therefore if He *did* speak on it, the Bible must be wrong and we should (must) ignore that section. An example from Isaiah 14:12–15 shows the error of believing your opinion overrules God — it didn't work out well for the guy trying it.

If you've ever had the opportunity to watch an illusionist live and in-person, you can stare directly at him, and you *know* he didn't saw the person in half, yet that's what you observed and witnessed. Will you believe your lying eyes? Or logical thinking skills?

Peter states an idea you might think strange at first, but in light of the previous makes 100% sense.

> *For we have not followed cunningly devised fables, when we made known unto you the power and coming of our Lord Jesus Christ, but were eyewitnesses of his majesty. For he received from God the Father honor and glory, when there came such a voice to him from the excellent glory, This is my beloved Son, in whom I am well pleased.*   2 Peter 1:16–17

Peter was *there* for most of Jesus' events, yet he tackles this vital subject and it's important because it applies to *us*, not just those who watched Jesus 2000 years ago, as he continues with a strange idea.

> *We have also a more sure word of prophecy; whereunto ye do well that ye take heed, as unto a light that shineth in a dark place, until the day dawn, and the day star arise in your hearts*   2 Peter 1:19–21

Peter states he was *there* for the events of Jesus' life, yet don't believe his eyewitness account, look to the more sure word of prophecy, and tosses in the additional thought if you want to be a smart person, you would do well to heed prophecy over what he saw — if you want to be smart in Peter's sense, don't believe gossip, unsubstantiated conspiracies, political nonsense, misquotes, or even your eyes.

Without diverting into a detailed analysis (others have), considering all the prophecies of Jesus and making guesses as to the probability of each (i.e. what are the odds of a person being born in Bethlehem?), obtaining a composite probability and considering the result, it's mathematically *impossible* for Jesus not to be who He said He was when viewed through a prophetic lens.

The probability numbers become more than the number of atoms in the universe, as if you marked a single atom somewhere in the universe, and you must pick the correct one on the first try. It rounds to zero — which explains why critics try to late-date Daniel and others for example, they know math proves prophecy and the Bible.

Trust. The. Math.

In the end, almost everything reduces to math. Economics, politics, pandemics, science, biology, and knowing the Bible all boil down to math.

The Bible demonstrates logical principles, which often are misunderstood (and misused).

> *If there arise among you a prophet, or a dreamer of dreams, and giveth thee a sign or a wonder, And the sign or the wonder come to pass, whereof he spoke unto thee, saying, Let us go after other gods, which thou hast not known, and let us serve them; Thou shalt not hearken unto the words of that prophet, or that dreamer of dreams: for the LORD your God proveth you, to know whether ye love the LORD your God with all your heart and with all your soul.*
>
> Deuteronomy 13:1–3

Even *if* a "prophet" arises, performs miracles or predicts the future, but contradicts God's Word, he remains a false prophet. Don't believe your eyes, believe God's Word.

Another fashionable trend remains "updating the Bible for modern times" — a bad idea as God remains constant, yet many state portions of God's Word don't apply today, or the scientific rules governing the cosmos since its creation don't apply either.

Principle #1 — Miracles do NOT Validate a Prophet

The magicians in Egypt duplicated Moses' miracles ... up to a point. Pharaoh failed to understand miracles can't be used to validate a true prophet of God. Deuteronomy 18 repeats a similar warning, but from a different perspective.

> *But the prophet, which shall presume to speak a word in my name, which I have not commanded him to speak, or that shall speak in the name of other gods, even that prophet shall die. And if thou say in thine heart, How shall we know the word which the LORD hath not spoken? When a prophet speaketh in the name of the LORD, if the thing follow not, nor come to pass, that is the thing which the LORD hath not spoken, but the prophet hath spoken it presumptuously: thou shalt not be afraid of him.* Deuteronomy 18:20–22

Here's where math comes in — Deuteronomy 13 proclaims a false prophet can perform miracles (which we know from Egypt) so DO NOT use that to validate; Deuteronomy 18 sets the standard for God's prophets as 100% accuracy — if a claimed prophet's events do not come to pass, he's not a prophet from God.

Principle #2 — Failure of prophecy Means a False Prophet

In math terms the Converse of a statement is not necessarily true. It *may* be, but you don't know it and it must be proved apart from the original idea.

- If A, then B
- Converse: If B, then A
- Inverse: If Not A, then not B
- Contrapositive: If not B, then not A

From the original statement, only the last can be assumed as true. The contrapositive of Deuteronomy 18 obtains the statement often repeated in Christian circles: A true prophet of God states prophecies which *always* come true with 100% accuracy. It's logically equivalent to Deuteronomy 18.

A simpler example might provide clarity. Suppose we say "If I am on the couch, then I am in my house" we can logically form the following statements:

- If I am in the house, then I am on the couch.
- If I am not on the couch, I am not in the house.
- Contrapositive: If I am not in my house, I am not on the couch.

It's obvious the converse and inverse may — or may not — be true, as a person could be in the kitchen, for example, or be sitting on the couch.

Back to Peter. Peter says you would do well to head math and logical analysis; don't be anti-science, anti-logic, or anti-math — those positions contradict the Bible's teaching. Peter provides the answer to a frequent and troubling question — why send a prophet when they won't heed the message?

> *And he said unto me, Son of man, I send thee to the children of Israel, to a rebellious nation that hath rebelled against me: they and their fathers have transgressed against me, even unto this very day. For they are impudent children and stiff-hearted. I do send thee unto them; and thou shalt say unto them, Thus saith the Lord GOD. And they, whether they will hear, or whether they will forbear, (for they are a rebellious house,) yet shall know that there hath been a prophet among them.* Ezekiel 2:3–5

Sure, people are rebellious and not many listen, but then they are without excuse when they *know* a prophet and God's message has been among them. Certainly true, but a more troubling question remains, why send the prophet when the Lord knows *nobody* will listen, as God tells Jeremiah.

> *Since the day that your fathers came forth out of the land of Egypt unto this day I have even sent unto you all my servants the prophets, daily rising up early and sending them: Yet they hearkened not unto me, nor inclined their ear, but hardened their neck: they did worse than their fathers. Therefore thou shalt speak all these words unto them; but they will not hearken to thee: thou shalt also call unto them; but they will not answer thee.* Jeremiah 7:25–27

Two reasons for sending prophets to stiff-necked rebellious people:

1. So *they* know a prophet has been among them.
2. As Peter says, so *we* validate the math.

Jeremiah writes more than most of the prophets, and he's one the Lord told the people won't accept the message; a reason besides the obvious of warning the people of Jeremiah's day *must* be involved, and Peter reveals it. We wouldn't have the message if the Lord told Jeremiah "don't bother with them, they won't listen" — we need Jeremiah's writing as Peter says trust the math of the prophets. Daniel *lived* Peter's words:

> *In the first year of his reign I Daniel understood by books the number of the years, whereof the word of the LORD came to Jeremiah the prophet, that he would accomplish seventy years in the desolations of Jerusalem.* Daniel 9

Daniel acknowledges two things: Jeremiah was a prophet, and he takes what Jeremiah said literally — 70 years are almost up. Notice no chapter exists on *trust the math*, but it's everywhere (here a little, there a little), and math's logical rules are explicit in the Bible.

Daniel foreshadowed what Peter would say much later: trust the math, and take prophecy literally. Daniel also lived Peter's next thought.

> *Knowing this first, that no prophecy of the scripture is of any private interpretation. For the prophecy came not in old time by the will of man: but holy men of God spoke as they were moved by the Holy Ghost.* 2 Peter 1

It's not private, but out in the open. Logical rules are available to anyone who *wants* to learn. Sadly, some don't, but it's not because it's secret or unavailable. Daniel didn't read Jeremiah and wonder, what does 70 years mean?

> *But there were false prophets also among the people, even as there shall be false teachers among you, who secretly shall bring in damnable heresies, even denying the Lord that bought them, and bring upon themselves swift destruction. And many shall follow their pernicious ways; by reason of whom the way of truth shall be evil spoken of.* 2 Peter 2:1–2

Victims are those who don't trust math, and many follow them. Commonly called tin-foil hat people, flat-earth, science deniers, and those in similar states of denial.

If people abandon logic, thinking, and science they'll wander — slowly at first — and end up far from the truth (read that: far from God and the Bible). False teachers *will* be in the church. One way to uncover them is they don't trust the math — they can be anti-science, anti-math, anti-logic, fail to modify their position when new evidence appears, fight and screech for their opinion, and become hostile to anyone who questions their idea or dares ask for evidence.

Questions are *always* acceptable on *any* subject as truth can withstand scrutiny (it's fine to discuss flat-earth theory, but it will be a short conversation). Those becoming hostile when legitimate questions come up (or fail to modify their position when evidence demands) provide a clue they don't have reality backing up their opinion.

Trust the math.

At 3 AM or any other time.

Appendix D

Frames of Reference

ABOUT AD 1900 SCIENTISTS BELIEVED everything had been figured out; little remained to discover. Sure, some details required further study, but for the most part we understood the world around us. Then along comes this Einstein guy and messes up the whole thing! Einstein is famous for two things — Relativity and Quantum Physics — plunging scientists into a world of doubt and uncertainty. Let's look at *one* of these two (Relativity) and see why it troubles people so. The other (Quantum Physics) is extremely interesting in its own right, but is a subject for another time (no pun intended).

First, consider the following diagram, and remember, *there will only be one line of Physics in the following discussion*, so if you are of the type thinking "I can't understand Physics stuff," hang on.

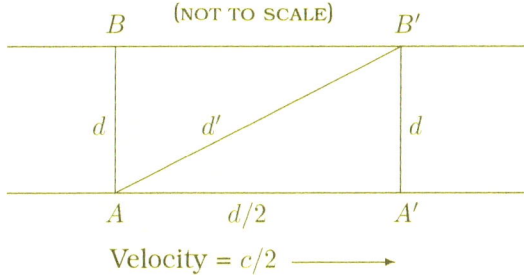

You and a friend ride motorcycles, represented by A and B. You travel from point A to point A' at $1/2$ the speed of light, or $c/2$. At point A you shine a flashlight toward your friend, at point B (notice the picture is not to scale).

From your point of view, *neither of you is moving since your speed matches*. This is familiar to anyone who has ridden in a car. If someone pulls up alongside you as you travel down the road, if they match your speed it appears to both of you as if you sit motionless in a parking lot. In either case, both you and your friend see the light travel along the path noted by d. For you both, *your forward motion is irrelevant to your perception of the event as you both exist in the same reference frame*.

Now consider someone standing along side the road, watching you go by. Since you and your friend move, they see you travel from A to A'. What path would the light take to them? Looking at the picture above, the answer is d'. This should also be familiar to anyone who has ridden in a car. Imagine throwing a ball out the window of a moving car. Since the car is moving, as you throw the ball, it still travels forward as it falls, doesn't it?

Before we continue, be sure you understand the diagram and the previous two paragraphs. Neither assume any understanding of Relativity or Physics, just recalling your experiences, however, they are critical to understand before continuing.

OK, now the fun begins! Once again, we must recall some of our experiences. Suppose you travel in a car at 60mph for 1/2 hour. How far have you traveled? How do you know? The answer is the following equation: $d = v * t$ (distance equals speed multiplied by time). Thus 60mph * 1/2 hour = 30 miles. But you already knew this (see, you know much more about Physics than you thought).

Lets apply the previous equation to our paths d and d' above. We thus have $d = v * t$ and $d' = v' * t'$. Fair enough? (Remember, d, v, t are for you and your friend riding the motorcycles, and d', v', t' are for your friend watching you go by). Notice by looking at the picture, that $d' > d$. In the interest of completeness, I shall now prove $d' > d$.

Using some geometric properties of a right triangle (the famous Pythagorean theorem where $a^2 + b^2 = c^2$) yields the following:

$$(d')^2 = \left(\frac{d}{2}\right)^2 + d^2$$

Lets perform the squares to get:

$$(d')^2 = \frac{5d^2}{4}$$

Taking the square root of both sides yields:

Frames of Reference

$$d' = \frac{\sqrt{5}d}{2}$$

The square root of 5 is about 2.2. Thus $d' > d$, which is what I asked you to believe. We don't really care about the *exact* ratio (it will vary depending on the velocity of the motorcycles), all we are interested in is for the moving motorcycles, $d' > d$.

Consider all we know:

$$d = v * t \quad (D.1)$$

$$d' = v' * t' \quad (D.2)$$

$$d' > d \quad (D.3)$$

Combining inequality and equations yields the following:

$$v' * t' > v * t \quad (D.4)$$

OK, I promised only one line of real Physics, and here it is:

Every observer measures the same value c for the speed of light[*]

This was Einstein's proposal. Simply put, it means everyone measures the speed of light as equal. What does that mean for our little example? That $v' = v = c$. Thus, inequality becomes:

$$c * t' > c * t$$

Which simplifies to the following shocking result:

$$t' > t \quad (D.5)$$

Remember what t represents, *time*. This means for our observer watching us go by, their time appears *longer*. Does this mean for our friends on motorcycles they experience a "slowdown" of time? It does not. If two atomic clocks are placed one on a motorcycle and the other with the person standing along the road, synchronized, and allow the motorcycles to ride by, when they come back we notice the clocks are no longer synchronized! *It is the very nature of time itself that has changed, not the accuracy of the clocks.*

Time is not an absolute property — it varies.

---

[*] Tipler, *Physics, Third Edition Volume 2*, page 1107

But, beloved, be not ignorant of this one thing, that one day is with the Lord as a thousand years, and a thousand years as one day. 2 Peter 3:8

Relativity is a recent discovery (1900's), so how would Peter have known about it thousands of years ago? Only by inspiration of the Holy Spirit. Yet another reason to take your Bible seriously.

Appendix E

Which Bible Translation?

Introduction

Many issues divide the Body of Christ today. Baptism, communion, pre-tribulation rapture verses post-tribulation and more all frequently cause division in the Church. Satan loves to divide and conquer; it's sad we fight among ourselves instead of the real enemy.

One of satan's clear strategies from early in Genesis becomes casting doubt on God's word. Recall in the garden satan's words "Has God really said?" confusing Eve and causing her to sin. Satan realizes casting doubt on what God actually says can be a winning strategy for him — what could cause more confusion than casting doubt the Bible in your lap isn't the exact Word of God?

This strategy continues today with the Bible translation debate. Is the King James really the best translation? What about ye Olde English? Shouldn't I use a newer translation? As usual many views exist, and unfortunately some people involved become rather militant. I've actually been told if you're witnessing to someone and they become saved, but you didn't use King James Version it didn't count. That's absurd.

However, in view of satan's strategy of creating doubt in God's word the translation and preservation of the Bible becomes critically important; you can't dismiss the concept and use whatever translation you pick off the shelf. Balance is required; getting that balance requires effort on your part — you need to do some homework. Fortunately acquiring a basic familiarity with the issues can be done briefly, paying dividends in your Bible Study.

Anyone translating between languages quickly understands it's *impossible* to completely and accurately translate between languages. The translator must attempt different wording to convey the original idea; sometimes it's impossible to express the idea of one language in another. As such, the translation is *never* as good as the original; it's always a compromise of sorts and subject to the personal ideas of the translator (which is why we must understand the personal ideas of the translator).

The idea we can have a *perfect* translation is gone — they *all* have problems. Understanding which translations have which problems is important. In the following discussion, we'll take a brief and summary look at issues affecting translation, and how those issues impact various translations. Understanding these issues is important to understand the advantages and disadvantages of the translation in your lap.

Issues Affecting Translation

When considering Bible translation, many issues arise but for simplicity we'll stick to two; these main issues concern you as a Christian trying to understand the Bible translation debate.

1. What you're translating *from*. Two main lines of Greek texts exist with differences between them. You also must consider if what we have today was handed down to us faithfully accurate to the originals.

2. *How* you translate what you've got. In other words, do you attempt to translate literally, or use more paraphrasing?

Textual Issues

PRESERVATION OF THE BIBLE

Written 2,000 years ago, do we have correct and accurate copies of the original New Testament? A quick glance of the following chart[*] illustrates the accuracy of the New Testament as it has been passed down to us, compared to other ancient writings.

---

[*] Eastman and Missler "The Bible: An Extraterrestrial Message" page 10

Which Bible Translation? 213

Document	Date	Copies	% Purity
Homer's Iliad	800 BC	643	95
Herodotus	480 BC	8	?
Plato's Tetralogies	427 BC	7	?
Caesar's Gallic Wars	44 BC	10	?
New Testament	50-95 AD	25,366	99.5

If we don't accept the validity and accuracy of the Bible, we must throw out much more than the Bible. Do we doubt writings with considerably less sources? The existence of George Washington? With considerable manuscript evidence, the Bible stands apart from other ancient writings.

Norman Geisler, a world renowned Bible scholar echoed this when he states: "Only 400 words of the NT are in doubt, whereas 764 lines of the Iliad are questioned. This five percent textual corruption (in the Iliad) compares with one-half of one percent of similar emendations in the New Testament"*

So the Bible has been preserved through the centuries for us as originally written; we can be confident our copies are very nearly perfect. Many differences exist in spelling or other minor issues only.

TEXTUAL HISTORY

Two main lines of Greek texts exist, diverging in minor but important ways. The text used almost exclusively until the 1800's was Textus Receptus. However, manuscript discoveries in Alexandria changed some scholars' views.

In 1525, Erasmus compiled the first Greek text using texts from Byzantium, which had been in use previously for centuries, forming the basis for what would later be called Textus Receptus.†
This is the main text the KJV translators used, although they likely had the other Alexandrian texts available (Codex Siniaticus, etc). They obviously felt the Alexandrian text base (later to become Westcott-Hort) was unsuitable.

Scholars Westcott and Hort compiled a Greek New Testament starting in 1853 and finished 28 years later, relying heavily on

---

* Eastman and Missler "The Bible: An Extraterrestrial Message" page 11–12
† Chuck Missler, "How we got our Bible", page 17

the Alexandrian Codex Vaticanus and Codex Siniaticus, changing the traditional Greek in over 8,000 places.* We'll treat all these Alexandrian texts as similar and refer to them collectively as Westcott-Hort (not technically correct, but for our purposes it's close enough). How they edited the text, the reasons why and their background becomes critical to understanding the newer translations derived from Westcott-Hort's work.

The KJV and NKJV (and more recently the MEV) are the only modern translations using the Textus Receptus Greek text. All the others (NASB, NIV, etc) use the Westcott-Hort or Alexandrian texts. After studying these a bit, it becomes apparent they've all been edited for theological reasons; the influence of early Gnostic heresy is unmistakable in Westcott-Hort's text.

For our purposes (even though it's not exact) we'll treat Textus-Receptus, Byzantium, and Majority Text as equivalent, and Westcott-Hort, Alexandrian, UBS, and Nestle-Aland as equivalent also.

GNOSTIC INFLUENCE — WESTCOTT AND HORT

Early in church history a heretical group sprang up called the Gnostics, accepting the Greek idea of dualism between spirit and matter.† All matter in Gnostic teaching was evil; since all matter is evil, Jesus really didn't have a physical body and no physical resurrection occurred. The Gnostics also believed they had special knowledge, leading to spiritual elitism in the early church.

The Gnostic's teaching on the evilness of material leads to two errors. On one side was a form of asceticism — denying yourself is the path to heaven (the extreme puritanical view). On the other side, your body (since it is evil) doesn't matter. If you do drugs or party it really doesn't matter since your body is evil anyway.

The Gnostic heresy Jesus didn't have a body denies His death, physical resurrection, and thus His atonement for our sins. The apostle John wrote his first letter (1 John) in part to combat the Gnostic heresy. John writes he saw and handled Jesus — Jesus had a physical body. Even more, John warned anyone stating Jesus did not come *in the flesh* is not of God.

> *Hereby know ye the Spirit of God: Every spirit that confesseth that Jesus Christ is come in the flesh is of God: And every spirit that confesseth not that Jesus Christ is come in the flesh*

---

*   Chuck Missler, "How we got our Bible", page 18
†   "Nelsons New Illustrated Bible Dictionary" page 500

Which Bible Translation?

> *is not of God: and this is that spirit of antichrist, whereof ye have heard that it should come; and even now already is it in the world.* 1 John 4:2-3

Just by John's one statement all Gnostic heresy is debunked. Why then is academia so enamored by it? Why would Westcott-Hort follow such heresy when it so obviously contradicts Biblical teaching? Why have we allowed people who obviously rejected Biblical teaching edit God's Word?

Westcott and Hort edited the original Greek as they compiled their edition, but as we shall see, both were heavily influenced by Gnostic philosophy. These Greek texts are usually footnoted in your Bible as "the oldest and best manuscripts." Yes, they're the oldest, but are they the best? Westcott and Hort had strange theological views — do we trust them with God's Word? Consider the words of Westcott and Hort themselves.

> *But the book which has engaged me most is Darwin ... My feeling is strong that the theory is unanswerable.*[*]
>
> *No one now I suppose holds that the first three chapters of Genesis, for example, give a literal history—I could never understand how anyone reading them with open eyes could think they did.*[†]
>
> *Christians are themselves in a true sense "Christs".*[‡]
>
> *I am inclined to think that no such state as Eden (I mean the popular notion) ever existed, and that Adam's fall in no degree differed from the fall of each of his descendents.*[§]

These are their views. They're entitled to them, of course, but do they agree with your Bible reading? In light of John's warning about Gnostic heresy, can we trust these men to compile an accurate Greek text? As we'll see in the examples, they allowed their un-orthodox views to influence their compilation of the Holy Scriptures — in some ways that simply make no sense.

A key issue is the integrated nature of the Bible; it's designed to be used as a whole and complete message. As soon as you edit

---

[*] F.J. Hort, *Life of Hort*, Vol I, page 416 (Chuck Missler, "How we got our Bible", page 19)

[†] *Life of Westcott*, Vol II, page 69 (Chuck Missler, "How we got our Bible", page 19)

[‡] B.F. Westcott, *The Epistles of St. John*, page 73 (Chuck Missler, "How we got our Bible", page 19)

[§] F.J.A. Hort, *Life of Hort*, Vol I, page 78 (Chuck Missler, "How we got our Bible", page 19)

parts, contradictions and other problems arise we'll see in the examples section. No way exists for Westcott-Hort (or anyone else) to edit the Biblical text and keep it consistent.

Translational Issues

Once you decide on the textual base (Textus Receptus or Westcott-Hort), you must decide exactly how to translate — literal or paraphrase? Both have pros and cons, but mostly you want to know where on the scale your translation is. If you've ever picked up a Greek-English interlinear, you know it can be difficult to read, as this example shows.

> so For loved God the world, so as the Son of Him, the Only-begotten, He gave, that everyone believing into Him not may perish, but have life everlasting.*

So the question isn't quite literal vs. paraphrase, but how much paraphrasing does the translator do? A translator trying to remain literal will do the minimum required to put the sentence into grammatically correct English and no more, while a paraphrase tries to convey the *idea* of the original without using the exact wording of the original, perhaps taking into account cultural or other differences.

Weights and measures provide one simple example. How many people know what a cubit is? Or that 4 cubits make one fathom? Or 1 firkin is about 9 gallons? In a more literal translation, these quantities translate as-is, and it's up to you to understand what they are. In more of a paraphrase translation, these appear in more modern measures. It's easiest to show this issue with examples.

Examples

LITERAL VS PARAPHRASE

Examine 2 Timothy 2:15 in two translations and how the literal verses paraphrase problem presents itself.

> *Study to show thyself approved unto God, a workman that needeth not to be ashamed, rightly dividing the word of truth.* (KJV)

---

*   John 3:16 *Interlinear Greek-English NT, 3rd Edition*, Jay P. Green

"Rightly divide" in the Greek is orthotomeo (from orthos) — you might recognize as similar to the math term orthogonal which means a right angle. So the KJV is literal. But do you know what it means? If you have a math background you understand orthogonal as precise, an exact right angle. The KJV accurately and literally translates the Greek. Now consider the NIV.

> *Do your best to present yourself to God as one approved, a workman who does not need to be ashamed and who correctly handles the word of truth (NIV)*

"Correctly handles" is not literal, but for many people brings the truth of the verse out better. But notice instead of "Study" the NIV uses "Do your best" which completely changes the meaning and makes it less clear. Study implies dedication or devotion, while just doing your best can mean a lot less. John chapter seven provides another example.

> *His brethren therefore said unto him, Depart hence, and go into Judaea, that thy disciples also may see the works that thou doest. For there is no man that doeth any thing in secret, and he himself seeketh to be known openly. If thou do these things, show thyself to the world.* John 7:3-4 KJV

What you might miss is Jesus' brothers picking on Him a little. Since they didn't believe Jesus was God, they're actually baiting Him to show His stuff. Now compare the New Living Translation.

> *Jesus' brothers urged him to go to Judea for the celebration. "Go where your followers can see your miracles!" they scoffed. "You can't become a public figure if you hide like this! If you can do such wonderful things, prove it to the world!"*
> John 7:3-4 NLT

In these two examples you can see both the advantages and disadvantages of literal and paraphrase translation. Most often you want literal translation, but sometimes referring to a paraphrase proves advantageous.

TEXTUAL

For these KJV and NKJV represent Textus Receptus, and the NIV (and also the NASB or the New American Standard Bible) represent Westcott-Hort. Most "modern" translations are influenced by

Westcott-Hort, even if they don't follow exactly the full changes Westcott-Hort made. Some translations include the changes as footnotes, others include in the main text.

> *(Matthew 18:11 NKJV) For the Son of Man has come to save that which was lost.*
>
> *(Matthew 18:11 KJV) For the Son of man is come to save that which was lost.*
>
> *(Matthew 18:11 NIV)* deleted

NIV deletes entirely, while NASB brackets it as probably not in original text. Why delete this verse? Perhaps if you believe (as Westcott) we're all true Christs and don't have need of salvation.

> *(Matthew 25:13 NKJV) Watch therefore, for you know neither the day nor the hour in which* **the Son of Man is coming**.
>
> *(Matthew 25:13 KJV) Watch therefore, for ye know neither the day nor the hour wherein* **the Son of man cometh**.
>
> *(Matthew 25:13 NIV) Therefore keep watch, because you do not know the day or the hour.*

That's a bizarre one. Why would I keep watch if I don't know what time it was? But it's not the time, it's the time of Jesus' return you don't know. We are taught to always be on the lookout for Jesus' return — it can come anytime.

> *(Mark 2:17 NKJV) When Jesus heard it, He said to them, "Those who are well have no need of a physician, but those who are sick. I did not come to call the righteous, but sinners,* **to repentance**.*"*
>
> *(Mark 2:17 KJV) When Jesus heard it, he saith unto them, They that are whole have no need of the physician, but they that are sick: I came not to call the righteous, but sinners* **to repentance**.
>
> *(Mark 2:17 NIV) On hearing this, Jesus said to them, "It is not the healthy who need a doctor, but the sick. I have not come to call the righteous, but sinners."*

Another fun one. Jesus didn't come to call the righteous, but sinners. For what? An invitation to dinner? To Saturday's football game? (NASB has similar edit to NIV).

> *(Acts 8:37 NKJV) Then Philip said, "If you believe with all your heart, you may." And he answered and said, "I believe that Jesus Christ is the Son of God."*
>
> *(Acts 8:37 KJV) And Philip said, If thou believest with all thine heart, thou mayest. And he answered and said, I believe that Jesus Christ is the Son of God.*
>
> *(Acts 8:37 NIV) deleted*

If you didn't believe Jesus was God, you certainly wouldn't want it in your text so you delete it. NASB brackets as not in original text.

> *(Ephesians 3:9 NKJV) and to make all see what is the fellowship of the mystery, which from the beginning of the ages has been hidden in God who created all things* **through Jesus Christ**;
>
> *(Ephesians 3:9 KJV) And to make all men see what is the fellowship of the mystery, which from the beginning of the world hath been hid in God, who created all things* **by Jesus Christ**:
>
> *(Ephesians 3:9 NIV) and to make plain to everyone the administration of this mystery, which for ages past was kept hidden in God, who created all things.*

NIV has God creating all things, NOT Jesus — which you wouldn't want to say if you accept Gnostic heresy. Here Westcott-Hort directly contradict Paul in Colossians 1:16-17 who attributes creation to Jesus. In Colossians 1:17, Paul even states Jesus holds the atoms of the universe together. (NASB has similar edit to NIV).

> *(1 Peter 4:1 NKJV) Therefore, since Christ suffered* **for us** *in the flesh, arm yourselves also with the same mind, for he who has suffered in the flesh has ceased from sin,*
>
> *(1 Peter 4:1 KJV) Forasmuch then as Christ hath suffered* **for us** *in the flesh, arm yourselves likewise with the same mind: for he that hath suffered in the flesh hath ceased from sin;*
>
> *(1 Peter 4:1 NIV) Therefore, since Christ suffered in his body, arm yourselves also with the same attitude, because he who has suffered in his body is done with sin.*

Jesus didn't just suffer, he suffered and died *for us*. NASB similar to NIV.

*(Revelation 11:17 NKJV) saying: "We give You thanks, O Lord God Almighty, The One who is and who was and **who is to come**, Because You have taken Your great power and reigned.*

*(Revelation 11:17 KJV) Saying, We give thee thanks, O Lord God Almighty, which art, and wast, and **art to come**; because thou hast taken to thee thy great power, and hast reigned.*

(Revelation 11:17 NIV) saying: "We give thanks to you, Lord God Almighty, the One who is and who was, because you have taken your great power and have begun to reign.

Denying the return of Jesus. (NASB has similar edit to NIV). In these few examples, you can see how Westcott-Hort personal theology (or lack thereof) influenced their compilation of the Greek text. Some changes contradict other areas of the Bible, while others make no sense at all. Since the Bible is inerrant, it must be Westcott-Hort making the mistakes.

King James Version

King James Only

Some claim the KJV as the only true Bible, claiming the translators of the KJV were divinely inspired just as Peter, Paul and John were, placing it on the same level as the original Greek. Unfortunately, no basis for this exists as anyone who has ever translated anything soon finds, it's *impossible* to accurately translate one language to another. Even worse, Greek is one of the most rich languages, with English one of the worst.

My father tells me a story of someone who was KJV-Only and said when he finished reading another translation, he tossed it on the coffee table. But when he finished reading the KJV, he reverently and gently placed it back from whence it came. That's idolatry.

We could continue to debate the KJV-only crowd, but I think most people don't hold such a view, and as such it isn't worth the time to continue the discussion. Just be aware some people hold this view, and from time to time you will encounter them.

The KJV is definitely a good (best) translation, although it's not the only translation that has use.

Olde English

Some would throw away the KJV due to it's old English. Certainly that *can* be a valid reason, but shouldn't preclude your use of it. Just as when studying any subject (Math), certain terminology must be learned. The KJV is no different. Remember you're reading text 2,000 years old from a different culture — it's going to be different.

The first problem pops up with archaic words. Dictionaries exist if you need help (Webster's 1913 edition is freely available online), but you'll quickly become accustomed to the vocabulary. The bigger issue is words you *think* you know, but changed meaning over time. These present a real problem, and unless you're aware of them you'll definitely encounter problems with the KJV.

> *For this we say unto you by the word of the Lord, that we which are alive and remain unto the coming of the Lord shall not prevent them which are asleep.*   1 Thessalonians 4:15 KJV

Any new translation will translate "prevent" as "precede". The word prevent changed meaning between 1611 and now. If you didn't know this verse makes no sense.

> *For the mystery of iniquity doth already work: only he who now letteth will let, until he be taken out of the way.*
> 2 Thessalonians 2:7 KJV

"Let" has changed meaning to "hinder". Again, any recent translation will correctly translate this verse (both of these verses are changed in the NKJV as well).

The other point people have with old English stems from "thees" and "thous" in the KJV. However, a reason does exist for these in the text; it's to differentiate singular and plural. Consider the following chart:*

	Nominative	**Objective**	**Possessive**
1st Singular	I	Me	My
1st Plural	We	Us	Our
2nd Singular	Thou	Thee	Thy
2nd Plural	Ye	You	Your
3rd Singular	He	Him	His
3rd Plural	They	Them	Their

---

*   https://av1611.com/kjbp/articles/bacon-theethou.html

Why is this important? Consider Luke 22:31-32.

> *And the Lord said, Simon, Simon, behold, Satan hath desired to have you, that he may sift you as wheat: But I have prayed for thee, that thy faith fail not: and when thou art converted, strengthen thy brethren.* — Luke 22:31-32 KJV

Here you can easily see Satan asked for much more than Peter — perhaps the entire group! However, Jesus prays for Peter *himself*. This distinction is easily missed in other translations (including NKJV).

Comparison of Translations

So how do we rate the various translations? The following chart provides a guide for modern translations, showing which textual base they follow and a rough guide of how literally they translate the original Greek.

Translation	Text Base	Literal Scale
KJV	TR	1
NKJV	TR	1
NASB	WH	1-2
NIV	WH	4
NLT	WH	6
The Message	?	9

Literal scale goes from 0 as a perfect literal (much like a Greek-English interlinear) to 10 which is a complete paraphrase — the translator reads a paragraph and translates it without trying to be literal.

It's important to know just because the newer translations are marked as Westcott-Hort does not necessarily imply they follow *all* of Westcott-Hort. Each translation has different ways of handling it. Some footnote, some delete, some ignore Westcott-Hort changes in some areas.

Recommendations

Use the King James or New King James for primary use, study and reading as it comes from the preferred Textus Receptus Greek Text. However, referring to a New Living Paraphrase in some cases will assist with meaning. These two translations provide a solid foundation for Bible Study.

Most importantly, understand *all* translations have problems. It's important to understand the strengths and weaknesses of the Bible translation you use. In the event you're using another translation, it does *not* mean to throw it out or stop using it. Several people I have considerable respect for use something besides KJV/NKJV.

Conclusion

You must have balance — no translation is 100% perfect, they all have problems. This does not mean the Bible has errors or inconsistencies, just that translation is imperfect. It's important to understand how your translation came to be, and what methods were used in its creation. Most importantly, you are encouraged to study on your own.

Appendix F

Deutero-Isaiah Hypothesis

I'VE REFERRED TO THE DEUTERO-ISAIAH HYPOTHESIS, but while the idea you might have heard of, why it's bunk may not be commonly known. The deutero-Isaiah hypothesis claims Isaiah didn't write the book bearing his name — actually multiple authors wrote different parts and those anonymous authors became compiled much later into one book called Isaiah.

What should a person do? The problem arises when strange theories cause people to fall away from faith, after failing to check out the scholarship for themselves (after all, who wants to read hundreds of pages of boring PhD thesis?). But of course, that assumes the validity of their theory — don't fall for the lie a PhD behind scholarly writing implies their bloviating contains any truth whatsoever. In the case of the deutero-Isaiah hypothesis, it's pure junk as the Gospel of John reveals.

> *But though he had done so many miracles before them, yet they believed not on him; That the saying of Isaiah the prophet might be fulfilled, which he spoke, Lord, who hath believed our report? And to whom hath the arm of the Lord been revealed?* John 12:37–38

A simple quote from John's gospel. Almost every Bible (and many readers) recognize the quote as from Isaiah 53: Who hath believed our report? And to whom is the arm of the Lord revealed? Simple so far, but continue reading in John:

> *He hath blinded their eyes, and hardened their heart; that they should not see with their eyes, nor understand with*

their heart, and be converted, and I should heal them. These things said Isaiah, when he saw his glory, and spoke of him. John 12:40–41

Not as many people recognize that quote, but it's from Isaiah 6:

And he said, Go, and tell this people, Hear ye indeed, but understand not; and see ye indeed, but perceive not. Make the heart of this people fat, and make their ears heavy, and shut their eyes; lest they see with their eyes, and hear with their ears, and understand with their heart, and convert, and be healed. Isaiah 6:9–10

John quotes from both "halves" of Isaiah — chapter 6 and 53. But who wrote them? Should we return to the deutero-Isaiah hypotheses and spend hours in boring research? Don't fret over the authorship of Isaiah, as sandwiched between John 12:38 and John 12:40 lies verse 39:

Therefore they could not believe, **because that Isaiah said again...**

Oops. John quotes from both "halves" of Isaiah, *and attributes them to Isaiah.* So who wrote Isaiah (*all of it*)? Isaiah. You don't need to waste hours reading hundreds of pages of so-called scholarship — John told you who wrote Isaiah. If you believe the inspiration of John as he wrote it settles the authorship of Isaiah (if you don't believe in the inspiration of the Holy Spirit and the inerrancy of the Bible you've frankly got much bigger issues than the authorship of Isaiah). Only liberal theology denying Biblical inerrancy and inspiration could possibly accept strange ideas like multiple authors of Isaiah.

You can toss the deutero-Isaiah hypothesis on the scrap heap of pseudo-scholarship once and for all. Don't waste time with it — it doesn't matter if someone wrote 500 pages espousing the scholarship, it's a useless and contradictory position you don't need to waste time with — the deutero-Isaiah hypothesis proves someone hasn't read the book they claim to be an expert on.

Simply read the Bible, it destroys so-called scholarship from people claiming to be experts, but in reality simply failing to read (and understand) the whole of it.

Appendix G

Post-Modern Philosophy

POST-MODERNISM DENIES ABSOLUTE truth (perhaps you've heard the slogan "that's truth for *you*"). Post-modern philosophy embraces experience and feelings over reason and logic, group-think and consensus instead of truth. Truth becomes relative and not absolute — some actually proclaim no absolute truth exists — an idea they proclaim absolutely (as the only absolute truth), demonstrating how circular and illogical their thought process is.

Post-modernism employs the dialectic process, using group-think and consensus to arrive at "truth." If you think that's not a good idea, you're correct, as for most people the thought of negotiating what $2+2$ equals sounds bizarre (it doesn't just sound bizarre, it *is*). How does this work in practice? Consider the following strange definition of sin.

> *From time to time, I have been asked in the academic classrooms where I have taught to define what I mean by sin. I always respond by saying, "Sin is what diminishes the humanity of another person and of the self."**

Suppose you told someone they were living contrary to God's law (adultery, drunkenness, etc). According to the previous definition of sin a Christian speaking truth sins, as it has the possibility to make the person feel sad. Boo hoo hoo. Send a Hallmark card instead.

Remember David when he murdered one of his men? What did he say to God in Psalm 51 — "Against thee, thee only, have I sinned,

---

*   http://www.redletterchristians.org/what-do-you-mean-by-sin/

and done this evil in thy sight." No mention of "dehumanizing," the offense is *always* against God, even if effects are felt here on earth.

Redefining sin removes God from the equation, reducing sin to whatever you want it to be — it's not constant, but whatever "diminishes the humanity" of a person. Not only is God not involved, but neither is *truth*. If speaking the truth bums someone out, that's sin on your part. Yet sin is against God — it's not about dehumanizing another person or yourself. Those may be *results* of sin, but they're most definitely not the *definition* of sin.

Where is the absolute inerrant Word of God? Nowhere to be found — only whatever man decides. A perfect example of post-modern value relativism, and the removal of God from what they call "Christianity" — reducing Christianity to a man-centered philosophy changing day to day.

I can hear you now; that's an isolated case, it doesn't happen that often. Really? Consider the current fad of "social justice" sweeping through the church. You'll quickly discover social justice contains nothing more than repackaged post-modern philosophy. First off, we need to define terms. What is social justice?

> *Social justice is based on the concepts of human rights and equality and involves a greater degree of economic egalitarianism through progressive taxation, income redistribution, or even property redistribution.*[*]

> *Economic egalitarianism is a state of economic affairs in which equality of outcome has been manufactured for all the participants of a society. It is a founding principle of various forms of socialism, communalism and cooperative economic organization.*[†]

In short, social justice attempts to manufacture a society with everyone having equal amounts of property, money, and everything else. Specifically, it's not equality of *opportunity* they seek (a fair and level playing field), it's equality of *outcome* — an outcome forced by confiscation and redistribution if needed. If you think that sounds like Marx's "from each according to his ability, to each according to his needs" you're quite correct.

---

[*] http://en.wikipedia.org/wiki/Social_justice (accessed Nov 12, 2011, though Wikipedia changes a lot.)
[†] http://en.wikipedia.org/wiki/Economic_egalitarianism (accessed Nov 12, 2011, though Wikipedia changes a lot.)

As a political idea, you might agree or disagree with it — that's fine. However, when someone claims Christians should support such an idea as your Christian duty, ask them where Jesus or any New Testament author claimed the church should lobby for forced confiscation of a person's income or property for the sole purpose of redistribution and equality of outcome (not fairness). You'll get a deer-in-the-headlights look, because they *know* it's not there, yet in their next breath they'll tell you it's your Christian duty to support it anyway. Tilt.

Some even go so far as to change the definition of the Gospel to include redistributive ideas — another case where post-modern philosophy runs straight into conflict with the Bible, as Paul exactly defines the Gospel.

> *Moreover, brethren, I declare unto you the gospel which I preached unto you ... For I delivered unto you first of all that which I also received, how that Christ died for our sins according to the scriptures; And that he was buried, and that he rose again the third day according to the scriptures ...* 1 Corinthians 15

Strange. No mention of social justice in any form at all. How can it be integral to the Gospel? It's not, as those people aren't using the Biblical definition of the Gospel, they're using some alternate gospel and not telling you about it. Recall Paul's warning about alternate gospels.

> *But though we, or an angel from heaven, preach any other gospel unto you than that which we have preached unto you, let him be accursed. As we said before, so say I now again, If any man preach any other gospel unto you than that ye have received, let him be accursed. For do I now seek the favor of men, or God? Or do I seek to please men? For if I yet pleased men, I should not be the servant of Christ. But I make known to you, brethren, that the gospel which was preached of me is not after man.* Galatians 1:8–11

According to Paul, where should post-modern philosophical ideas changing Biblical definitions end up? On the scrap heap. It's left to the reader to examine each idea and question the person asking *why* they're abandoning the Bible, and what they want to replace it with. They'll be slippery about it of course, but force them to define terms, and you'll discover some people use the same words but with totally different meanings.

You need to understand post-modern philosophy because new fads in the church use post-modern thought as those groups seek to redefine the Bible to suit whatever purpose they're actually trying to achieve — whatever that purpose may be, it certainly isn't Christianity. As post-modern philosophy infects the church, you must be able to recognize bizarre non-Biblical ideas for what they are — lies, distortions, heresy, and a denial of God's absolute Word. And we state that absolutely, in spite of post-modernism claiming absolute truth doesn't exist.

Post-modern philosophy and the denial of absolute truth allows heretics to creep into the church and deceive many. They will *never* identify themselves as such ("hi, I'm a heretic and I'm here to move you away from God's Word"), and will even use normal Christian words such as sin, justice, redemption, hell, salvation, and more, but their ideas remain in conflict with the Bible, and you'll notice a subtle shift (sometimes not even subtle) away from God's inerrant Word towards whatever ideas they want to replace the Bible with.

Appendix H

Buzzword Bingo

PEOPLE THROW AROUND THE WORDS heretic and apostate. When discussing heresies it's important to know what the words *mean*, as well as what they *don't*. Christians tend to use them as an insult — when someone gets mad and wants to say something nasty, they throw out the h-word. Some misunderstand what heresy means — it's not an insult as it speaks to a belief, not character. What is heresy, and its similar cousin, apostasy?

Heresy

Heresy involves what a person believes (knowledge), and how or what they promote.

> *Religious belief opposed to the orthodox doctrines of a church ... rejection of a belief that is part of church dogma.*[*]

Heresy simply means ideas conflicting with accepted foundational doctrine. In the case of Christianity, that means the Bible. It says *nothing* about the character or morality of a person. They could be Sister Teresa or Satan himself.

Consider an example. Perhaps you've heard of "social justice," with some claiming it's the essence of the Gospel. Is that true? In this case, it's not a matter of opinion, it's a matter of *fact*, because Paul defined the Gospel for us.

---

[*] Agnes (2007, page 667)

> *Moreover, brethren, I declare unto you the gospel which I preached unto you ... For I delivered unto you first of all that which I also received, how that Christ died for our sins according to the scriptures; And that he was buried, and that he rose again the third day according to the scriptures.*
>
> 1 Corinthians 15

That's the Gospel, *according to the Bible*. If someone claims social justice or some other idea represents the essence of the Gospel, they've made a fundamental error, and an error of opinion regarding foundational doctrine. A heresy — those supporting such ideas are *heretics*.

The heretic, therefore, is nothing more than someone accepting or promoting heresy. It's not an insult or derogatory, it describes their beliefs as at odds with orthodox doctrine (i.e. the Bible); in the case of social justice, conflicting with Paul. Orthodox doctrine can also mean what we logically derive *from* the Bible. However, if an idea conflicts with the Bible, it has to go.

Heretic doesn't imply they're bad people, it doesn't mean they're evil. They may be the nicest people you'd want to live next door. They're simply wrong, and in the case of social justice, *as a matter of fact*, not opinion. A difference exists between a matter of fact and a matter of opinion (conclusion). A matter of fact states your fingerprint exists on the bloody knife. A matter of opinion (conclusion, or interpretation) states that fingerprint proves you're guilty of murder.

Apostasy

Similar to heretic, many sling this around as an insult. While the heretic could be corrected by instruction and education, the apostate generally involves a willful abandonment.

> *An abandoning of what one has believed in, as a faith, cause, or principles.**

That desertion could be willful, or due to improper teaching. An apostate, therefore, is one forsaking his religion. For example, someone who now claims to be an atheist. Heretics proclaim their religion, while promoting factually false doctrine; the apostate walks completely away from it.

---

* Agnes (2007, page 66)

Again, it doesn't mean they're bad people, only they've decided to abandon their religion for some reason. Freedom and liberty (which God gave) means you're free to believe or not believe anything you want. That doesn't make it true, of course, as John Loeffler says "your failure to be informed does not make me a wacko," words applying to those misunderstanding heretic and apostate.

Words Are Important

Communication can only be possible if everyone uses words the same way. If I say put the book on the table, you understand what I mean because we all use *book* and *table* the same way. Problems arise when people fail to use words correctly. The church displays this problem when liberal theology proponents redefine words. How does this happen? Something called post-modern philosophy, sometimes referred to as value relativism, or you have your truth and I have mine.

Terms like Gospel, Jesus, salvation, and judgment hold specific meanings; if someone changes those meanings from what everyone else uses, they can sound thoroughly orthodox while speaking from the pit of hell.

If you really want to insult someone (not a good idea, civil discourse is always the goal), these words won't get the job done; they say little about a person's character, only their beliefs. Calling someone a heretic isn't an insult; used properly it describes their beliefs as contradictory with traditional doctrine.

Whether you choose to believe heresy, is of course, up to you.

Appendix I

Five Bible Commentators You Should Listen To

WITH SO MANY RESOURCES, HOW DO YOU quickly gain an *overall* understanding of the Bible, current events, cults, science, logic, and application? We provide five choices to begin your study; it's the minimum you should have in your library.

1. Chuck Smith

Chuck Smith provides an incredible foundation for future study. He's not the most technical, the most specialized, or the most involved with current events, but if you want a framework for Bible study Chuck's the guy to provide it. Best of all, you can get his entire Bible commentary for less than $30 on MP3, and his radio program "The Word for Today" runs on radio stations everywhere.

2. Jon Courson

Jon possesses the unique ability to tell you a 15 minute story from his life, and just about the time you're wondering *why* he's wasting so much time on it he'll provide one Bible verse, and make a one-sentence comment, and you'll be left thinking *now* I understand that verse.

If you like a laid-back, conversational style with lots of personal stories and application, you'll love Jon Courson. His entire Bible commentary is available for about $100 on MP3, and Jon's radio program "Searchlight" frequently airs on many radio stations.

3. Walter Martin

Walter Martin is *the* expert on cults. If you don't have his book "The Kingdom of the Cults" get a copy — it is *the* definitive study on the issue. Walter's book is so far above anything else you'll ever hear or read, it's like the Space Shuttle compared to a Yugo.

4. Chuck Missler

If science is your bag, Chuck Missler has it covered. For a general introduction on relativity, quantum mechanics, probability, and more, see the "Beyond Collection," as Chuck frequently discusses science and its relationship to the Bible. His radio program "66/40" is available as a podcast and at https://khouse.org.

5. John Loeffler

John Loeffler isn't so much a Bible commentator, but if you want to understand current events and how they relate Biblically, John's *the* guy to listen to. He frequently covers political, educational, and logical issues with the overall theme of *what is true*, not what is popular. As John says

- The herd almost always runs in the wrong direction
- Your failure to be informed doesn't make me a wacko
- Reality votes last

References

Agnes, M. (Ed.) (2007). *Webster's New World College Dictionary* (4 ed.). Wiley Publishing, Inc.

Coulter, A. (2006). *Godless*. Crown Forum.

Courson, J. (2003). *Jon Courson's Application Commentary, New Testament*. Thomas Nelson.

Feynman, R. (1964). *The Feynman Lectures on Physics*, Volume I. Addison-Wesley.

Lewis, C. (1969). *Mere Christianity*. The Macmillin Company.

Lucado, M. (2005). *Thomas Nelson*. Thomas Nelson.

Martin, W. (2003). *The Kingdom of the Cults*. Bethany House Publishers.

McGee, J. V. (1982a). *Thru the Bible*, Volume III. Thomas Nelson.

McGee, J. V. (1982b). *Thru the Bible*, Volume V. Thomas Nelson.

Missler, C. (2008). *Hebrews*. Koinonia House.

Sewell, M. (2009). The Hitchens Transcript. *Portland Monthly* http://www.portlandmonthlymag.com/arts-and-entertainment/category/books-and-talks/articles/christopher-hitchens/. Accessed 2012-07-16.

Smith, C. (2000). *Calvary Chapel Distinctives*. The Word for Today.

Taunton, L. (2007, 12). Richard Dawkins: The Atheist Evangelist. *byFaith* http://byfaithonline.com/richard-dawkins-the-atheist-evangelist/. Accessed 2012-07-19.

Zodhiates, S. (1992a). *The Complete Word Study Dictionary New Testament*. ANG International.

Zodhiates, S. (1992b). *The Complete Word Study New Testament*. ANG International.

www.ingramcontent.com/pod-product-compliance
Lightning Source LLC
LaVergne TN
LVHW041915070526
838199LV00051BA/2622